LITERARY CRITICISM AND PHILOSOPHY

YEARBOOK OF
COMPARATIVE CRITICISM

VOLUME X

Literary

Criticism and

Philosophy

Edited by

Joseph P. Strelka

THE PENNSYLVANIA STATE
UNIVERSITY PRESS
University Park and London

Library of Congress Cataloging in Publication Data
  Main entry under title:

  Literary criticism and philosophy.

    (Yearbook of comparative criticism; v. 10)
    Includes index.
    1. Criticism—Addresses, essays, lectures.   2. Litera-
ture—Philosophy—Addresses, essays, lectures.
I. Strelka, Joseph, 1927–   .   II. Series.
PN85.L573   1982   801'.95   82-10137
ISBN 0-271-00324-3   AACR2

CONTENTS

PREFACE

The interrelationships between literary criticism and philosophy are manifold and far-reaching. First, the very foundation of literary scholarship—its principles so to speak—are established by philosophical means. The definition of the subject matter of literary scholarship as well as the nature of its aims, its epistemological possibilities, is to a great extent of a philosophical nature. This becomes eminently clear through the work of the Polish philosopher Roman Ingarden (for the first time made available for a larger audience in English by Eugene Falk's excellent book *The Poetics of Roman Ingarden*[1]).

It fell to a philosopher, namely Roman Ingarden, to establish more clearly than ever before the identity of a literary work of art. He showed that it was a multifaceted structure of four interrelated layers: the layer of sound-formation, the layer of meaning-units, the layer of presented objects, and the layer of schematized objects.[2]

As far as the philosophical foundation of the basic process of cognition is concerned, Ingarden did further pioneering work by establishing a phenomenological theory of epistemology.[3] While his establishment of the identity of the object of the literary work has not been seriously challenged, some theories advanced by other scholars, while differing significantly from Ingarden's, do not entirely contradict his multi-layered process of cognition and indeed, at least in some respects, complement it: e.g., the theories of Eric Donald Hirsch Jr.[4] and Paul Ricoeur[5] and several others who try to adapt the methods of the philosophical circle, of "hermeneutics," to the task of modern literary scholarship.

There is one more essential point that is part of the very foundation of literary scholarship and that has been and could have been developed only from a philosophical perspective: literary scholarship, as a humanstic discipline differing from the natural sciences, is by its very existence concerned with the problem of values, the theories of beauty, and various other aspects of aesthetics. (It was Roman Ingarden again who developed a remarkable theory of literary values.[6] From a different viewpoint, a theoretical foundation of aesthetics[7] as well as a theory of the practical implications of aesthetics for criticism[8] has been given by Harold Osborne.)

Second, besides the theoretical foundation of literary scholarship, practical criticism itself, i.e., the methods of literary scholarship, has been influenced by philosophy and was based on philosophy from early times. Not by accident was one of the oldest theories of literary genres developed by Aristotle and not by accident were the practical methods and the craft of criticism, in different ways, related to philosophy. One of the most crucial dialogues about the task of contemporary criticism, between Murray Krieger and W. K. Wimsatt, bears—also not by accident—a title as philosophical as "Platonism, Manichaeism, and the Resolution of Tension."[9] Since it grows out of theoretical consistency, the philosophical implications are inevitable.

Third, to the extent that philosophical ideas are implied within the literary works themselves, it is the aim of criticism to expose them and to show their function and meaning within the text. The aesthetic truth that, in literature as in any other art, the "how" is essentially more significant than the "what" has at times been overstated to such an extreme degree and with such onesidedness that it has led to practical error. It is too far-fetched to be acceptable, for example, when George Boas claims that "the ideas in poetry are usually stale and often false and no one older than sixteen would find it worth his while to read poetry merely for what it says."[10] And one just cannot take T. S. Eliot seriously when he announces that "neither Shakespeare nor Dante did any real thinking."[11]

As a matter of fact there exists a problem of truth and meaning in literature which, in spite of the fact that it refers not to empirical but to aesthetic truth, is full of philosophical considerations. One of the more interesting books of criticism in the last years has been devoted to the truth of poetry.[12] Richard Kuhns has shown truth to be a value of tragedy and has dealt not only with art as a defense of moral values but also with several other affinities between philosophy and literature.[13]

One of the most genuine philosophical considerations of the problem of truth in literature is the aspect of subjective artistic—or essayistic—truth versus objective, scientific truth. There are, however, many other aspects. One of the most difficult is the critical revelation of hidden philosophical thoughts and meanings in literary works of art. The works from Dante to James Joyce open up a wide range of possibilities.

In addition there exists the case of the philosopher who turns deliberately to literary forms—like the German Salomo Friedlaender—in order to express his philosophical thoughts in literary genres,[14] or the case of the philosopher-poet, who—like Nietzsche—wrote beautiful poems.

Needless to say, it is impossible to cover all the aspects of the affinity between literary criticism and philosophy in one volume. Contributions

are to be found, however, regarding the most important issues. After a
general introductory article by Morris Weitz on "Literature and Philosophy," there are three contributions dealing with the principles of literary scholarship and the very foundations of criticism: John Fizer explains
the epistemological theory of Roman Ingarden, Kurt Müller-Vollmer
clarifies the philosophical implications of literary interpretations, and
Eugene Falk takes up the problem of aesthetic values.

The second part of the book is concerned with the philosophical considerations of criticism itself. Jürgen Naeher tries to analyze the philosophical concept of criticism, Robert Magiola takes up an essential issue
of the Freiburg phenomenological school, Edward Wasiolek shows the
philosophical implications of establishing a sound and meaningful con-
textualism, and Meir Sternberg as a kind of Neo-Neo-Aristotelian establishes a theory of motivation as foundation of a functional model of
literary structure.

The third part of the volume presents articles concerned with philosophical problems inherent in literature itself and to be discovered and
brought to light by literary criticism. Frank Gado is concerned with the
"philosophical" in a wide sense and distinguishes in his refinement several kinds of aspects. Alain Mercier is concentrating on one particular
kind of philosophical content of (French) literature, namely esoteric traditions. M. E. Grenander, finally, is applying Neo-Aristotelian criteria
to Shakespeare's *Macbeth*.

Besides a nice cross section of the most important aspects of the
interplay of literary criticism and philosophy, the articles make significant contributions to literary scholarship. I deeply regret that such a fine
man and scholar as Morris Weitz was not able to see in print the last
piece he ever wrote. He died before the volume could appear.

JOSEPH STRELKA

Notes

1. Eugene Falk, *The Poetics of Roman Ingarden* (Chapel Hill, 1981).
2. Roman Ingarden, *Das literarische Kunstwerk* (Tübingen, 1965).
3. Roman Ingarden *Vom Erkennen des literarischen Kunstwerks*, (Tübingen, 1968).
4. Eric D. Hirsch, *Validity in Interpretation* (New Haven and London, 1967).

5. Paul Ricoeur, *Le Confit des Interpretations* (Paris, 1970).
6. Roman Ingarden, *Erlebnis, Kunstwerk und Wert* (Tübingen, 1969).
7. Harold Osborne, *Theory of Beauty* (London, 1952).
8. Harold Osborne, *Aesthetics and Criticism* (London, 1955).
9. "Platonism, Manichaeism, and the Resolution of Tension," in Murray Krieger, *The Play and Place of Criticism* (Baltimore, 1967, p. 195–218).
10. George Boas, *Philosophy and Poetry* (Wheaton College, Norton, Massachusetts, 1932), p. 9.
11. T. S. Eliot, *Selected Essays* (New York, 1932), pp. 115–116.
12. Michael Hamburger, *The Truth of Poetry* (New York, 1970). Cf. especially pp. 21–41. Cf. also Käte Hamburger, *Die Philosophie der Dichter* (Stuttgart-Berlin-Köln-Mainz, 1966).
13. Richard Kuhns, *Structures of Experience* (New York-London, 1970), pp. 3–47 and 132–174
14. Cf. Joseph Strelka, *Auf der Suche nach dem verlorenen Selbst* (Bern und München 1977, pp. 38–53.

BASIC PHILOSOPHICAL FOUNDATIONS OF
LITERARY CRITICISM

Morris Weitz

LITERATURE AND PHILOSOPHY: SENSE OR NONSENSE*

Is there really anything new to be said about the relation between literature and philosophy? Of course, one can always invent a new piece of nonsense. Certain contemporary styles of literary criticism and theory prove the point; the ever-present possibility of nonsense provides a virtual guarantee of novelty. Indeed, this seemingly inexhaustible potentiality of novelty in nonsense ought in all consistency to enjoin certain enterprising contemporary linguistic theorists to postulate, along with their innate mental structures that purportedly explain the generation of new sense, another, more powerful, structure that alone could account for our unlearned capacity for limitless nonsense.

In exploring the relation between literature and philosophy, I shall aim at something new, without nonsense—or more realistically perhaps—at a nonsense that transgresses the limits of sense by trying to say what can only be shown, if it can be shown at all, rather than at that kind of prevalent nonsense that violates both the syntax and the semantics of intelligible critical discourse.

Literature and philosophy, then, to begin, is traditionally at any rate but one species of the genus art and truth, of which another important species, especially from Wordsworth to I. A. Richards, is poetry and science. Much has been written on both the genus and its species, though not as much on literature and philosophy as one might have expected. Plato and Aristotle, among the ancients, raise the problem directly and fully, as does Sir Philip Sidney some 2000 years later. But in between there is very little: art and truth, not literature and philosophy, becomes a central issue, along with other problems concerning the arts. More surprising, there is equal neglect of the problem of how

*I wish to dedicate this essay to the nursing staff of Beth Israel Hospital, Feldberg 5, Boston, Massachusetts.

literature relates to philosophy from Sidney to Croce and I. A. Richards. The great figures of neoclassicism and of romanticism, both English and continental, have much to say about poetry, literature, criticism, and truth in literature; and some, especially the nineteenth-century German philosophers, explore voluminously the nature of art and the nature of philosophy and reality, but they are especially illuminating when they turn from abstract discussions of literature and philosophy to their concrete analyses of tragedies as examples of philosophy in literature. Even Matthew Arnold, in spite of his abiding concerns for both criticism and literature as the best that has been thought and expressed, is not directly worried about the problem of literature and philosophy. It is therefore only in the modern period, beginning with Croce and encompassing I. A. Richards, some of the New Critics, and early Santayana in his *Three Philosophical Poets*,[1] that Plato's ancient quarrel is revitalized and new answers offered as to the proper relation between literature and philosophy. Thus, in spite of the antiquity of the problem, the disciplinary rubrics Philosophy and Literature, Philosophy of Literature, and Philosophy in Literature, each of which derives from Plato's quarrel, are mainly contemporary approaches, without the solid historical grounding of other, philosophical, including aesthetic, problems.

What, now, does the tradition say about the relation between literature and philosophy? Plato begins the debate. He revives what he refers to as the ancient quarrel between poetry and philosophy; so presumably, the problem of the relation between literature and philosophy is older than Plato. Plato distinguishes poetry from philosophy. Poetry—neither he nor Aristotle has or coins a word for literature, though Aristotle fumbles for such a word at the opening of the *Poetics*—is the making of certain kinds of object that include painting, sculpture, music, and of course drama. Philosophy, though a dialectical activity, makes nothing; instead it seeks to grasp the forms: the ultimate entities of reality. What we call literature, what he calls (a species of) poetry, aims at and produces illusions or perspectives of imitations of the real. Philosophy, alone, aims at and grasps the real. Whatever the nuances, subtleties, or deviations may be in Plato's writings (some commentators even regard him as the supreme poet or maker), Plato never wavers on his fundamental and irreducible dichotomy between literature (epic, tragedy, comedy) and philosophy. In effect, he resolves the ancient quarrel not by joining literature and philosophy but by rendering them asunder once and for all as the irresolvable difference between literature as falsehood and philosophy as truth. They cannot be friends; the putative truth-claims of literature remain just that—pretenses to truth about reality that give us instead (harmful) falsehoods.

Plato does more than divorce literature from philosophy; he also introduces the powerful idea that literature is purely emotive (as well as impurely cognitive). Unlike his successors, he does not identify poetry or literature with the noncognitive, that is, as neither true nor false, only with expressive language; but he does state for the first time the important doctrine that literature, though a tissue of lies and falsehoods, is emotive. And because he regards the emotive as harmful since it is false, his rejection of literature and of any legitimate relation between literature and philosophy is complete and definitive. Whatever modifications he offers in his whole *corpus*, one of the footnotes Plato bequeathes to western thought and literary criticism is that literature can no more be married to philosophy than falsehood can to truth. It is this footnote that serves perennially as the major text in the ensuing discussions about the relation, if any, between literature and philosophy. Moreover, it is not entirely clear, even after 2500 years, that Plato's separation and his accompanying characterization and castigation of literature, together with his antecedent description and exaltation of philosophy, have been decisively refuted.

Aristotle, not Plato, in some of his dialogues according to some of his commentators, is the first to answer Plato. He agrees with Plato that philosophy seeks truth and, when it finds it, is true; and that philosophy (the contemplative life) is best. But he disagrees with Plato on what the real is that truth captures, since for him, the forms or universals that Plato dissociates from their instantiation, at least in the ordinary world of things in space and time are, he claims, precisely in this ordinary world as its generic characteristics. Philosophy, thus, seeks, among other things, the universals in things (καθόλου), not the dubious universals beyond things (εἴδη) that Plato postulates. He also agrees with Plato that literature (poetry—ποιητική) is imitative but, in a master stroke of deduction from his conception of the real, he restricts the imitative to artifacts rather than, as Plato does, construing the imitative as coextensive with all objects, artifactual and natural.

Poetry, then, Aristotle says (and literature, he implies), because it comprises imitative artifacts, contains truth. Poetry (literature) seeks and, when successful, finds a variety of basic καθόλου. He says in a famous passage that poetry (literature), which unlike history deals with what might happen, is "more scientific and serious than history": poetry can give general truths (τὰ καθόλου), history, only particular facts.

Poetry is more like philosophy than is history. But does this compliment extend to poetry (literature) as philosophy, so that both literature and philosophy aim at and achieve the same things, namely, truth about reality? Aristotle's hierarchy of the intellectual virtues in Book VI of the

Nicomachean Ethics suggests otherwise: that philosophy, which involves σοφια, differs from literature, which is merely τέχνη, a virtue that requires general truths for its proper practice but that is not, as wisdom is, directly concerned with them. Literature may be better than history; but it is not quite as good as philosophy.

Nevertheless, left-handed compliment or not, Aristotle's tribute to poetry (literature) as a repository of truths about the general or shared features of human actions and experiences is the first of many attempts to join literature with philosophy to the enhancement of the first without a necessary denigration of the second. He asks and answers affirmatively: Does literature contain philosophy, that is, general truths about general things? His answer rests upon his denial of the reality of transcendent forms. Hence, if Plato is correct that these forms constitute a necessary condition for the existence of anything else and that there is no philosophy and no truth without these forms, Aristotle's specific reply to Plato's challenge collapses. Literature cannot be joined with philosophy if the objects and truths of the latter differ radically from the imitations and opinions of the former.

Nevertheless, Aristotle's doctrine that literature can and does contain certain truths of the highest ontological order and is therefore philosophical in that sense remains a possibility and a possible defense of the joining of literature and philosophy. Transcendent forms or not, the world as we all live in it exemplifies certain generic features. Why cannot literature include these and by doing so incorporate philosophy?

After Plato and Aristotle, there is further probing into fundamental problems regarding the arts. Plotinus, Horace, Longinus, Augustine, and Thomas Aquinas, among others, introduce or debate many questions that we today recognize as aesthetic, that is, as philosophical problems about the arts. However, to repeat, there is little—I believe, perhaps in ignorance—that is of major importance on our topic of the relation between literature and philosophy until Sir Philip Sidney's *An Apology for Poetry* (1595).

This essay, in my judgment as profound in its implications as it is scintillating in its presentation, is typically Renaissance as it returns to the ancients for the union of literature and philosophy and just as atypically a naissance as it anticipates certain later, mostly modern, doctrines that divorce literature from philosophy. It obviously borrows from Aristotle and Horace; but it also implicitly points to a conception of literature that does not *state* truths but *shows* them instead, and thereby employs language that is neither true or false nor purely emotive. Literature, on this conception, contrasts sharply with philosophy, which *affirms* truths and is thereby a use of language that in its capacity to state truths (or falsehoods) differs completely from the language of literature. The ostensible emphasis on the feigned fictions and the moral efficacy of literature, stressed by both Sidney and his commentators, becomes incidental in his essay to the implicit main arguments for the two contrary possibilities of literature in relation to philosophy.

Sidney, following Aristotle and Horace, defines poetry as an art of imitation: "that is to say, a representing, counterfeiting, or figuring forth—to speak metaphorically, a speaking picture; with this end, to teach and delight." To which he adds later: ". . . it is not rhyming and versing that maketh a poet . . . But it is that feigning notable images of virtues, vices, or what else, with that delightful teaching, which must be the right describing note to know a poet by. . . ."[2]

Whether Sidney offers two definitions of poetry, one that emphasizes teaching and delight, the other, morality, or what is more likely, one definition that specifies the moral or "what else" as what poetry teaches, he does define poetry in a manner that allows it to compete with philosophy.

To be sure, Sidney does not define philosophy. However, it is clear from what he does say about it that he construes philosophy in the traditional terms of (true or false) doctrines about what is, may be, or should be, comprising as it does metaphysics, natural philosophy, and morals. Moreover, philosophy is, like poetry, an art—a practice—whose function is to proclaim truths, including but not identified with truths about how we are to live: it too claims to teach.

Sidney next locates the difference between literature and philosophy not in *what* they teach but in *how* they teach. Philosophy teaches by abstractions, morality in particular, by abstract precepts. Literature teaches by examples, by richly fabricated, feigned notable images. Philosophy proceeds by way of definition, division, and distinction, each dry as dust, that can be understood only by those few who already understand or who are too old for it to make a difference in their actions; in regard to morals, philosophy provides only knowledge of virtue, with no guide as to its practice. Poetry (literature), on the other hand, furnishes richly concrete examples that can move us to be virtuous, not merely to know the virtues. Shifting from considerations of what should be to what is, even here, Sidney claims, literature beats philosophy in their common game of getting at the essences. Consider, for example, anger. The philosopher, Sidney says, analyzes and defines it, the Stoics in particular as "a short madness." The dramatist [Sophocles], on the other hand, brings an Ajax on the stage, portrays him as whipping and slaughtering sheep, thinking them to be Greek soldiers, beaten and destroyed. Tell me, Sidney asks: "if you have not a more familiar insight into anger than finding in the Schoolmen [or the Stoics, or any other philosophers] his genus and difference." Poetry, thus *is* philosophy, but philosophy rendered richly concrete. Sidney concludes: "the poet is indeed the right popular philosopher."[3]

Poetry, then, according to Sidney, not only makes virtue attractive, but also makes truth accessible. It differs from philosophy not in its concern with truth, since it conveys all the truths that philosophy does, but it conveys the truth more effectively. What Sidney strongly suggests, then, is that both philosophy and literature contain truths: about what should be and about what is. So they can be, are, and should be joined. Where they differ is that philosophy states whereas literature shows truths. And because showing is more revealing and more moving than saying, literature is superior. Examples, richly invented one might add, are more vivid, convincing, and appealing than abstractions, however persuasively argued. Poetry, Sidney sums up in his defense of poetry against its detractors, is not ". . . an art of lies, but of true doctrine."

How, now, we may ask, can poetry (literature) be an art of true *doctrine* if poetry shows but does not state truths? Are feigned notable images, indeed any image or representation, true doctrine?

Sidney offers an answer: ". . . I think truly, that of all writers under the sun the poet is the least liar, and, though he would, as a poet can scarcely be a liar . . . for the poet, he nothing affirms, and therefore never lieth."

If poetry affirms nothing—contains no statements, true or false, about the world as it is or should be—how can it be an art of true doctrine? It cannot. Poetry (literature) can show what is or what should be, but it says, states nothing true (or false).

On this view, literature and philosophy are radically distinct. The first is an art of representation, the second, an art of statement. Truth (and falsity) belong to philosophy, not to literature. The dramatist can still show us anger as a short madness, but he cannot, without affirmation, state what it is or present an insight into or a true doctrine of anger as a short madness. Should he do so, on Sidney's second account of poetry, the dramatist abandons poetry, unconcerned with truth, for philosophy, concerned only with truth. Literature differs from philosophy no longer as competing modes of truth but as radically distinct modes, the one as neither true nor false but feigned representation, the other as either true or false statement. Sidney cannot have it both ways: either literature and philosophy can, are, and should be joined in their mutual quest for affirmed true doctrine or they cannot, are not, and should not be united in their separate quests for feigned fictions and true doctrine.

If, as Ben Jonson puts it,

> For he knows poet never credit gained
> By writing truths, but things like truths, well feigned,[4]

or as Francis Bacon says, "poetry is feigned history," then what Sidney implies in his essay, with Jonson and Bacon, is close to Archibald MacLeish's admonition, centuries after Sidney:

> A poem should be equal to:
> Not true . . .
> A poem should not mean
> But be.[5]

Plato claims that Poetry (literature) pretends to be true and always fails. Aristotle counters that literature pretends to be true and often succeeds. Sidney agrees with Aristotle in one mood but rejects both Plato and Aristotle in his other mood. What, now, are some of the other positions on the relation between literature and philosophy that are formulated or suggested by the tradition?

Wordsworth's Preface to the Second Edition of the *Lyrical Ballads* (1800) is, I think, the first new document, after Sidney, on the relation between philosophy and literature, as indeed it is the first major statement on the opposition of science and poetry.

To praise the originality of the Preface, however, is in no way to discredit the importance of Boileau, Dryden, Pope, Johnson, and other neoclassicists; rather, it is to suggest that their contributions lie elsewhere. On the generic issue of art and truth, they remain Aristotelians and because of their acceptance of the delight as well as the instruction of literature, they are good Horatians too. Boileau's "Rien n'est beau que le vrai: le vrai seul est aimable";[6] Corneille's commitment to *le vraisemblable* and to *le nécessaire*; Dryden's insistence on drama as "a just and lively image of human nature, representing its passions and humours, and the changes of fortune to which it is subject, for the delight and instruction of mankind;" Pope's

> First follow nature, and your judgment frame
> By her just standard, which is still the same.
> Unerring NATURE, still divinely bright,
> One clear, unchang'd, and universal light;[7]

Lessing's adherence to art as *Nachahmung* and to the mimetic principle even as he challenges the doctrine of *ut pictura poesis*; and Johnson's "Nothing can please many, and please long, but just representations of general nature"[8]—whether they epitomize their individual author's views on the relation of art and truth or do not—are but variations on the Aristotelian *cum* Horatian theme of art as delightful instruction in general truths about nature. These authors may differ about art and truth and they disagree about nature. But they never demur from the requirement, hence legitimacy, of literature joined with philosophy in the common pursuit of truth about the world. Thus, the whole neoclassic aesthetic, diverse as it is, concurs on the main thesis that literature and philosophy, though distinct in their aims and effects, can be joined without the detriment at least of literature but without any obvious enhancement to philosophy.

Wordsworth's Preface is "a systematic defence of the theory upon which the Poems [*Lyrical Ballads*] were written."[9] Both the theory and its defense are universally recognized as the first of the great credos of English Romanticism, the second being Coleridge's *Biographia Literaria* (1817). The Preface contains much of importance to historians on the proper subjects of diction in Wordsworth's experimentations with poetry. Of central concern to us, however, is what he says or implies about poetry and its relation to philosophy. In regard to this topic, of major significance is his shift from the putative opposition of poetry and philosophy to his stated quarrel between poetry and science, the latter of which he identifies with "matters of fact"; although even here, he projects a future of reconciliation once science divests itself of its purely quantitative approach to recognize the intrinsically subjective, qualitative content of true scientific knowledge.

It is this theme of reconciliation and unification of human faculties and of nature that pervades Wordsworth's critical theory and poetry. Human feelings, passions, and emotions, directly experienced and subsequently enlarged by an imagination that modifies and synthesizes our sensations, images, feelings, and thought, make up poetry and its unified vision of a unified and ordered world.

There is thus for Wordsworth a true picture of poetry that corresponds to the truth about the world: its richly concrete qualitative unity. Wordsworth introduces a number of complications and qualifications but the gist of his theory, and that which has most relevance to us, is that poetry in its verbal, imaginative unity expresses and reflects the nonverbal concrete order of the world. Poetry is a philosophically true rendition of the philosophically true character of the world. His *Lyrical Ballads*, unlike much traditional poetry that he even questions as poetry, are natural expressions of the true unities of feeling and thought—not artificial, ornamental, contrived metric or nonmetric composition—of certain concrete orders of feeling and thought in the world. Poetry—his poetry—is expression that delights as well as avers philosophical truth about reality

Thus, it is not accurate to reduce Wordsworth's theory to the idea that poetic truth is emotional knowledge or a transcendent vision or revelation of the nature of things. For he believes that poetry is straightforward linguistic expression that in its closeness to real speech is natural, therefore true to this speech, and that it is truly about man in nature. Wordsworth employs both "true to" and, more important, "truth about," in his statement about the nature of poetry in relation to the world. Poetry is true in the sense of "natural" or "true to" our expression of contemplated passion and, at the same time, is "true about" these experiences. This, I think, is the correct as well as fairest interpretation of Wordsworth's contribution to the relation between poetry and philosophy as he promotes their union in the same way that he seeks unity and synthesis in all things. At any rate, this is how I read the relevant portions of his Preface and especially its marvelous, frequently quoted, remarks: the poet ". . . has a greater knowledge of human nature, and a more comprehensive soul, than are supposed to be common among mankind." "For all good poetry is the spontaneous overflow of powerful feelings," to which he adds the important qualification: "it takes its origin from emotion recollected in tranquillity: the emotion is contemplated till, by a species of reaction, the tranquillity gradually disappears, and an emotion, kindred to that which was before the subject of contemplation, is gradually produced, and does itself actually exist in the mind."[10] ". . . Poetry is the most philosophic of all writing: . . . its object is truth, not individual and local, but general, and operative; not standing upon external testimony, but carried alive into the heart by passion; truth which is its own testimony . . . Poetry is the image of man and nature . . . the poet writes under one restriction only, namely, the necessity of giving immediate pleasure to a human Being . . ."". . . The Man of science seeks truth as a remote and unknown benefactor; he cherishes and loves it in his solitude: the Poet, singing a song in which all human beings join with him, rejoices in the presence of truth as our visible friend and hourly companion. Poetry is the breath and finer spirit of all knowledge; it is the impassioned expression which is in the countenance of all Science."[11]

Like Coleridge (and others), we may reject much of the Preface, especially Wordsworth's naive view that poetic diction is the ordinary language of ordinary men; but what remains hard-headed and unsentimental, perhaps even unromantic in its rejection of any pathetic fallacy, is Wordsworth's very clear theory about how one kind of poetry (that he takes, rightly or wrongly, to be the only kind) is, as poetry, true to one kind of reality (again, that he takes to be the only kind). If the world is a particular kind of concrete unity, then a poetry that expresses, imitates, or represents it is true in precisely the sense that a poetry (or poetic pretense) that rejects or distorts this unity is false. In the end, Wordsworth's argument for the union, not identity, of poetry and philosophy rests upon his specific, not so implausible, theory and philosophy of the world itself. We can ask no more of an adequate theory of the relation between poetry (or literature) and philosophy, even if we cannot share the metaphysics that sponsors and supports it. Wordsworth, like Johnson, believes that poetry provides knowledge of certain general truths about general facts. To call this claim to knowledge irrational intuition or revelation is to do injustice both to the English language and to Wordsworth; to label it "insight" is to commend it as knowledge, not to applaud or castigate it as something higher than or different from knowledge. Finally, to claim, as some commentators do, that Wordsworth identifies truth with sincerity and thereby changes the question "Does poetry (literature) contain truths about the world?" to "Is poetry sincere?" is to conflate the poetic process with its product. The poet is sincere, true to himself, his feelings, and thoughts; but his poetry is true (or false), as he is sincere, when and only when it expresses and communicates to others the requisite unity of feeling and thought that constitutes reality.

Coleridge, like Wordsworth, celebrates the union of poetry and philosophy. He says of Wordsworth's poetry that it is "the union of deep feeling with profound thought,"[12] which he generalizes into a principle in his assessment of Shakespeare: "No man was yet a great poet without being at the same time a profound philosopher."[13]

But Coleridge challenges Wordsworth's theory of poetry and his philosophy of nature. Wordsworth, he claims, is wrong in his naive theory of poetic diction and he is inadequate in his metaphysics in that he neglects the fundamental organic character of reality. More important, however, than these two objections is Coleridge's deep feeling and profound thought that Wordsworth does not grasp the full significance of union as an organic fusing of elements rather than as a mechanical juxtaposition of compatible, even if discordant, elements. For the defining principle of union to Coleridge is the secondary imagination that he struggles, perhaps in vain, to formulate and clarify, an imagination that germinates rather than fructifies (that he calls the primary imagination). In this regard, Coleridge relates to Wordsworth as Kant's Second Edition Deduction of the Categories in the *Critique of Pure Reason* does to the First Edition Deduction. Kant, too, sees that without the (Second Edition) transcendental synthetic unity of apperception as the noncategorical, nonconceptual basis, there can be no unifying principle of experience that can overcome the limitations of his First Edition Threefold Synthesis of Knowledge.

The analogy to Kant is meant to be exact. Coleridge realizes that Wordsworth's (and traditional) conceptions of the imagination as a synthesizing faculty cannot account for the originative and organically unifying "permeative, blending, and fusing" power of the imagination. Coleridge's theory of the secondary imagination, vague and maddeningly brief as is his account of it, is nevertheless the absolute center of Coleridge's theory of poetry (literature) and of a philosophy that purports to be a true metaphysics of art and nature; and, most important for our topic, of the very role of philosophy in literature.

Although Coleridge comes close to identifying art and nature, both being like growing plants; the concept allows him to hold on to a mimetic view of art as an imitation of the processes of nature; and although he comes close to identifying poetry and philosophy, he refuses to do so. Poetry, he contends, gives us pleasure, derived both from its separate parts and as individual wholes; philosophy, like science, on the other hand, seeks only truth about the world, however organic that truth must be about an organic world. Poetry, alone, seeks a union—a fusion, not a juxtaposition—of passion, truth, and pleasure. It is, says Coleridge in one of his occasional pieces, the "union of passion with thought and pleasure which constitutes the essence of all poetry."[14]

There is little to say in favor of Coleridge's organicism as the fundamental metaphysical principle, derived no doubt from Schelling's aesthetic philosophy of nature. We can safely ignore it, even though Coleridge does not, contending that the organic in art replicates the organic in nature. But this view presupposes that art and nature are themselves organically or internally related, which they are not.

On the other hand, there is everything to say for Coleridge's organicism as a fundamental aesthetic principle. That each item in a work of art is interrelated, as a harmony of concordant and of discordant elements, and that this unifying, processive character can best be explained by an imagination that permeates, blends, and fuses is one of the few great contributions in the history of aesthetics or the philosophy of art.

As attractive as Coleridge's organic theory of art is, it is in its application by him that the theory comes to glorious life, as his criticisms of the dramas of Shakespeare—even as the (for the most part) reports and marginalia they are—so beautifully reveals. For me, as for many others, his Shakespearean criticism is one of the great moments in the history of literary criticism. All of it, whether we quarrel with parts of it, for example his treatment of Hamlet, or with the whole of it, is replete with his aesthetics of organicism. He sees each of the plays as germinating from the first scenes and as individual organic wholes, growing like a plant, being born and being nourished by an imagination that fuses everything, even the discordants, that Keats is later to refer to as the disagreeables that evaporate in the work "from their being in close relationship to Beauty and Truth." Omnipresent Deity or not, Shakespeare, for Coleridge, is the supreme example of the union of passion, pleasure, and thought.

We cannot here go into the details of his assessment of Shakespeare. In any case, I have done this elsewhere. Suffice it to say that, for Coleridge, philosophy—profound, true thoughts about the world—enters into literature exactly as do the other elements of character, plot, dialogue, etc. Of course literature relates to philosophy: it joins them not by juxtaposing them but by fusing them into an organic whole that is the individual work of art. Coleridge sees as clearly as anyone before or after him that the relation between philosophy and literature is one in which the philosophy is in the literature, when it is, in exactly the same sense in which the other distinguishable but not separable elements are, germinating and contributing to the whole interrelated work. No wonder that he celebrates the union of poetry (literature) and philosophy! It is also he who invents and legitimizes Philosophy in Literature as a proper discipline with a proper subject. We can applaud the achievement without accepting the dubious union of art and nature that Coleridge insists on. Literature can be organic without the nature it depicts being itself organic and organically related to the literature that depicts it. Moreover, I think that Coleridge agrees with me: for the two principles of his criticism of Shakespeare—that the dramas are illusory and enjoin a willing suspension of disbelief that he calls poetic faith and that the dramas are true to life (which feature enjoins belief, not suspension of belief or disbelief)—are themselves as discordant as they are fundamental. Is Coleridge able to reconcile these disagreeables as he believes Shakespeare and poetry do? I think not. In the end, Coleridge is terribly torn between the organic in art as a replication of the organic in nature and the organic in art as a deviation from the organic in nature. Both art and nature may grow like plants; but in art the growth is accompanied and fused by a pruning secondary imagination, a power that is entirely lacking in the plant of nature. No one, I submit, is more aware of this difference than Coleridge, as his specific exegeses of the various movements in the plays of Shakespeare show again and again.

After Coleridge's Copernican Revolution against traditional conceptions of the relation between literature and philosophy, a revolution that locates the planet of philosophy in the universe of literature rather than, as the tradition has it, a planet revolving around and being attracted to

or repelled by the independent planet of literature—indeed, a revolution that is less vulnerable than Kant's "Copernican Revolution" or, for
that matter, as it has turned out, Copernicus'—the offerings on our topic
are slim, at least in comparison with Coleridge's. Lamb, Hazlitt,
Shelley, De Quincey, and J. S. Mill provide addenda to the problem of
poetry (literature), truth, science, and philosophy. Hazlitt's view of poetry as the language of the imagination that ". . . is not the less true to
nature, because it is false in point of fact; but so much the more true and
natural, if it conveys the impression which the object under the influence of passion makes on the mind" ("On Poetry in General") is worth
noting. So is De Quincey's famous distinction between the literature of
knowledge and the literature of power, the latter of which "is a rarer
thing than truth—namely *power* or deep sympathy with truth."[15]
Shelley's "A Defence of Poetry" is a great paean to poetry which claims,
without much argument but with much eloquent exhortation, that poetry reaches after eternal truth, that Shakespeare, Dante, and Milton,
for example, "are philosophers of the very loftiest power," that poetry
"is at once the center and circumference of knowledge," and that "Poets
are the unacknowledged legislators of the world."[16] Mill's essay,
"Thoughts on Poetry and its Varieties" (1833), ten years before his
Logic, is of great fascination because it is written by a philosopher who,
as a no-nonsense nominalist, rejects the traditional search for real definitions of the genus differentia or essence variety and yet who, in his
writing on poetry, lays down as exact and real a definition of poetry as
has ever been given, in which he reduces poetry—"true poetry"—to the
soliloquizing lyric, meant to be not heard but overheard, and best exemplified in Shelley, not Wordsworth, where all is the truth of human
feeling. In a language that out-romanticizes the romantics, Mill characterizes poetry—its inner essence—as the "delineation of the deeper and
more secret workings of human emotion," as "feeling confessing itself to
itself, in moments of solitude," as "the natural fruit of solitude and
meditation," as "impassioned truth," in which the truth of poetry "is to
paint the human soul truly," not "to give a true picture of life," and,
finally, as "Feeling itself, employing Thought only as the medium of its
expression." As audacious and legislative as his definition of poetry is,
his application of it to the purely poetic as against the oratory of music,
especially to the *Dove sono* in Mozart's *The Marriage of Figaro*—"Who
can imagine 'Dove sono' *heard*? We imagine it *over*heard"—redeems
all.[17]

Only Keats, among the romantics after Wordsworth and Coleridge,
makes a major contribution. His notion of negative capability is on a par
with Coleridge's notion of the secondary imagination as the germinating

and integrating force of literature. However, because his notion applies more to the difference between philosophy in literature as against the philosophy in philosophy than it does to the relation of literature and philosophy—our present topic—I shall return to his notion later, as one of the brilliant ways of understanding the difference not between literature and philosophy but the difference between philosophy in literature and the philosophy in traditional philosophy.

Of the continental theorists I have said and will say nothing about the French and Italians, although Leopardi's radical dichotomy between poetry (literature) and philosophy is worth remembering: "the more poetry is philosophical, the less it is poetry . . . Philosophy wants truth, poetry falsity and illusion. Philosophy harms and destroys poetry . . . There is an unsurpassable barrier, a sworn and mortal enmity between them, which cannot be abolished, reconciled or disguised"[18]

The Germans are another story. From Lessing and earlier writers, through Goethe, Schiller, Schelling, the Schlegels, to the philosophers Hegel, Schopenhauer, and Nietzsche, there is a running concern for the metaphysics of art, poetry, literature, life, nature, reality, and of philosophy itself. There may even be some profoundly new ideas on the relation of literature to philosophy. But I must leave this possibility to the future historian who has yet to write the first book on this fascinating, for the most part neglected, subject. For me, as I have already indicated, the great contribution of these Germans to the problem of how literature relates to philosophy is not in their abstract metaphysical speculations, brilliant as they are, but in their concrete discussions of the tragic in the tragedies they discuss. Hegel, for example, shows how the dialectic works best in philosophy and literature when he applies it to some of the ancient Greek tragedies, especially his exemplar, *Antigone*. Here we are offered full illustrations of how philosophy joins with literature. Nevertheless, because these philosophers are more interested in the metaphysics of tragedy as an abstract philosophical problem than they are in elucidating the tragic in the tragedies they discuss, like most philosophers who deal with literature, they commit the heresy of paraphrase, by abstracting the tragic from the tragedies in order to explore the tragic rather than the actual literary tragedies. As a result, they do philosophy of literature, not philosophy in literature. A. W. Schlegel, perhaps, is the great exception, as his lectures on Shakespeare's tragedies amply testify. But then he is a critic, not a philosopher.

This brings us to Arnold and the moderns. Arnold has many memorable words and phrases, among them "touchstone," "sweetness and light," and "culture and anarchy"; there are also many memorable ideas, such as his notion of literature "as the best that has been thought and said," his definition of criticism as "a disinterested endeavour to learn and propagate the best that is known and thought in the world," his statement of the function of criticism and of the critical power in all knowledge as "to see the object as in itself it really is," and his conviction "that poetry [literature] is at bottom a criticism of life."[19] In his essay "Literature and Science," Arnold meets their quarrel with an attempt to reconcile them through the reminder that both are in the same business of acquiring and transmitting knowledge. Presumably this would be his answer too to Plato's ancient quarrel between philosophy and poetry.

Unless we become bewitched by any of these words, phrases, or ideas, and treat them as touchstones of Arnold's achievement as a critic, each of them is, even if memorable, vulnerable, and some of them, such as his ideas of literature, criticism, and poetry, are downright unacceptable. It is not so much that these doctrines are false, which they are; rather, that if they are (taken to be) true, they reduce poetry, literature, and criticism to mockeries of what they so heterogeneously are.

What about Arnold's (implicit) idea of the relation between literature and philosophy, once we skip over his facile reconciliation of literature and science and look elsewhere? I know of no essay in which he tackles the problem head-on. However, there is an answer or at least the suggestion of one in his essay on Wordsworth, in which he introduces his selection, *Poems of Wordsworth* (1879).

Poetry, he begins, ". . . is nothing less than the most perfect speech of man, that in which he comes nearest to being able to utter the truth. It is no small thing, therefore, to succeed eminently in poetry." To this he adds: ". . . the noble and profound application of ideas to life is the most essential part of poetic greatness. . . . A great poet receives his distinctive character of superiority from his application under the conditions immutably fixed by the laws of poetic beauty and poetic truth, from his application, I say, to his subject, whatever it may be, of the ideas 'On man, on nature, and on human life.' "[20]

Many poets meet this criterion, including, Arnold contends, Wordsworth, at least in his best poems. Indeed, Arnold claims, Wordsworth is superior to any of his contemporaries, English and continental, because "he deals with more of *life* than they do; he deals with *life* as a whole, more powerfully." However, it is not, as some say, Wordsworth's philosophy of life, but his poetry about man, nature, and human life, that makes him great. We read him not for his abstract ideas but for ". . . the extraordinary power with which Wordsworth feels the joy offered to us in nature, the joy offered to us in the simple primary affections and duties: . . . the extraordinary power with which, in case

after case, he shows us this joy, and renders it so as to make us share
it. . . ." Arnold concludes: "Wherever we meet with the successful balance in Wordsworth, of profound truth of subject with profound truth of
execution, he is unique." It is therefore his poetry that "is the reality,
his philosophy . . . is illusion."[21] And what is true of Wordsworth, Arnold suggests, is true of all great poetry, that its reality is in its concrete
criticism of life, not in its abstract statement of philosophical ideas.

As consistent as Arnold's criteria of poetic greatness in Wordsworth
are with Arnold's overall conception of poetry as a criticism of life, and
as dubious as these criteria may be as unchallengeable ones or as sole
criteria of poetic greatness, Arnold implies at least the central idea that
the great difference between literature and philosophy—both deeply
concerned with truth—is that the truth of literature lies in the truth of
concrete execution of ideas whereas the truth of philosophy is abstract.
And if this is so, Arnold, in the end, simply reiterates one version of the
relation between literature and philosophy: both deal with truth, the
one with its concrete immediacy of feeling, the other with its abstract
remoteness of thought. There is truth in literature, but no philosophy.
Philosophy and literature, therefore, remain distinct. Coleridge's implicit contention that there can be philosophy in literature, just as there
can be character, plot, or dialogue in drama, is forsaken for the more
traditional view that though poetry may be more philosophical than
history in its general truths, it is not less philosophical than philosophy.
Instead, poetry is not like philosophy or philosophical at all. Philosophy
in literature must be an illusion.

That there is or can be philosophy in literature is an illusion is also the
cardinal tenet of at least two of the moderns who deal with the relation
of literature to philosophy: Benedetto Croce and I. A. Richards. And, if
my reading of Arnold is correct, Arnold anticipates the modern radical
divorce between philosophy and literature as much as he sums up one
version of the Aristotelian tradition. For both Croce and Richards present powerful indictments against the joining of literature and philosophy in any harmonious way. Whether their arguments for their indictments are as powerful as their indictments is another story. Croce makes
his case by demanding a radical distinction between art and philosophy
in his hierarchy of knowledge; Richard makes his case by insisting upon
a radical distinction between the two fundamental uses of language: the
emotive versus the symbolic or descriptive or referential. Croce's not
implausible conclusion[22] that art (literature) is not philosophy—that the
expressive, intuitive is not the conceptual—rests upon the entirely implausible premise that the aesthetic, the intuitive, the expressive—that
is, art—is nonconceptual, a kind of unmediated immediate experience, a

knowledge by acquaintance, which because it is intuition without conceptualization, is incoherent. Richards' equally plausible conclusion[23]
that science or philosophy and poetry are two distinct kinds of utterance, the one, true-false, the other, affective, rests upon the unacceptable premise that there are these two radically distinct and different
kinds of utterance. Richards' emotive-symbolic distinction, a direct influence on both Logical Positivism and C. L. Stevenson's metaethics,
reduces the many different kinds of use of utterances—what today we
call Speech Acts—to an arbitrary two and an equally arbitrary radical
division between them. For there are many different kinds of uses of
language whose variety cannot be reduced to any dichotomy of expressing or emoting and describing or referring.

But deeper than this objection is that Richards, like the Positivists,
Stevenson, and others, simply assumes that the convention for construing sentences as statements and therefore as true-false scientific or
philosophical claims is fixed in such a manner that one can easily distinguish the sentences of literature from the sentence-statements of science
and philosophy. It may very well be that there is such a convention for
converting the sentences of science and philosophy into statements. But
although there is a similar convention for reading the sentences of literature as sentences, not statements, the convention Richards subscribes
to, it is precisely this convention that is debatable and exchangeable;
indeed, it goes right to the heart of the whole problem of philosophy
and literature. With the sentences of science or of philosophy, we do not
ask, Are they statements? That they are is built into our notions of
science and philosophy. But with the sentences of literature—of poems,
dramas, novels—there is this question, "Are they, or at any rate some of
them, statements?" To say that literature is not philosophy or science,
on Richards' or any linguistic account, is in effect to deny that the
sentences of literature are in any sense statements. This denial purports
to be based upon the description of the function of the sentences of
literature. It is nothing of the kind; the denial is not the factual dis-
claimer that the sentences we read in literature are statements, it is the
normative recommendation not to take them as statements, which we
may accept or reject, an option not open to us with the sentences in
science or philosophy.

Richards' program, then, and the whole dichotomy between literature
and science or philosophy conflates the injunction against the reading of
a certain class of sentences as statements with a mythical factual description of that class, that it contains no statements. Whether the sentences
in literary works are or are not statements revolves around two equally
powerful conventions, unlike the one convention that governs the sen-

tences of science and philosophy. There may be no philosophy in literature. But the argument that there is none cannot rest on the incoherent
premise of Croce's nonconceptual immediate knowledge or the confused
and arbitrary premise of Richards' emotive as against symbolic use of
language.

So much for our brief and ever so cursory survey of some of the major
traditional positions taken on the relation between literature and philosophy. These range from the view, best stated by Plato, reiterated by
Sidney in one of his moods, and most recently revitalized by Croce and
Richards and their numerous, if diverse, followers, that literature and
philosophy are radically distinct enterprises which cannot be joined
without the detriment of both and without the enhancement of either,
to the view, first stated by Aristotle, repeated by Sidney in his major
mood and by many others in different ways, that they can be joined
without compromising either and perhaps with the enhancement of
both. In between are views that literature, as insight, revelation, or
intuition, is the higher philosophy; that literature is concrete philosophy; that literature includes or may include philosophy; and so on. And
throughout there hovers the whole problem of art and truth. Rather
than entering once again into this interminable debate, I wish now to
argue for the aesthetic legitimacy of philosophy in the works that contain
it. I want to defend the presence of philosophy in literature and the
happy joining of them. This is my topic, the academic subject of which is
Philosophy in Literature. I shall say no more about the topics of philosophy and literature or philosophy of literature, except that, at least to me,
as academic subjects, Philosophy and Literature and Philosophy of Literature are closer to academic entrepeneurism and philosophical imperi-
alism than they are to genuine subjects of inquiry. As academic subjects,
the first strikes me as a part of the history of ideas, and the second as the
exploitation of literature for the promotion of concrete examples for
philosophy. Neither, I think, serves the purpose of enriching our understanding of literature as works of art.

I understand by Philosophy in Literature two related theses: (1) that
some works of literature, certainly not necessarily all, contain philosophical ideas that are as integral to these works as any of their other
constituents; and (2) that there is a place in literary criticism for the
aesthetic articulation of these ideas. More specifically, I find it fruitful to
ask of any work of literature: "Does it have any philosophical ideas?" If it
does, "How do they get into the work?" and "What aesthetic contribution do they make to the work?"

In asking the first question, we must distinguish between a philosophical theme and a philosophical thesis. For example, a novel, say,

Anna Karenina, may have many philosophical themes, among them that we are not to blame, hence not to be judged, for what we do—a theme that is voiced by all the major characters; or that *laissez-faire* is the best philosophy of life, which is exemplified by Oblonsky. But it is not always clear that a philosophical theme, however much it is expressed, serves as a philosophical thesis; neither of these two themes, for example, can be convincingly read as Tolstoy's truth-claim about human life in *Anna Karenina*. In fact, the philosophical thesis, at least on my reading of the novel, is not even expressed on the printed pages of the novel but must be elicited from the plot in relation to the other elements. I am also aware of powerful and persuasive arguments by modern aestheticians against the distinction between theme and thesis in literature. All of these arguments, I believe, rest, as do the arguments against the distinction between sentence and statement in literature, on a confusion of the factual question "Are there philosophical theses (statements) in literature?" with the normative question "Ought we, when the plot, characters, dialogue, authorial interpolations, tone, and themes are described and explained in a certain way, to construe one or other of the themes (sentences) as *a* or *the* philosophical thesis (statement) in the whole work?" In regard to this normative question, it seems to me that there is no compelling reason for a negative reply and every good reason for an affirmative answer, provided that we are able to accommodate false as well as true philosophical theses (statements) in those works that have or imply them.

My model for philosophical literary criticism is, of course, Coleridge's organic aesthetics (without the metaphysics). My more immediate model is a form of the imagistic criticism of Shakespeare's plays. Traditionally—though the tradition is quite recent—the imagistic approach to Shakespeare displays the same conflict over reductionism as philosophy in literature in contrast to philosophy abstracted from—philosophy of—literature, best seen in the work of Caroline Spurgeon and Wolfgang Clemen. Both of these fine critics explore the imagery of each of the plays. Spurgeon, however, reduces the whole meaning of the play to its dominant image; Clemen, on the other hand, regards the imagery as but one aspect of each of the dramas, sometimes central, sometimes not, but, in any case, a contributing element to the whole drama, which cannot be reduced to any central element, including the imagery. For him, as for Coleridge (and others), the play's the thing, not the imagery. So, too, for me, the literary work is central, not its philosophical theme or thesis, which may or may not be dominant (or even present) in any particular work.

In a number of essays I have tried—by way of examples, the only way philosophy in literature can vindicate itself—to practice philosophical literary criticism as a branch of literary criticism, not as a part of philosophy. Whether successfully or not, I have tried to show that Voltaire's *Candide*, Shakespeare's *Hamlet* and *King Lear*, Tolstoy's *Anna Karenina*, Proust's *A la recherche du temps perdu*, and Eliot's *Four Quartets* contain philosophical themes and theses: how these are brought into these works and what aesthetic difference these make to the works. This enterprise, I hope, justifies philosophy in literature, both in literature and philosophy, without reducing the one to the other and with the one interrelatedly contributing to the other. I have also tried to show, again by example, this time with another of Shakespeare's great tragedies, *Antony and Cleopatra*, that there can be and are great works of literature without philosophical theses. (I am also convinced that there can be and are great literary works, lyrics, for instance, that have no and need have no philosophical themes. Literature without any philosophy is therefore possible and, indeed, actual, in spite of certain philosophers' dogma that *all* art, including literature, must be philosophical and true.)

Let me now attempt to show how certain literary works not only contain philosophy but a philosophy that in its truth gets at the facts of nature and experience in a way that philosophy proper that deals with the same facts presents falsehoods about them. To reverse Plato's charge, then, I wish to argue that some philosophy can be said to be false in competition with some philosophy in literature that is true.

I begin with that paradigm of both philosophy and literature, tragedy. To say that x is a tragedy or that y is tragic is, whatever else it is or comes to include in its reference, an indisputable example of a statement about a literary work and a statement about human life. In any case, there exists a number of dramatic works by Aeschylus, Sophocles, and Euripides that are ancient Greek tragedies, and that serve to locate the home base of the concept of tragedy. Now, however these have been analyzed and assessed, from Plato and Aristotle to the present, they are, each of them, indisputable members of the class of tragedy. They are paradigms of the genre of tragedy. But because they are paradigms, they need not be such in virtue of some paradigm set of properties that they all share and must share in order to be legitimate members of the genre. It is this unwarranted assumption, reinforced by Plato's dogma that things called by the same name must have a common defining core, that has, from Aristotle on, given rise to competing theories of tragedy, each of which holds that it and it alone captures the essence of all the paradigms. The assumption implies that if x is an indisputable, paradigmatic, home-base example of dramatic tragedy, then *why* x is tragic can also be answered definitively by a paradigmatic property. But the fact is that agreement on paradigm examples of dramatic tragedies has never yielded an agreed-upon set of paradigm properties common to and determining the tragic in these tragedies. Thus, as absurd as, for example, "Is *Oedipus Rex* a tragedy or tragic?" is, "Why is *Oedipus Rex* a tragedy or tragic?" is as alive today as it was to Aristotle. What this suggests is that these ancient Greek tragedies are tragedies even though the tragic in them is variously interpretable and not necessarily some univocal, defining tragic property that guarantees their being tragedies.

Now, however variously interpretable the tragic is in the extant tragedies of Aeschylus, Sophocles, and Euripides, one thing is clear and cannot be denied: that these dramas show, say, or imply something about a tragic fact in the world of man's existence. Greek tragedy, whatever else it is, is a metaphysical view about a nondramatic tragic fact in the world, which exists independently of its mimetic depiction in the tragedies. Whether this tragic fact is fate, transgression of moral or theological law, human fragility or vulnerability, the celebration of the mystery of human life, or *arete* shining through *hamartia* and suffering, transcending them; that is, however variously interpretable all of the tragedies are as a group or even severally, they point unmistakenly to an undeniable, irresolvable tragic fact in the world. Aeschylus, Sophocles, and Euripides make or imply metaphysical statements about the tragic in their dramatic tragedies, even if these statements or the critical commentary about them do not reduce to a univocal claim about what is really tragic. Each of them, all of them, characterize the tragic fact that—whether homogeneous or (as I think) heterogeneous—*is* a fact in the world, undeniable by any putatively true picture or description of the world. The tragic exists as an ultimate, brute, sometimes brutal, ontological fact. Our three dramatists make truth-claims about this tragic fact that, however, disagreement is possible on exactly what it is, cannot be eradicated or rejected.

Now, if we turn from the Greek tragedies to the Greek philosophers, what do we find in regard to this ultimate, irreducible tragic fact? Plato reluctantly recognizes the tragic in the world—suffering, evil, etc., as constituents of the world of appearances or becoming—but argues that it can and must be overcome by reason. Aristotle restricts the tragic to the stage, construing it only as a representation of the passage from happiness to misery, a passage that also reason can overcome. If we agree that the tragic, however variously conceivable it is, is something irredeemable—a brute fact in the world—then surely Greek tragedy proclaims a philosophical truth about the world that Greek philosophy denies. Greek tragedy, thus, is not only a clear case of philosophy in literature, or a conception of what is tragic in life as a constituent in the tragedies, but is also, I think, a striking victory of literature over philosophy in the common pursuit of truth about the way things are.

Aeschylus, Sophocles, and Euripides dramatize the tragic fact that may be understood but cannot be overcome, not even by resignation, acceptance, or reason. Both Plato and Aristotle agree that there is such a tragic fact however they describe it or explain it away, but they deny that it is ultimate and cannot be overcome by the dialectic of human reason. Who is right? It seems to me that, on this issue of the power of reason being strong enough to mitigate, or to overcome, or to transcend the tragic in human life, that Plato and Aristotle speak falsely or naively in a way that our three tragedians speak truly and realistically about the world and man's destiny in it. If there is anything tragic in the world, the Greek literature of tragedy speaks more *philosophical* truth than Greek philosophy. Aristotle, thus, should have said: "Poetry may be more philosophical than history but it is not, at least when it comes to philosophical claims about the καθόλου of the tragic, less true than philosophy, it is more." In this ancient quarrel between philosophy and poetry, the poets win: by honesty, by truth, by knowledge. Greek tragic poetry is philosophically true; Greek philosophy of tragedy is false. Here in Greek tragedy, philosophy in literature integrates and, if only philosophy could learn from it, enhances philosophy as much as it does literature by expanding the range of philosophical truths about the world.

What about Shakespeare, another paradigm of literature and, for many, of philosophy as well? Is there a philosophy or philosophical thesis in Shakespeare's work? Wholesale affirmative as well as negative answers have been equally disastrous. That Shakespeare presents a unified system of ideas about life and the world simply will not stand up to the diversity of ideas in his plays. That Shakespeare has no philosophy, offers no profound claims about man, a view put forth by no less a poet and critic than T. S. Eliot in his contrast of Dante as a poet-thinker with Shakespeare as a dramatist-poet, is also suspect when we turn to some of the individual plays. *Hamlet* and especially *King Lear* dramatize themes and suggest theses that in their profundity are not only philosophical but rival, as the writers of Greek tragedy did their philosophical contemporaries, the naive and pragmatic optimism and pessimism of his age.

We may also ask of Shakespeare, "Are any of his tragedies without a philosophy, that is, without a thesis about man in his world?" *Antony and Cleopatra*, I think, is a great tragedy which contains a number of philosophical themes but no implicit or elicitable philosophical thesis or universal claim. Thus, in the sense that *King Lear* may be convincingly interpreted as a philosophical drama about man's worth in an indifferent universe, or that *Hamlet* may be seen as a drama with its thesis about man's ability to raise all the important questions without his being able to find any of the answers, *Antony and Cleopatra* is not a philosophical drama: it neither makes nor includes any general claim about man and his world. Rather it is a tragedy of two particulars who instance no universal applicable to all.

There are many themes, some philosophical in any traditional sense of philosophical, in the dramas of Shakespeare. None of the plays, not even the tragedies, reduces to these themes; neither do the themes add up to a unified system; nor do the theses, to a unified philosophy. There may be a unifying quality in Shakespeare's work—what Dryden characterizes as the "largest and most comprehensive soul" and Johnson, as "inexhaustible plenty"—but there is no unifying philosophy. Shakespeare is, when he is, a philosophical poet, not a poet with a philosophy. His themes and theses, homogeneous as they may be, are not univocal. In each of the plays, especially the tragedies, there may be themes and theses, most implied by the totality of the elements in the play; but any philosophy in Shakespeare must be distinguished from any philosophy of Shakespeare. In *Hamlet* and *King Lear* the philosophical themes and theses are central or at least are among the controlling elements of these dramas. In *Antony and Cleopatra*, the philosophical theme of generation and corruption, of coming into being and passing away, is as important as anything else in the play. But there is no philosophical thesis, hence, no philosophy in *Antony and Cleopatra*.

The German philosophers are not the only ones to attribute a unified philosophy to Shakespeare. Tillyard, Theodore Spencer, and Duthie, among many others, invest an overall thesis in all the dramas of Shakespeare. Their claim raises the problem of conflicting philosophies in the same literature and just how one is to decide which, if any, is the philosophy in the literature under discussion. Their claim is this: that the doctrine of the universe as a great chain of being is the pervasive doctrine in all the plays, such that without knowledge of this doctrine, Shakespeare's philosophy and work are lost to us. Now, according to this doctrine, first enunciated by Plato in his *Timaeus*, perfection is a kind of cosmic completeness and hierarchical order, which in its completeness includes disorder as a necessary constituent of a larger order.

The "order-disorder synthesis," as it is called, is certainly a dramatic feature in many of Shakespeare's dramas, especially the tragedies, the histories, and maybe in some of the comedies, for example, *The Taming of the Shrew*. But is it and its related doctrine of perfection as completeness pervasive or even present in the whole of Shakespeare? In *Antony and Cleopatra*, Shakespeare dramatizes the theme of perfection but of a kind of perfection that can find no secure place in the platonic universe as cosmic completeness and order. Instead, the play revolves around or at least includes a kind of perfection in love that destroys itself at the very moment of completion.

The world of *Antony and Cleopatra*, vast as it is, encompasses infinite variety but also gaps in nature. The traditional notion of perfection as variety can accommodate the one but not the other, for these gaps are among the inexplicable missing links in any chain of being. Both the variety and the gaps, however, are linked to the rhythms of transformation, of one thing becoming another, of perennial generation and corruption. The images of the play especially, whether those of normal, to be expected transformations, or of abnormal, surprising, indeed inverted, transformations, such as an Antony "That grew the more by reaping" (V, ii, 88) or a Cleopatra who "makes hungry,/Where most she satisfies" (II, ii, 237–238), reinforce the variety. One, but only one, form of this variety of generation and corruption, of the inexhaustible rhythms of nature and experience, is the love of Antony and Cleopatra, confined to them, that generates a ". . . nobleness of life . . . when such a mutual pair,/And such a twain can do't" (I, i, 36–38). In their relationship, but not in love universal, there is a coming into being (the intensity of fire) of a love (the rarefaction of air) that, though it transcends the baser elements of earth and water, self-destructs in its very perfection. The sustaining implicit image of the play, then, is not that of a Nile that begets fertility, then famine, but of a Nile that in its abundance of fertility destroys itself.

One kind of perfection, in a world of many perfections and imperfections, thus, is a love that corrupts itself in its fullness of generated being. In *Antony and Cleopatra* Shakespeare dramatizes this *infima species* of the genus of perfection. He does not reduce this variety or even this perfection to the traditional conception of perfection as (ordered, hierarchical, complete) variety. Indeed, he shows, as he does with many traditional philosophical ideas, how the dramatist as artist may have a truer sense of reality than the philosopher, and in particular, in *Antony and Cleopatra*, that there is a variety of perfections and imperfections but that there can be no resolution of this variety into some fictitious, metaphysical perfection in variety.

Othello also shows that Shakespeare is as much interested in the varieties of perfection as he is in the orthodox perfection in variety. Here, too, I think, Shakespeare dramatizes a kind of perfection that, though rooted in the disorder of the traditional order-disorder synthesis and dichotomy, is nevertheless a perfection that is more real than any nebulous perfection of a cosmic order.

The traditional interpretation of *Othello* is that it is essentially the tragedy of a man who is unable to cope with sexual jealousy. On this reading Act III, scene iii is not only the numerical but the dramatic center of the play: the temptation of Othello and the gulling of him by Iago. It is Othello's inability to deal with his jealousy that reveals his *hamartia* which, played upon by Iago, breaks him and, in doing so, produces the requisite pity and fear along with Othello's final regeneration and suicide.

Fundamental to this orthodox interpretation and its many variants is the notion of a kind of defect or imperfection in Othello that buttresses the centrality of the third scene of the third act and that gives a unifying direction to the whole play.

But there is another, I think, stronger possibility, suggested by Brabantio's explanation to the Senators of Othello's seduction of Desdemona. It is incredible, Brabantio says, that Desdemona should "fall in love with what she fear'd to look on" (I, iii, 98). Othello, therefore, must have conjured her.

> It is a judgment maim'd, and most imperfect,
> That will confess perfection so would err
> Against all rules of nature, and must be driven
> To find out practices of cunning hell
> Why this should be.[24]

Here Brabantio refers to Othello's cunning hell in winning his daughter, and he implies that any other explanation is maimed.

What, now, if one understands these lines not as a causal explanation of Othello's successful wooing but as a critical interpretation of the whole play? Then the judgment that *Othello* is about a "perfection [that] so would err/Against all rules of nature, and must be driven/To find out practices of cunning hell/Why this should be" is far from maimed and imperfect but instead a sound overall reading of *Othello* as a kind of perfection flawed and destroyed by the cunning hell of Iago, with the Why of it unresolved in Iago's last

> Demand me nothing, what you know, you know,
> From this time forth I never will speak word[25]

as answer to Othello's

> Will you, I pray, demand that demi-devil
> Why he hath thus ensnar'd my soul and body?[26]

I do not know whether Shakespeare intended us to take Brabantio's lines in the way they so stunningly suggest. Nor can I endorse the claim that would find in thse lines an unconscious or supersubtle clue to their real meaning. All I insist on is that Brabantio's observation, without his negative assessment, embodies the best interpretation I have yet encountered of the meaning of *Othello*. If it strikes anywhere near the heart of the play, it explodes completely the traditional interpretation. Perfection flawed is hardly compatible with the tragic flaw.

That *Othello* is a tragedy of the flawing of perfection—of a chrysolite as fragile as it is strong and rare, chipped away at until it is smashed—illumines much in the play, the details and of course the vindication of which we must forgo here. Suffice it to say that the data of the play, especially the crucial III, iii, point as much to perfection being flayed and flawed as they do to an inherent fault being painfully mined.

When we turn to Desdemona, however, the evidence points only one way. That she is a perfection in the Elizabethan and in our sense of "flawless" is one of the *données* of the play. Hers is a perfection flayed but not flawed, in this case by Othello's cunning practices on her fidelity. Her consecration of soul (I, iii, 254) to Othello remains intact, never wavering, not even at the moment of Othello's strangling of her. As admirable as her unswerving faith in Othello is, what is truly remarkable in her perfection, however, is that it represents to her, as well as to everyone else in the play, and probably to the Elizabethan audience, too, a perfection founded on and sustained by the disorder, hence imperfection, of her downright act of violence in marrying Othello (I, iii, 249).

The marriage—the love of Othello and Desdemona—brief as it is, is then another kind of perfection, wholly different from the love and perfection of *Antony and Cleopatra*. The latter generates its own corruption; the former is generated in a violation of traditional perfection as variety—"against all rules of nature"—yet is a perfection that is destroyed not because it is a form of imperfection in any cosmic order of things, but because of Iago's wickedness, festering and fructifying in the very pit of disorder.

In *Othello*, Shakespeare consecrates part of his art—we cannot speak of his soul—to a perfection of a marriage in love that is not inherently flawed, as it must be according to the orthodox order-disorder schema, but is instead a perfection flayed and flawed, destroyed ultimately by the terrible imperfection of Iago. This reversal of a traditionally conceived imperfection of a miscegenated marriage into a kind of perfection that violates all the rules of conventional philosophical conceptions of perfection as ordered, hierarchical being is as remarkable as any-

thing in the play. That Shakespeare, who probably shared with Brabantio and his Elizabethan audience negative views contrary to the positive view he dramatizes of a recognized form of imperfection into the
highest kind of perfection, is a supreme instance of the negative capability (that Keats finds so abundantly in him) the irresolution of doubts
that extend even to Iago's motives for his demonic malignancy. Great
alchemist that he was, he transmutes the dross of orthodox imperfection into the gold of a real perfection of a marriage in love that leaves
his critics as baffled as Othello ("Why he hath thus ensnar'd my soul
and body?") by Iago's

> Demand me nothing, what you know, you know,
> From this time forth, I never will speak word.[27]

The creator of *Othello* remains as enigmatic as his creation. But the
perfection of an imputed imperfection remains as clear as ever: as one of
the great themes in Shakespeare, even without any univocal philosophical thesis about the nature of perfection in the world. *Antony and
Cleopatra* and *Othello* together and by themselves prove beyond a
doubt that there is and can be a philosophy in Shakespeare's dramas that
must be elicited from the plays, Not imposed upon them by critics who
are too knowledgeable about the ideational history of the Elizabethan
age and not sufficiently sensitive to the artistry of its leading poet.

Keats says of Shakespeare's plays that, like all great poetry, dramatic
or other, they have "negative capability." Keats means by this the capability "of being in uncertainties, mysteries, doubts, without any irrit-
able reaching after fact or reason." The poet, he adds, should not be
"incapable of remaining content with half knowledge." Again: "We hate
poetry that has a palpable design upon us." We do not want ". . . to be
bullied into a certain philosophy."

If to Keats' "negative capability" we add "affirmative or positive capability"—the refusal to remain in uncertainties, mysteries, doubts, the
obsession with certainty, being content only with full knowledge—then
we have a distinction as illuminating as any between philosophy in
literature and philosophy in philosophy plain or proper. Literature, in
seeking philosophical truth about the world and the range of human
experience in it, is the depiction of the ultimately irreducible complexity
or multivalence of experience, a complexity which cannot yield any
simple formula. Philosophy proper, on the other hand, seeks a truth that
reduces these complexities to universal formulas and which thereby
attains a knowledge relieved of doubts.

Now, if it is true, as I think it is, that much, perhaps most human

experience—the appetitive, the emotional, the intellectual, and especially the moral—does not reduce to simple formulas, then that range of
discourse which embodies this claim is true to experience in a way in
which that range of discourse which quests after certainty and simple,
univocal answers is false. If literature, or at least most of it, exemplifies
the first kind of discourse and philosophy the second, then literature is a
truer philosophy than philosophy proper. Keats is profoundly right: it is
negative, not positive, capability that reflects human experience, its
inexhaustible, irreducible range. Literature is philosophically true in its
implication of negative capability; philosophy proper is philosophically
false in its affirmation of positive capability. Once more, literature can
be understood as the victor in its perennial competition with philosophy
to depict correctly the nature of human experience.

This is not to imply, however, that all literature realizes Keats' negative capability or what he calls in another letter "making all disagreeables evaporate, from their being in close relationship with Beauty and
Truth." Much of literature is, when it contains philosophical themes or a
philosophical thesis, as direct a statement about the essences of things as
is traditional philosophy. Any good *roman à clef*, such as Camus's masterpiece *L'Étranger* with its devastating Cartesian nihilism as the fundamental theorem of human experience and destiny, would be truly absurd without its affirmative capability. Literature with or without negative capability, then, is still literature; the question is not whether it is,
but which has the better claim to knowledge into the way things actually
are? Thus, Keats' notion and my generalized contrast cannot state by
themselves a definitive criterion for distinguishing literature and philosophy. Negative (or negative as against positive) capability serves (1) to
remind us of the kind of true, philosophical knowledge that some literature (but no traditional philosophy) offers; and (2) to suggest that certain
general truths or καθόλου—namely, that there may not be these universals in vast areas of human experience—can better be learned from
literature. This may be the lesson Proust's narrator learns in his quest
for the creation of a philosophical novel in which the search for the
essences, stated in the last volume, leads only to the dissolution of
essences, narrated and dramatized in all the previous volumes, from *Du
côté de chez Swann* to *Le temps retrouvé*. Or it may be the lesson
taught, if only we listen, by Michel's story in Gide's *L'Immoraliste*: that,
though there may be univocal answers of the typical traditional ethical
kind to moral questions regarding the extreme cases (for example, of a
life with the body denied or the mind and will suppressed), the univo-
cality of the moral as against the immoral evaporates in the disagreeables
of those middle cases of human life in which our moral choices affect

others, such as Marceline, Michel's wife. Gide's bitter fruit of a novel that quenches no one's thirst ends as it starts, except that the title grows a question mark which though invisible is there for all who would see to see. His novel remains a great challenge to traditional philosophical morals and ethics and their fundamental conviction that all questions about right and wrong, of what is moral as against immoral, have and must have definitive answers. Gide dramatizes the dubiety of this traditional conviction. He does not proclaim it false, he shows that it is naive and facile; and he implies that it is itself wrong: life is simply not that simple. His philosophy of morality—a philosophy of negative, not positive, capability and, in any case, a philosophy in the novel, to be related to all the other elements, including the geographical split between the north and the south of Europe, so important to Michel's physical and spiritual travels in looking for but never finding himself, not a philosophy to be abstracted from the novel, Gide's other novels or his journals—may not satisfy moralists and philosophers, ever questing for certainty. But it does satisfy those who are more concerned with truth than they are with unequivocal answers to basic moral problems.

One final example: In his *The Hedgehog and the Fox: An Essay on Tolstoy's View of History* Sir Isaiah Berlin reminds us of the parable of the fox who knows many things and of the hedgehog who knows one big thing, and goes on to distinguish between the seeker of multiplicity and the seeker of underlying unity, a division that, on the fox side, parallels Keats' negative capability and which Berlin applies to writers and thinkers. Tolstoy, he says, is the supreme fox in his novels, and a supreme hedgehog in his beliefs.

> Tolstoy perceived reality in its multiplicity, as a collection of separate entities round and into which he saw with a clarity and penetration scarcely ever equalled, but he believed only in one vast, unitary whole. No author who has ever lived has shown such powers of insight into the variety of life . . . No one has ever excelled Tolstoy in expressing the specific flavour, the exact quality of a feeling . . . the inner and outer texture and 'feel' of a look, a thought, a pang of sentiment, no less than that of the specific pattern of a situation, of an entire period, of the lives of individuals, families, communities, entire nations. The celebrated life-likeness of every object and every person in his world derives from this astonishing capacity of presenting every ingredient of it in its fullest individual essence, in all its many dimensions, as it were . . . an event fully present to the senses or the imagination in all its facets, with every nuance sharply and firmly articulated.
>   Yet what he believed in was the opposite. He advocated a single embracing vision; he preached not variety but simplicity, not many levels of consciousness but reduction to some single level—in *War*

and Peace, to the standard of the good man, the single, spontaneous, open soul . . . .[28]

As magnificent as Berlin's assessment of Tolstoy's achievement as a
novelist is—the full quotation reveals a texture as rich as Tolstoy's—and
as accurate as Berlin's overall conflict he finds in Tolstoy the novelist and
Tolstoy the thinker or essayist may be, I think he has missed Tolstoy's
union of the hedgehog and the fox in at least *Anna Karenina*, Tolstoy's
supreme achievement and perhaps the European novel's supreme achievement. For while it is true that the dominant tone of *Anna* is that
largess that Berlin so beautifully details, a largess that celebrates the
abundance of nature and life, covering a variety of human experiences
from eating and dancing to marrying and having children, it is not
outside the novel that Tolstoy seeks the unity underlying this largess,
but in the novel and, in particular, I think, in the implicit significance of
the two most important, if not absolutely central, events in the plot of
the novel, the suicide of Anna and the conversion of Levin. What ties
these events together—if they are not tied, the novel fails as an organic
whole, with everything left dangling after Anna's suicide—must be itself
tied to the principle underwriting the largess. I believe it has something
to do with the principle of creativity or fertility in nature, that some call
God, but that Levin recognizes in the secularly sacred, through Fyodor,
the peasant, and that Anna aborts in her refusal to give Vronsky more
children and a legitimate family. I am hesitant about how best to state
this principle without doing violence to Tolstoy's insight; but I am convinced that in *Anna Karenina* Tolstoy joins the hedgehog with the fox,
just as he joins a particular philosophical thesis about the principle of the
good with the multiplicities of goods that there are in the world and
which he presents and lingers over in his great work. Nature, of course,
cannot mate the hedgehog and the fox; perhaps neither can most of us,
including most artists and thinkers. But Tolstoy as artist-thinker does
mate them in *Anna*. His genius transcends both nature and God, as it
partakes of the very principle of creativity that unites the multiplicity of
the good in *Anna*. It also enables him to offer the strongest example of a
literature and a philosophy in literature in which his richly endowed
negative capability both accommodates his richly stringent positive capability and is itself its finest product.
    In this essay I have hardly scratched the surface of the various possi-
bilities of philosophy in literature. Much remains to be done on many
works of literature that almost cry out for an account of them that
includes the philosophical themes and theses which enrich the totality of
these individual works without at the same time reducing the work to a

philosophical nugget, to be extracted from the work and exploited as an example of some philosophical problem. As I hope my examples show, a literary criticism that elucidates the philosophy in the literary works that contain it as an integral, aesthetically contributing part of them is as legitimate and self-justifying as any branch of literary criticism, so long as the whole of the literary work is kept in focus. Without engaging in futile discussion about what criticism is, or what philosophy or literature is, so that these crucial concepts are rendered precise and even definable, we begin with the paradigms. We know that there are works of literature, philosophical writings, and essays in literary criticism. No true definition of literature, philosophy, or criticism is needed or even possible. Nor would such definitions serve as criteria for distinguishing the clear, indisputable cases from the marginal ones. That myth, that these concepts—indeed, that all concepts—rest on clear, precise definitions of them, the Plato-Frege myth we may call it, is not, as western thought has assumed, an overall necessary condition for intelligible discourse, and certainly not for the discourse of literature, philosophy, and criticism. The late work of Wittgenstein explodes this myth forever.

But Wittgenstein, in both his early work and his late work—in the *Tractatus Logico-Philosophicus* and *Philosophical Investigations*—challenges as radically as anyone has ever done the very possibility of the union of literature and philosophy, especially as I have been promoting it. For one of the assumptions of the legitimacy of philosophy in literature is that both philosophy and literature, whatever else they are, are fundamentally engaged in the making of truth-claims about the world. Both, that is, are capable of embodying and proclaiming ideas or doctrines, whether ontological, anti-ontological, moral, psychological or, as Sidney puts it, "what else" about the world. Both, but especially philosophy, purport to be true doctrine or system about how things actually are. That philosophy is the search for doctrinal truths about the world, however philosophers differ on what these truths are, is a proposition shared by every philosopher in the tradition from Plato to early Wittgenstein.

In the *Tractatus*, Wittgenstein claims, although in avowed violation of his strictures on what can be said or shown, that philosophy, unlike science, is not a series or system of truth-claims about anything. Rather it is an activity, not a theory or doctrine of anything (*Tractatus* 4.112). Whatever the changes, whether radical, as I believe they are, or continuous, as some commentators contend, Wittgenstein never wavers on this fundamental point, reiterating it, again as central, in the *Investigations* (paragraph 109).

As activity, not as doctrine making, Wittgenstein changes his mind on what this activity is but not on philosophy as an activity, that is, as neither ontological nor anti-ontological, neither common sense nor science.

That traditional philosophy is nonsense also remains intact from the *Tractatus* to the *Investigations*. In the *Tractatus*, nonsense is either trying to say what can only be shown (*sinnlos*) or trying to say what cannot be said, because it violates the syntax of the one language of science or because it has no syntax at all (*unsinnig*). In the *Investigations*, nonsense is misconstruing grammatical remarks for ontology or anti-ontology or it is the violating of the logical grammar of concepts.

In both works philosophy functions therapeutically, to expose the nonsense that results when we transgress the limits of language. One but only one of these bits of nonsense would be the attempt to impose on literature a philosophy or to pursue what I have been calling philosophy in literature: to find true or false statements in a use of language that at least so far as its philosophical aspects are concerned is vacuous nonsense. That there is no such thing as philosophy in literature is no true or false doctrine either; rather it serves as a reminder of the inability of philosophy to function in a doctrinal capacity and as a further reminder of the function of sentences in literature. It is therefore, on Wittgenstein's view, philosophy in literature that is nonsense, not literature.

So devastating and radical is Wittgenstein's conception of the nonsense of traditional philosophy, it is no wonder that he has critics as avid in their objections as he has followers who proclaim his the greatest revolution in the history of philosophy. Revolutionary or not, nihilistic or not, Wittgenstein offers the most powerful indictment ever against traditional philosophy and its history. But he also offers philosophy a choice it has not had before: either to recognize and accept what he says about the inadequacy of traditional philosophy as true-false doctrine or to continue producing more nonsense. The choice is this, then: doing philosophy his way or else doing it another way; if he is right, there is no other way!

In discussions of contemporary painting, art historians and critics distinguish between traditional representational art, formalism, and abstractionism. The distinction parallels that of philosophy as traditional ontology, logical atomism of the sort that Russell formulated in his middle period of 1914–1918, in which both language and facts are logically reduced to their ultimate corresponding, isomorphic logical forms, and Wittgenstein's further restriction of philosophy to logical syntax (in the *Tractatus*) and logical grammar (in the *Investigations*), with no regard, in either case, for the correspondence of language to fact or for the nature of the facts themselves, which inquiry properly belongs to the sciences anyway. Philosophy's sole concern is with language: in the

Tractatus, with the syntactical rules that determine and govern the formation and functioning of the (only) language of science; and in the *Investigations*, with the rules, syntactical and semantical, exact or inexact, that govern but do not determine the formation and the functioning of any language that is operative rather than idling.

Abstractionism also contends that traditional representational painting is, as painting, plastic or pictorial forms that may not include representations, neither the harmful nor the harmless, to be dissolved into their plastic or pictorial equivalents, as the Formalists allowed, but is pure nonrepresentational forms, which constitute the essence of painting in its purest, undefiled state. The essence of painting is the purely plastic or pictorial: lines, colors, textures, shapes, designs, etc. It is this that is proprietary to painting, that gives it its uniqueness among the arts; and it is this that makes abstract painting autonomous, that is, independent of all else, including the heteronomous mimetic connections with the world. The autonomy of painting, like that of music, consists in this rejection of all the heteronomous elements that tie painting to the world. And because it accepts the abstract in good traditional or formal painting, Abstractionism is not a subtraction from painting, rather an art stripped of all its unessentials and irrelevancies.

Now if by the autonomy of painting we mean, as we should, not the doctrine that art exists for its own sake, but rather that it exists independently of the world and is not a replication of it, however realistic or ideal, then perhaps we may say of Wittgenstein's exclusive concern with logical syntax or logical grammar that he, too, is an abstractionist in philosophy, practicing an activity that is also purely autonomous, again not in the sense of doing it for its own sake, but in the sense of doing it independently of the heteronomous promotion of true-false doctrine about the world, or even in the semiheteronomous search for the logical forms of language and fact. Like the Abstractionist, Wittgenstein centers on what is proprietary to philosophy, its logical syntax or logical grammar that parallels the plastic or pictorial forms sought by the Abstractionist.

Where he differs from his Abstractionist counterpart is in his denial that the proprietary is the essence and that this essence, without the encumbrances, is what makes traditional philosophy or formal analysis philosophical. There are no essences or, better, we need not assume that there are essences in order to explain the intelligibility of discourse and thought about the world; and it is certainly not true that traditional philosophy and formal analysis are ultimately logical syntax or logical grammar. What they are are conflations of bad logical syntax or grammar with ontology: clouds ". . . of philosophy condensed into a drop of grammar" (*Investigations*, Part II, xi, p. 222e).

Further, although Wittgenstein does not, like Abstractionism, sever the semantic or mimetic connection with the world, since for him language reaches out to the world in the *Tractatus* and is in the world in the *Investigations*, he does sever the connection between philosophy and putative doctrine about the world. So his emphasis, like that of the Abstractionist, is on the syntax rather than the semantics of his discipline, where in each case the painting or the philosophy exists autonomously, independently of their heteronomous uses, whether for bad, as in representational painting, or for good, as in science.

Quite independently of the parallel I have drawn (whether accurate and illuminating, especially for those outside of philosophy, in the arts, and whatever the ultimate convincingness of Abstractionism as a theory of true painting), at least the beauty of Wittgenstein, especially as it applies to our problem of the relation of literature and philosophy, is in his pristine rejection of any such subject as Philosophy in Literature: not, as Richards has it, because of the exclusive use of emotive language in literature, but because of the nondoctrinal character of philosophy. The vulnerability and arbitrarily legislative character of Abstractionism in art vanishes in the striking, shocking truth of Wittgenstein's devastating attack on the traditional conception of philosophy. This, accompanied by his equally striking substitution of logical syntax, then logical grammar, for philosophy, reduces our concern throughout for a proper, fruitful joining of literature and philosophy to but one more piece of traditional nonsense that requires treatment, not further futile effort.

What, now, of literature? Without asking what its essence is—in any case a question as futile as it is fatuous—but instead beginning with some of the paradigms, of which there are plenty, we ask what, if anything, is proprietary to literature? Or is it, too, autonomous, independent of its heteronomous, mimetic connections with the world? That literature is the unique use of sentences to create a world—a heterocosm—not to imitate the one we have, that it consists of sentences alone or of a self-referring use of language, in which the syntax of literature, not its semantics, is all-important, is certainly a possible view and indeed one argued before with much force from neoplatonist aestheticians to A. C. Bradley in the history and theory of literary criticism. But, as we have seen, this view is after all only one option, certainly not the dire implicative conclusion of Wittgenstein that, since philosophy is logical syntax or logical grammar, there cannot be anything like philosophy in literature, unless it is itself logical syntax or logical grammar or nonsense. If Wittgenstein is right that acceptable philosophy is elucidation of those concepts that traditional philosophy has nonsensically misconstrued, we have no other option than his of repudiating Philosophy in Literature. There is nothing so stringent in literature; for with literature, there is the other option, again as we have seen, of construing the sentences of literature, or at least some of them, as statements, as truth-claims about the world and therefore as heteronomous, with nothing proprietary to it. That literature is in the world and about the world is as valid as that though it is in the world, it need not be about the world. Instead, literature is the creation of possible worlds: pieces of fiction, not pieces of truth in fiction.

As attractive as the first option may be—of literature as autonomous, in which the mimetic ingredients are to be rendered nonmimetic, as aspects of presentational structures rather than as representational structures, as the creation of worlds that satisfy the imagination and that may even invite new possibilities for future human actions, the latter fortuitous, not indigenously heteronomous, because this option is just that, and not a conclusion drawn from true premises against statements in literature—this option vies with the more orthodox option that literature, of all the arts, is mimetic: in as well as about the world. In the end, then, that literature contains certain sentences which sometimes are read as statements—whether as attractive as its rival—is the option that is the more conventional and natural, and to be rejected only by a recommendation to convert literature, which does not function as an abstract art, to abstract art, as some convert the painting in all painting to abstract art, and both to the abstract art of music. Nevertheless, stringent and truncated as it is, the autonomy option—is cannot be or be regarded as a thesis about literature as literature—is as possible as it is plausible and attractive. And, once accepted or chose, it gives us the final answer to our question about the proper relation between literature and philosophy: that there is none. How could there be, since both are complete strangers to each other, inhabiting entirely different worlds?

So, how shall we decide between these two options? If literature is taken to be autonomous and if philosophy is autonomous and *cannot* be taken as anything else, provided Wittgenstein is right; and if literature is proprietarily the creation of nonmimetic, fictional worlds, made up out of sentences alone and philosophy is proprietarily the formulation of the logical syntax of the language of science or the elucidation of the logical grammar of the conceptual life, then there is literature and there is philosophy but neither contains truth-claims about the world and us in it. If, on the other hand, philosophy is autonomous and literature is not, or not taken to be, then literature but not philosophy contains statements, including truth-claims about the world. But these truth-claims cannot be philosophical. What, then, are they? Only statements about matters of fact, some particular, some general. Literature, on this heteronomous view, can be said to be close to history and perhaps to science although, when one thinks about science, full of theories, models, hypotheses, laws, but very little on matters of fact except as reports on relevant confirming or disconfirming data, already invested with theory, literature being like science seems very remote indeed. So we are left with literature being close to history and those sciences that emphasize reporting on matters of fact: sciences or, some say, pseudosciences such as sociology or psychology. In any case, this comparison of literature to disciplines that concentrate on matters of fact rather than on matters of science or philosophy is likely to please no one, not even Aristotle, who complimented literature as being more philosophical than history.

My subject, Philosophy in Literature, and my above vindication of it, is viable, then, only within the classical conception of philosophy as true-false doctrine and system about the world, a conception that Wittgenstein shows is nonsensical and which verdict I accept, since I agree with him in his resolution of philosophy into logical grammar, done either badly, as in the tradition, or well, as in the *Investigations*. Nevertheless, if classical philosophy—ontology and the rest—is misguided, disguised logical grammar, poorly practiced, there remains one reminder that may yet salvage our battered subject of Philosophy in Literature, and that is to return to the original sense of philosophy as the love of wisdom. Construed as philosophy, as ontology, formal analysis, logical syntax, or logical grammar, wisdom is also nonsense. But wisdom is none of these. I do not know what it is; again we must fall back on the paradigms, not a buttressing definition that states its essence as true doctrine. I know wisdom is not philosophy as ontology, logical grammar, etc.; I also know it is not science or history or sociology or psychology or matters of fact. I am also convinced that, though not true-false doctrine, wisdom is close to knowledge, without at the same time being a form of or identical with knowledge. It is what it always was, and it will not go away; some philosophers had it; perhaps even some scientists or lesser beings who are more than prudent, sagacious, sensible. But artists, especially writers of literature, have it; it may even be what is proprietary to literature. And it may still be characterized as nonsense (*sinnlos*) in trying to show what cannot even be said, but it is not nonsense (*unsinnig*) as violation of logical syntax or logical grammar. Wisdom and wisdom in literature is the kind of nonsense we can live with, and since nothing else has it, it is the kind of nonsense we need if we are to be more than philosophers, scientists, historians, or surviving masters of matters of fact. Philosophy in literature, then, is the presentation of wisdom, to be provided only by literature. If I have been able to show that and how some literature contains wisdom—which is all that is left of *philo sophia* (even though construed as philosophy, it is nonsense)—I am satisfied. Who can ask for anything more?

Notes

1. George Santayana, *Three Philosophical Poets: Lucretius, Dante, Goethe*. Cambridge, Mass.: 1910.
2. Philip Sidney, *Defense of Poesy*. In Hyder E. Rollins and Herschel Baker (eds.), *The Renaissance in England* (Boston, 1954), pp. 608 and 609.
3. Sidney, op. cit., p. 610.
4. Ben Jonson, Prologue to *Epicœne*, 1609.
5. Cf. also Archibald MacLeish mentioning to Mark Van Doren that Katsimbalis recited to him with great effect a poem of Seferis in Greek although he did not understand a word of it. In *The Dialogues of Archibald MacLeish and Mark Van Doren* (New York, 1964), p. 200.
6. Nicolas Boileau-Despréaux, "L'Art poétique." In his *Oeuvres divers* (1st edition, Paris, 1674).
7. Alexander Pope, *An Essay on Criticism* (London, 1713).
8. Samuel Johnson, "Preface to Shakespeare." In *Rasselas, Poems and Selected Prose*, ed. Bertrand H. Bronson (New York, 1958), p. 241.
9. William Wordsworth, *Selected Poetry*, ed. Mark Van Doren (New York, n.d.), p. 675.
10. Wordsworth, op. cit., pp. 684 and 693.
11. Wordsworth, op. cit., p. 688.
12. Samuel Taylor Coleridge, *Biographia Literaria*, ed. J. Shawcross, revised by G. Watson (London, 1956), Chapter IV.
13. Coleridge, op. cit., Chapter XV.
14. Coleridge, *Miscellaneous Criticism*, ed. T. M. Rayson (London, 1936), p. 277.
15. William Hazlitt, "On Poetry in General." In *Hazlitt on Literature*, ed. J. Zeitlin (New York, 1913).
16. Percy Bysshe Shelley, *A Defence of Poetry*. In *Shelleys Prose*, ed. D. L. Clark (London, 1954).
17. John Stuart Mill, "Thoughts on Poetry and Its Varieties." In *Dissertations and Discussions* (London, 1875).
18. Giacomo Leopardi, *Zibaldone de pensieri*, quoted from René Wellek: *A History of Modern Criticism 1750–1950*, vol. 2 (New Haven and London, 1955), p. 276.
19. *Selected Criticism of Matthew Arnold*, ed. Christopher Ricks (New York and Scarborough, 1972), pp. 92–117.
20. Ibid., pp. 368–369.
21. Ibid., pp. 379–383.
22. Benedetto Croce, *La Poesia* (Bari, 1936).

23. Ivor Armstrong Richards, *Principles of Literary Criticism* (London, 1955), especially pp. 261–271.
24. *Othello*, I, iii, 99–103.
25. *Othello*, V, ii, 304–305.
26. *Othello*, V, ii, 302–303.
27. *Othello*, V, ii, 304–305.
28. Isaiah Berlin: *The Hedgehog and the Fox* (1953), pp. 39–40.

Kurt Mueller-Vollmer

UNDERSTANDING AND INTERPRETATION: TOWARD A DEFINITION OF LITERARY HERMENEUTICS

I

The demise of New Criticism and the subsequent tide of structuralist and post-structuralist methodologies have resulted in a virtual abandonment of traditional methods of interpretation as a viable approach to literary studies. In contrast, the behavioral and social sciences have moved decidedly in the opposite direction during recent years. Social scientists from different fields and of differing orientation have frequently integrated into their methodologies interpretive procedures traditionally associated with the humanities. Interpretation has always been a key term in the debate concerning the nature of the human sciences and their relationship to the natural sciences. This debate, which began with Galileo and Vico, is far from over today. The "intrinsic" approaches of the New Critics and their Continental counterparts fostered a narrow view of interpretation as the purely literary and aesthetic exegesis of a literary work selected from the canon of high literature. This view has led to a neglect in literary studies of the essential role of the concept of interpretation within the wider spectrum of the human sciences and their respective methodologies.[1]

Although literary studies must be counted among the group of human sciences, it would be erroneous to assume that what is needed to remedy the present situation is to borrow boldly from the social sciences some of their recent tools of interpretation. This would amount to stuffing the already overflowing grab bag of approaches with still another "method" taken from elsewhere. Literary studies hold their own independent membership in the group of human sciences and have no reason to transform themselves into a subbranch of sociology. Methodological problems must be viewed in accordance with the nature and the practical requirements of each discipline. This does not mean the literary student should close the doors to other fields of learning. But if he does not attend to the methodological requirements of his own discipline, he faces the serious danger of obliterating distinctions essential to this discipline. A case in point is the relationship literary studies have developed in recent decades with the movement of philosophical hermeneutics in its diverse forms. The concepts of understanding and interpretation have been of central concern to this movement if we judge from the philosophy of Martin Heidegger and the hermeneutic views of Gadamer, Habermas, and their followers. Yet, under their hands, these concepts have become most problematic when we consider their actual usefulness within the context of literary hermeneutics.[2]

Far too long, at least since Dilthey's influential essay *The Rise of Hermeneutics* (1900),[3] students of literature have relied on philosophers and members of other disciplines to define for them hermeneutic principles and methods of their own enterprise. The following reflections have been undertaken in an attempt to clarify some of the intricacies and notorious confusions surrounding the concepts of understanding and interpretation as they have come down to us, and to prepare the ground for a literary hermeneutics appropriating what has been proven valid from the philological and philosophical traditions while remaining open to new developments in literary and other fields.

Views recently advanced by philosophers and social scientists in the Anglo Saxon world, while they exemplify certain traditional hermeneutic difficulties, also contain important new insights and distinctions that bear directly on the issues of literary hermeneutics. Thus concern for hermeneutic problems can be detected in Whitehead's philosophy, notably in his work *Modes of Thought* (1938),[4] and in G. H. Mead's attempts to delineate the sphere of the social sciences in terms of subjective perspectivism and social action, but it was not until the momentous impact of Wittgenstein's later philosophy in the 1950s, particularly his *Philosophical Investigations*, that a re-examination of the basic assumptions of the social sciences got under way. P. Winch's *Idea of a Social Science* (1958),[5] directed against the explanatory model of the behaviorist school and its reliance on a narrow causal mechanism of stimulus and response to explain social interaction, became the rallying point for intense and extensive discussions among philosophers and social scientists in England and the United States, as well as on the Continent. Taking his cue from the later Wittgenstein (who, having abandoned his quest in the *Tractatus* for a timeless metasystem of logico-linguistic rules, argued that clarification of linguistic usage required an analytic effort to uncover its semantic roots in a given social practice[6]), Winch defined sociology as fundamentally an interpretive science and thereby underscored the importance of the notion of understanding for all the human sciences.

In the hermeneutic tradition of the historical and social sciences on the Continent, from Droysen's *Methodology of History*[7] to Dilthey's *Construction of the Historical World in the Human Sciences*,[8] the notion of understanding has characterized methods germane to the human and cultural sciences (as opposed to the method of causal explanation found in the natural sciences). The present shift of the social sciences from explanation toward understanding and interpretation, however, was not inspired by the older Continental traditions but occurred quite independently from them.[9] Thus we find an emphasis, not on a transcendental analysis of the concept of understanding characteristic of traditional hermeneutic theory but on the nature of the objects under study (namely, human actions as they reflect goals and purposes).

The notions of ends (*telos*) and of purposeful action have played a predominant role in recent discussions—e.g. in Charles Taylor's important book *Explanation and Behavior* (1964). Critics have therefore referred to the representatives of this kind of action theory as the "new teleologists."[10] The position taken by Winch and those who follow him point directly at similar difficulties inherent in the concept of understanding of the hermeneutic school represented by Dilthey and his followers. For it is one thing to contend that human actions must be understood in terms of aims and purposes pursued by their agents, but quite another thing to try to understand the life of institutions over long periods of time, or the nexus among events not identifiable with any specific intention or volition, and which may even cancel out the original purpose of the act. In fact, the meaning of events often lies in intersubjective structures and forms of interaction quite removed from any individual's volition or intention.[11] More serious, from the point of view of literary hermeneutics, is the problematic nature of the relation between acts of understanding and interpretive explanation of social phenomena as seen by Winch and others. These two types of activity seem to fuse into each other to create that state of ambiguity and confusion also characteristic of the hermeneutic tradition.

Some recent views in sociology, particularly A. Cicourel's notion of "Cognitive Sociology"[12] and the role it accords to interpretation, are of potential importance to literary studies. Cicourel's starting point closely resembles A. Schutz's phenomenological analysis of the social life-world

as systems of meaning-endowed intersubjective acts.[13] He also draws
from recent development in linguistic and semantic theory in order to
establish a model for the comprehension of social processes as rule-
governed behavior. Cicourel's interpretation of these processes as manifestations of an underlying system of semantic rules or communicative
competence enabled him to avoid the pitfalls of the teleological action
theorists. The rules governing human behavior, he argues, are acquired
much in the manner of linguistic rules: "They both presuppose interpretive procedures" (*Cognitive Sociology* 52) that are "invariant properties
of everyday practical reasoning necessary for assigning sense to the sub-
stantive rules sociologists usually call norms" (*ibid*.). It is the task of the
social scientist to corroborate and make explicit these interpretive rules.

From the point of view of literary hermeneutics, two things are important in Cicourel's approach: first, the notion of a specific hermeneutic
competence that is closely related to linguistic competence (both types
of competence display certain universals or invariants); second, the distinction implied by the social scientist between two groups of phenomena, the understanding displayed by the participants of social interaction
which manifests a body of implicit interpretive rules on the one hand
and the explication (by the sociologist) of these rules on the other.
Literary hermeneutics makes similar distinctions. For instance, a given
text may be regarded as expressing a specific hermeneutic competence
that is related to and is to some degree itself of linguistic nature. This
process of understanding is clearly distinguishable from the acts of textual exegesis and the explicit interpretation that should be differentiated
from those tacit or implied acts of interpretation governing our primary
textual understanding. What is meant by these distinctions and how
they may enable us to cast light on the hermeneutic processes characteristic of literary studies will emerge from the historical discussion below.

Before we can turn to the history of the two concepts in question, we
must examine the position of the philosophical school of hermeneutics.
Its adherents claim to have uncovered the historical and ontological
roots of hermeneutics and to have laid new ground for the sciences of
man.[14] Indubitably, important new insights and a renewed interest in
the philosophy of these sciences have sprung from hermeneutic philosophy, yet, from the point of view of literary studies, these claims have
little value if they are held against the actual accomplishments of classical nineteenth-century hermeneutics. The twentieth century has wit-
nessed a radical shift away from the philological and textual concerns of
Schleiermacher or Boeckh toward a rather different emphasis. Philosophical hermeneutics has interpreted classical writers of the hermeneutic tradition in the light of its own very different goals and presupposi-

tions. There is no reason why literary students should not reverse this process and start looking at the hermeneutic tradition from their own viewpoint.

Beginning with Dilthey, the term "understanding" has assumed the meaning of a "category of life" (*Lebenskategorie*) or existential principle (*Existenial*) without ceasing to be considered a methodological concept. Those practitioners of hermeneutic philosophy who have followed Heidegger, however, have not been able to delineate clearly the difference between the existential and the methodological aspects of understanding. Consequently, the distinction between understanding and interpretation that was frequently ambiguous in classical hermeneutic texts has become all but obliterated. One recent writer, Bubner, has reduced hermeneutics itself to a "doctrine of understanding."[15] Dilthey, in contrast, had still maintained that hermeneutics should be both "the art and science of understanding *and* interpretation."[16]

Let us pause for a moment to examine the meaning Bubner has ascribed to the term "understanding." Like many other social scientists and philosophers in West Germany in the 1970s, Bubner has made an effort to accommodate the view of Heidegger and Gadamer with those of Habermas and his followers. Bubner writes:

> For hermeneutics "understanding" signifies a fundamental comprehension of truth which occurs through intersubjective communicative processes mediated by history. . . . The social and historical basis of understanding yields a deeper foundation for the cognitive labors of knowledge where theory is, as it were, embedded in the very praxis of life.[17]

What does all this mean? Behind an awkward mixing of metaphors, these statements reveal a certain ideological concern for the usage of currently acceptable terminology at the expense of critical distinctions. The "fundamental comprehension of truth" is familiar to the readers of Heidegger and Gadamer. "Intersubjective communicative processes" that are "mediated by history" have been derived from Habermas' social theories. The same is true for the "historical basis of understanding" in the next sentence, which is supposed to yield us "a deeper [than what?] foundation" because it is embedded "in the praxis of life" (Dilthey's expression). Echoes of Dilthey can also be heard in the following statement that proclaims understanding "as foundational because no intellectual effort can go beyond it".[18] Dilthey, however, had stated that "life" was the ultimate "given" beyond which no thought could reach, whereas understanding should be made the object of cognitive analysis. This was, in fact, one of the tasks that Dilthey had set forth for hermeneutics. If today's hermeneutic philosopher thus describes the "methodologically ordered and controlled types of scientific knowledge" as having been deduced from "elementary acts of understanding," his claim remains purely verbal.[19] He makes no effort to differentiate acts of understanding from interpretation, or to discuss the possibility of different modes of understanding in relation to specific objects in the human and social sciences.

If "understanding" and "interpretation" have become problematical for the student of literature, this has occurred because the body of knowledge contained in the classical hermeneutic texts has come down to us mainly through the filter of philosophical hermeneutics. Gadamer's influential work *Truth and Method (Wahrheit und Methode)*[20] has largely determined the usage of these terms in contemporary discussions on the Continent. Its influence can be seen not only among the followers of philosophical hermeneutics such as Bubner, but it also extends equally to social philosophers and sociologists who have aligned themselves with the theories of the Frankfurt school. In literary studies, the receptionist approach developed by Jauss and others has incorporated important notions from Gadamer's hermeneutics.

Gadamer denies an actual distinction between understanding and interpretation or explication (*Auslegung*). He claims that Romantic hermeneutics, despite its shortcomings, "taught us that, in the final analysis, understanding and interpretation are one and the same" (*Wahrheit und Methode* 366). (Whether this is really the lesson we ought to derive from Romantic hermeneutics, we shall see shortly.) On the other hand, Gadamer retracts part of his statement when he maintains elsewhere in his book that during certain "acts of immediate comprehension explication is only potentially contained in these acts" (376). Explication thus merely brings understanding to the fore. This means that, for Gadamer, "explication is not a means to aid understanding, but has itself entered into the meaning (*Gehalt*) of that which is being understood." In other words, "explication" has become part of the meaning that is understood.

Even if one temporarily suspends one's critical consciousness, Gadamer's argument is difficult to follow. What Gadamer has in mind when he speaks about explication is not what we have called "tacit" or implied interpretation but explicit interpretation. Thus, interpretation for Gadamer is always explication expressed through language: "Linguistic explication is the very essence of explication" (*Sprachliche Auslegung ist die Form der Auslegung überhaupt*).[21] It seems obvious, however, that understanding is not identical with interpretation. It certainly is not the same as articulated explication. The interrelatedness of these activities does not support the view of their identity. Gadamer is also aware of their difference when, at still another place, he speaks about an "inner connectedness between explication and understanding." But should it be left to the reader to decide whether the two terms in question refer to only one or several states of affairs?

A major feature of Gadamer's hermeneutic philosophy is that it establishes a relationship between the concept of understanding and human speech or linguisticality (*Sprachlichkeit*). The author of a recent book on literary hermeneutics praises Gadamer for having given a new and different turn to hermeneutics:

> Gadamer's most original contribution to the history of hermeneutics is his linguistic turn. In contrast with hermeneutic theories that view understanding as a psychological process . . . , Gadamer thinks of understanding as a linguistic phenomenon.[22]

The same author claims that previous theories—like those of Schleiermacher or Dilthey—have been oblivious to the linguistic nature of understanding. But he has ignored the fact that among the Romantics, both Humboldt and Schleiermacher grounded their concept of understanding in human speech, and also that they saw no reason for collapsing the distinction between understanding and interpretation. Gadamer, on the other hand, concluded from the linguistic character of understanding that it must necessarily find expression in verbal explication (Wahrheit und Methode 373). Indeed, explication for him is the realization of understanding itself (375): understanding finds its completion only in its verbal expression.

We have reached a crucial point in Gadamer's theory from where certain assumptions of the receptionist approach to literary history have originated. As the linguistic side of understanding, explication for Gadamer constitutes the actual fulfillment of the act of understanding. But he goes one step further and declares that this fulfillment is "nothing but the concretion of meaning itself." If explicating a text and speaking about its meaning lead to "the concretion" of its meaning, as Gadamer maintains, then the meaning of the text can be seen as lying only in its explications. This historical chain of such explications is what Gadamer calls the tradition (*Überlieferung*). Literary works live through their explications (their receptions) and form part of an historical continuity which, sustained by a speech community, is itself of a linguistic nature.

Because he equates understanding and interpretation, however, Gadamer's position remains ambiguous. On the one hand he wants to maintain the normative character of a text for each historical act of understanding or interpretation; on the other, he claims the life of the work to be embedded in its historical interpretations. If by interpretation is meant explication (explicit interpretation), we face a serious dilemma in this respect. The meaning of the text would, as Jauss and his followers have maintained, be embodied in its explications, its receptions. This means, to put it bluntly, the upshot would be that there are essentially no meanings to be understood—only explications to be explicated.

Against this position, it must be argued that interpretations—i.e., explicatory statements about texts and textual meanings—do not constitute an embodiment of these meanings. No explication or exegesis of textual meanings ever replaces these or my understanding of them. For example, the concretization of a literary text through acts of understanding is one thing; the critic's statements about these acts or what is constituted through them, quite another. The interrelatedness of certain hermeneutic phenomena does not warrant the postulate of their identity; instead it calls for an investigation into the nature of their interrelatedness.

II

As hermeneutic categories, "understanding" and "interpretation" have evolved in close relation to each other. Sharing the same intellectual and historical contexts, they underwent changes and transformations as parts of different hermeneutic systems. This alone raises serious problems of interpretation: for example, the term "understanding," which shifts among a variety of different meanings, itself seems ambiguous. Fortunately, however, when we examine texts from the eighteenth and nineteenth centuries, we find that these shifts seem always to occur among three principal meanings of the term. Depending on the occasion, the term may refer to the operation of understanding something—a text, a spoken phrase—or it may refer to the understanding which a person might gain from reading a text of from listening to someone's words. But the term may also designate hermeneutic competence: the abilities and skills required for the proper understanding of speech or written words. Thus the student of hermeneutics will have to keep in mind that a given writer may use only the one term "understanding" while referring to any of its different aspects.

Chladenius, who wrote the first general theory of hermeneutics in the vernacular, *Introduction to the Correct Explication of Discourses and Writings* (1742),[23] employs the term understanding (*Verstehen*) synonymously with *Verständnis:* i.e., the understanding which one has of something. He believed that this understanding of a speech, a passage in a book, or an entire work could be attained with ease in certain cases or as the result of deliberate interpretive labors in others. For him, understanding was closely related to the concept of reason (*Verstand*). Words and texts are intelligible because of their rationality and reasonableness. Reason, or *Verstand*, carries two distinct meanings for Chladenius. First, it must be taken as the equivalent of "sense" or "meaning"—as in the meaning of a statement (he often speaks about the reason, *Verstand*, of linguistic utterances). Second, it denoted human reasoning or rationality as the precondition of any hermeneutic understanding. In essence, then, texts can be understood because of the rationality they represent. For Chladenius, as for the enlightened mind in general, hermeneutics was a "knowledge of reason" or "rational cognition" (*Erkenntnis des Verstandes*). The grounds for a correct interpretation (*Auslegung*) resided in reason itself: that of the interpreter and that embodied in the text or in the spoken word. Hermeneutics had to provide its students with a faithful listing and critique of the techniques and strategies which an interpreter could apply in order to reach the intended meaning of an utterance. Because understanding was seen by Chladenius as *Verständnis*, the actual comprehension of verbal meaning, interpretation (*Auslegung*) had to be distinctly set off against it:

> Interpretation (*Auslegung*) thus is nothing but teaching someone the concepts which are necessary for him to understand perfectly a given speech or piece of writing or to teach him to understand these. (p. 93)

Kant's Copernican Revolution of Thought brought about a new and different usage for the term understanding. From the transcendental viewpoint of the *Critique of Pure Reason*, understanding (*Verstand*) appeared as an underlying condition for the possibility of thought and experience. In his *Logic* Kant writes:

> To understand something (*intellegere*) means to know or to conceive of something through the understanding (*Verstand*) by means of our concepts.[24]

Thus understanding (*Verstand*) is the capacity for rational thought, denoting man's ability to know and recognize things for what they are. Understanding (*Verstehen*) is present in all thought and conscious experience as an expression of man's rationality, his rational competence (*Verstand*).[25]

Receiving his inspiration from Kant, Schleiermacher grounded hermeneutics in his own concept of understanding. Since then, "understanding" has become the cornerstone of hermeneutic theory. But few who followed in Schleiermacher's footsteps had sufficient grasp of what he had intended when he linked man's hermeneutic capacity with his capacity for speech. Schleiermacher's view of understanding arose from a profound and complex conception of language that belonged to what may be called the Romantic language paradigm—the most illustrious proponent of which was probably Wilhelm von Humboldt. Schleiermacher's and Humboldt's linguistic philosophies fell by the wayside when this paradigm was abandoned by subsequent generations of academic linguists and scholars whose work was guided by different concerns and interests.

Schleiermacher viewed understanding as an activity analogous to that of speaking.[26] It derives from man's linguisticality or speech capacity (*Sprachfähigkeit*)—that is, his knowledge of language (*Sprache*) and his mastery of speech (*Rede*). He thought that every human being was equipped with a basic linguistic disposition that had to be realized by aquiring a given language at a particular moment of its history, and by internalizing its grammatical rules. Men express their linguistic competence in speech-acts (*Sprechacte*) which produce utterances (*Rede*); similarly, their linguistic competence enables them to understand the utterances of others. According to Schleiermacher, therefore, speech-acts and acts of understanding, both grounded in the common linguistic competence of speaker and addressee, closely corresponded:

> Their correlation consists in that every act of understanding is the reverse of an act of speaking, and one must grasp the thought that underlies a given utterance.[27]

Into this scheme Schleiermacher introduced a distinction of potentially momentous importance for literary hermeneutics. Understanding an utterance (*Rede*) involved, he believed, the coalescence of two different elements (*Momente*). The student of hermeneutics had to distinguish these, even though they always necessarily occurred together. The first element concerned the understanding of speech in relation to language; the second considered language in relation to the speaker as an expression of his mental life. Man as producer of speech could thus be viewed not only as the location where language is articulated (finds articulation) in a given instance but also as a being whose cognitive life-stream finds expression in his speech. It is the nature of speech that it participates in two systems simultaneously: that of the interpersonal realm of language (*Sprache*) and that of the individual speaker's life process and internal history. Consequently, for Schleiermacher:

Understanding takes place only in the coinherence of these two moments:

1. An act of speaking cannot even be understood as a moment in a person's development unless it is also understood in relation to language. . . .
2. Nor can an act of speaking be understood as modification of the language unless it is also understood as a moment in the development of the person.[28]

To these two sides of understanding corresponded two distinct modes of interpretation (*Auslegung*)—which Schleiermacher called grammatical, and psychological or technical. If developed to their extremes, the grammatical interpretation would lead to the exclusion of the author, and the psychological and technical one would ultimately disregard the element of language. Under the label "psychological" or "technical interpretation," Schleiermacher would gather all those aspects of verbal understanding that are not strictly grammatical in nature but make up the individual character of an utterance (*i.e.*, how this utterance relates to its author's individuality, its particular genre, and the historical circumstances it embodies). Boeckh would later differentiate generic, individual, and historical interpretation more accurately. But when he placed grammatical interpretation *de facto* on par with the other interpretive modes, he obscured Schleiermacher's epoch-making accomplishment (namely, the grounding of the concept of understanding in linguisticality and language).

The implications of Schleiermacher's insights have scarcely been explored by literary students. These insights would make it possible, it seems, to accomodate and derive an entire spectrum of interpretive strategies—ranging from the structural and linguistic to the formalist, phenomenological, psychological, and sociological approaches—all from a single hermeneutic model.[29] Schleiermacher saw hermeneutics as "the art of understanding," where "understanding" is elevated to the art of a scholarly discipline. He thought hermeneutics should not, however, concern itself with the specific rules and principles of interpretation found in the hermeneutic treatises of the theologians or jurists of his time. Nor should it include the presentation of what it had brought to an understanding (*Darlegung des Verständnisses*).[30] The latter was relegated to the domain of rhetoric. Schleiermacher's view was essentially transcendental, aimed at the subjective and objective conditions underlying acts of philological (textual) understanding.

But the problem is whether hermeneutics, which is also the theory of the art of understanding (it is that which Schleiermacher actually presents in his *Hermeneutik*), is possible as he envisioned it. Can such

theory exclude from its agenda the element of presentation and still
fulfill its task? This seems rather doubtful. For the art of the philologist
consists mainly of generally accepted procedures, assumptions, verbal
stragegies, an institutionalized body of knowledge, and a tacit agreement
on standards for hermeneutic competence. The presentation of one's
understanding (Verständnis) is an integral part of the art in question.
Schleiermacher does not offer us a clear distinction between understanding and explication (Auslegung) or interpretation (Interpretation);
in fact he often implies that the art of understanding is really the art of
interpretation. Even so, he does not admit that interpretation as explication (Auslegung) is always presentation and thus discursive. The ambiguity that Schleiermacher imparted to the concept of understanding was
to endure until today. It is still evident in the title of one of the major
works devoted to the development of hermeneutics in the nineteenth
century, J. Wach's prodigious monograph, Das Verstehen (Understanding).[31] In this work, the author, one of Dilthey's students, treats understanding as the specific method of the human sciences.

   Almost forty years later, a new dimension was added to the concept of
understanding by the historian J. G. Droysen. Looking beyond the
purely rational meaning of an utterance, he expands the object of hermeneutic concern to include its expressive aspects as well—i.e., its
psychological, emotive, and spiritual (geistiger) content. He argues that
an utterance, in order to be fully understood, must be grasped as an
expression of something "internal," which reveals to the historian—
besides its obvious meaning—the attitude, intention, or state of mind of
its originator. If the historian bases his method upon understanding, as
Droysen maintains, he can do so only because what he understands
expresses man's inwardness (or inner nature). In his Historik he writes:

> The possibility of this understanding arises from the kinship of our
> nature with that of the utterances lying before us as historical mate-
> rial. A further condition of this possibility is the fact that man's
> nature, at once sensuous and spiritual, speaks forth every one of its
> inner processes in some form apprehensible by the senses, mirrors
> these inner processes, indeed, in every utterance.[32]

Droysen was the first to use the term "understanding" to define the
nature and method of the human sciences. These he considered historical in essence. He distinguished three methods of knowing, each characterized by its own mode of cognition:

>   . . . according to the objects and according to the nature of human
> thinking, the three possible scientific methods are: the speculative,

philosophically or theologically, the physical, and the historical. Their essence is to find out (*erkennen*), to explain (*erklären*), to understand (*verstehen*).[33]

These three methods did not appear to Droysen as three different paths to the same goal of knowledge, but like

> the three sides of a prism, through which the human eye, if it will, may, in colored reflection, catch foregleams of the eternal light whose direct splendor it would not be able to bear.[34]

In other words, Droysen recognized three independent and equally valid methods of knowing reality, represented by the three disciplines of philosophy, the natural sciences, and history.

Droysen's scheme became a principle source for the view, widely held since the latter part of the nineteenth century, of the dichotomy between the natural sciences (which engage in causal explanations), and the human sciences (which are believed to be identified with the "method of understanding"). Dilthey provided the theoretical underpinnings for this view and transformed Droysen's historical method into that of the human sciences (*Geisteswissenschaften*) in general.[35]

For the literary student, Droysen's work is important because of its rich content and the many insights it provides. Droysen clearly distinguishes, for example, between two aspects of understanding: process and result.

> We may distinguish the actual understanding itself (*Verständnis*) from the logical mechanism of the understanding process (*Verstehen*).

Even more important, he defines the historical method as "understanding by means of investigation" (*forschendes Verstehen*).[36] In other words, understanding *per se* does not constitute the historical method—except insofar as it is combined with the practice of the historian. This practice must rely on two procedures: criticism and interpretation. The first attempts to secure the truth-status and genuineness of the historian's sources and purported facts. The second is concerned with the evaluation and explication of historical facts according to specific modes and classes of interpretation. Consequently, interpretation itself, always explicit for Droysen, finds expression in the historian's account of his findings. It made sense, therefore, to include in the *Historik* a section with specific guidelines and rules of composition for the historian to follow in his writings. In order to function as a methodological concept, understanding had to find its appropriate form of expression; this was one of Droysen's important realizations. In this respect, Dilthey's version of the concept represents a step backward from Droysen. The discursive aspects of "understanding" and of "interpretation," which began to emerge in Droysen's hermeneutics, disappeared again and were replaced by another view of the matter.

Before examining Dilthey's position, we must focus on the contributions of the classical scholar and student of Schleiermacher, A. Boeckh. To him we owe the most comprehensive and carefully elaborated theory of interpretation in the nineteenth century from a philologist's pen. His *Encyclopedia and Methodology of the Philological Sciences*[37] fused the Romantic impulses with the philological tradition of classical scholarship from the humanists of the Renaissance to the classical scholars of nineteenth-century Germany. In this work, Boeckh defined philology as "knowledge of what is known" (*Erkennen des Erkannten*)[38]—in other words, knowledge of what has been produced by the human mind throughout its history. To know (that is, to re-cognize what has been known) means, for the philologist, to understand it. Having thus established philology's particular mode of cognition, Boeckh goes on to distinguish between: first, the act of understanding, its elements and its structure; and second, the result of this act—that which has come to be understood (*Verständnis*). In this instance, Boeckh's insights parallel those of Droysen. But Boeckh is also aware of the aspect of understanding that we have called hermeneutic competence. "Correct understanding, like logical thinking, is an art," he writes, "and therefore rests partly on semiconscious competence (*Fertigkeit*)."[39] It is the function of hermeneutic theory to make explicit what has been unconsciously present in the philologist's process of understanding. Hermeneutics is for Boeckh the "scientific-methodical development of the rules of understanding"[40] rather than the establishment of practical rules of interpretation.

But Boeckh is not clear about the relation between the acts of understanding and of interpretation. Despite his view of hermeneutics as the study of the underlying rules of philological understanding, he also calls the act of philological understanding "explication" (*Auslegung*) or "interpretation" (*Interpretation*). Boeck claims that, in order to understand a text, the philologist must rely on his application of four modes of interpretation: the grammatical, the historical, the generic, and the individual. Each modifies and presupposes all the other; each also represents a specific competence that the philologist acquires as part of his craft. It appears that Boeckh is speaking from the position of the classical scholar who seeks his basic task as that of bridging the historical gap between his own age and the world of the classical texts he studied. Hence, interpretation seems to him identical with explication (*Auslegung*), even though the process of understanding (*Verstehen*) depends in fact on numerous acts of tacit interpretation in order to reach an actual understanding (*Verständnis*) of a text. Boeckh, however, equates interpretation with explication and explication with understanding. He thereby levels again the distinction he had made in other parts of his work. Yet there are passages that seem to suggest another view, allowing the presence of tacit interpretive acts in textual understanding. At one point, Boeckh speaks of the process of understanding as a system of interpretive semiotic acts:

> Since the great mass of verbal tradition is fixed through written record, the philologist for his explication must understand (1) the sign of the signifier, i.e., the writing; (2) the signifier, i.e., the language, (3) the signified, i.e., the knowledge contained in the language.[41]

Nevertheless, Boeckh does not draw the obvious conclusions from these observations which would have led him to revise his concepts of understanding and of interpretation. The power of the classical hermeneutic paradigm and its systematizing force prevails over him.

Dilthey's hermeneutics represents a true watershed between nineteenth-century theories which were outgrowths of Romanticism, and our contemporary philosophical hermeneutic. Upon first glance, Dilthey seems to follow closely in the footsteps of his nineteenth-century predecessors. Like them, he places major emphasis on the concept of understanding; following Droysen, he believes that understanding, together with explication, should constitute the method of the human sciences. But a radical shift wrought with far-reaching consequences for literary hermeneutics is manifest in his position: Dilthey abandons Schleiermacher's idea that understanding is rooted in language and man's linguistic nature (an idea still present in Boeckh's view of "grammatical interpretation") and embraces a very different conception instead. Since Dilthey's own work in the humanities builds on the inspiration of Schleiermacher, and since he is known as the author of some imposing works on Schleiermacher (including his *Hermeneutik*[42]), this is a most curious development. In Dilthey's view, understanding as a methodological concept has its origin in the process of life itself: it is primarily a "category of life" (*Lebenskategorie*).[43]

In their daily lives, human beings find themselves in a social, cultural, and institutional environment, where they must act on the basis of a

practical understanding. Their actual behavior reflects their lived understanding and comprehension of the environment. Dilthey believed that
all "higher" or complex manifestations of understanding derive from
those lower or primitive forms of comprehension. The object of understanding is for him always a manifestation of human life, a "life-expres-
sion" (*Lebensäusserung*), just as understanding itself must be seen as an
expression of life. Thus understanding and the life-expressions at which
it is directed form part of our lived experience; they are *Erlebnisse* and
carry an inherent meaning.

The difficulty with Dilthey's position lies in the wide gap it leaves
between understanding as a "category of life" and understanding as a
critical concept in the human sciences, a gap that neither Dilthey nor
the adherents of philosophical hermeneutics have been able to bridge
satisfactorily. There is no doubt that Dilthey himself saw the need for a
methodological foundation of the human sciences, and that he was un-
willing to reduce the status of these sciences or of hermeneutics to that
of a quasi-theoretical consciousness for an existing "praxis." (That he
stubbornly insisted on standards of validation has earned him black
marks from the philosophical hermeneuticians, notably Gadamer and his
school.)

Dilthey did not specifically account for the aspect of competence in
understanding; he concentrated his attention instead on the process of
understanding and the structures displayed in it, and he derived an
epistemology from its analysis. He shifted the idea of competemce to the
level of interpretation. It is here—in Dilthey's statement that "understanding" in the human sciences "rests on a special personal talent"
(*besondere persönliche Genialität*) and that this talent is translated subsequently into the specific technique of the humanistic discipline—that
we find the traditional confusion between understanding and interpretation. "Understanding" has slipped into "explication"; combining Schleiermacher's concept of hermeneutics with Droysen's notion of explication, Dilthey defines explication as "the methodical understanding of
permanently fixed expressions of human life."[44] In other words, understanding becomes methodical, "scientific" (*wissenschaftlich*), when it is
directed at a specific class of objects—namely, those that can be considered objectivations of human life.

But what precisely is the domain of understanding, and what per-
tains to explication or interpretation alone? If one is not clear on this
matter, how can one define interpretation and explication in terms of
understanding?

It is noteworthy that Dilthey considered the "highest" forms of explication to be those dealing with life-expressions of a written nature:

Because our mental life finds its fullest and most complete expression only through language, explication finds completion and fullness only in the interpretation of the written testimonies of human life.[45]

Hence the human sciences should derive their proper awareness and theoretical stance from disciplines which, like literary studies, obtain their knowledge from the interpretation of the written records of human life. It seems doubtful from our perspective that literary studies could be made to carry in this way the burden of the unsolved problems of the human sciences unless they have first established a hermeneutic basis of their own. These same doubts apply to P. Ricoeur's recent attempt[46] to revitalize Dilthey's position by utilizing a model of text interpretation to establish principles and an outline for a general hermeneutics of the human and social sciences. Ricoeur is mistaken when he claims that his own conception of hermeneutics, which deals solely with the exegesis of written texts, is identical with Dilthey's notion of explication (*Auslegung*). For Dilthey, a student of Droysen, the human sciences included the interpretation of other, nonverbal phenomena. Ricoeur's own usage of the term explication vacillates between what we have called tacit interpretation and explication proper. Consequently, the relation between understanding and interpretation remains ambiguous. In fact, Ricoeur claims that understanding, never immediate, must always be preceded or accompanied by explanatory procedures; in other words, it is always linked to explicit interpretation. Ricoeur comes to this conclusion because he equates immediate understanding with emotional identification, something which he considers extraneous to textual interpretation.[47]

III

Explication does not, however, necessarily precede or accompany textual understanding. Ricoeur, like others before him, does not seem to realize that immediate understanding is not of the nature of emotional identification, and thus *eo ipso* untrustworthy. It springs rather from the interaction of different acts of tacit interpretation and manifests acquired hermeneutic competence. Dilthey's "complex forms of understanding" may be described in this way. An understanding of highly structured and complex verbal expressions always proceeds through manifold interpretive operations of which the interpreter is not consciously aware. They can, nevertheless, be made the object of a systematic study, as

Ingarden has shown in his descriptive analyses of the cognition of the literary work.[48] What he calls concretization—the comprehension of strictly literary and aesthetic texts—constitutes merely a special instance within the larger context of textual understanding. It would be a mistake, therefore, to try to define interpretation solely in relation to the works of a particular literary tradition—like, for example, modernist and symbolist poetry of the nineteenth and twentieth centuries, which P. Szondi has attempted in his literary hermeneutics.[49] The resulting view of interpretation is too narrow to accommodate works from other literary traditions. Furthermore, it does not allow us to determine the relationship of literary studies to the other human sciences.

Literary and textual understanding is hardly ever purely immediate or entirely the result of conscious efforts and methodical procedures. Rather, it is a combination of the two. If our understanding comes to a sudden halt, proves deficient, or requires validation, the art of the interpreter takes over. Schleiermacher's and Boeckh's modes of interpretation were simply an explicit formalization of procedures practiced at that time in their disciplines of theology and classics, but their distinctions also point toward certain hermeneutic invariants which literary hermeneutics must undertake to evaluate and incorporate into its own enterprise.

The positions we have examined have displayed discongruity and contrariety. Yet our critical analysis has shown that the two terms "understanding" and "interpretation" appear to circumscribe a specific set of phenomena which display a definite order and relationship among them. If these phenomena are seen together, they illuminate the nature and inherent structure of the hermeneutic operations and procedures found in literary studies. Understanding is the basic mode by which we comprehend the verbal meanings of spoken or written utterences. Literary understanding, in turn, manifests a specific competence of complex nature. It is made up of linguistic-semiotic, generic, psychological, and other classes of components that constitute what I have called tacit or implicit interpretation. This latter therefore specifies hermeneutic competence and facilitates the identification and delineation of its component elements.

An individual may acquire hermeneutic competence in two possible ways: as a member of a given culture or cultural group, he gains understanding of the language, customs, literary codes, and conventions of that culture; as a literary student and critic, however, he must enlarge and modify his competence consciously and "artificially" in order to conform with the requirements of his discipline. For the practitioners of nineteenth-century hermeneutics like Ast, Schleiermacher, Boeckh, and their followers, this meant the methodical acquisition of the philological craft that enabled them to understand those literary works and documents that were historically and linguistically removed from them. For this reason, as we have noticed, they identified explicit interpretation (*Auslegung*) with understanding itself. But *Auslegung* (explication) is not the external expression of an inward act of understanding. It is different in kind because it entails a reflexive stance *vis-à-vis* these acts and forms part of the discursive system of the discipline in which the philologist participates. Explication is the external manifestation of this participation.

Explicit interpretation, therefore, as the meaning of this term has evolved from our discussion, may designate two distinct but closely interdependent classes of operations and procedures. Each possesses its own sphere of objectives. The first consists of deliberate reflexive (nonverbalized) interpretive efforts; it constitutes the subjective element of the art of interpretation. The second, made up of verbal articulations and formalizations of these efforts, constitutes the link between the subjective and the intersubjective spheres of a humanistic discipline.

Among the nonverbalized, that is "subjective," explicit interpretive efforts, we can distinguish an entire spectrum of different operations which can be grouped around two basic directional attitudes. The one is concerned with bringing to critical consciousness elements and structures of the process of understanding itself; the other, in contrast, deals with the object to be understood: a text, a literary work, or any of its aspects. We can properly call the first hermeneutic reflexion. The second, on the other hand, consists of the interpretive labors required by any humanistic discipline and covers therefore a wide range of operations of different type and direction. However, this is not the place to attempt an analysis or a typology of the various reflexive acts of interpretation that occur in literary studies.

Interpretive efforts and operations, once we formalize them through verbal articulation, become explication, and thus, part of an actual system of critical discourse. In the same way as hermeneutic reflexion turns into hermeneutic theory proper, the praxis of the literary student, by its very nature, is pedagogical and communicative. It is embodied in the statements he contributes to the discourse of his discipline. Literary studies depend on explicit interpretation as their *modus operandi*.

To what extent should explicit interpretation be considered part of literary hermeneutics? This question, which must be asked, is important; answering it involves nothing short of a definition of literary hermeneutics and of its task and function in relation to literary studies and the human sciences. The danger exists today of considering hermeneu tics as one critical approach among many with an applicable "method" of its own. When Schleiermacher defined hermeneutics as the "art of understanding", he gave us an analysis of this art in his *Hermeneutik* and developed a theory of understanding which he thought would apply to all the humanistic disciplines. We have similarly attempted, although in a more rudimentary fashion, to identify and analyze different kinds of strategies and modes of interpretation, certain invariants, and their inherent order—all of which constitute the hermeneutic process in literary studies. These distinctions, not advanced for the benefit of any particular school of literary criticism, apply equally to all approaches which make use of interpretation (albeit with different aims and for different purposes).

Literary hermeneutics, then, is not a special school of criticism or a trend in literary scholarship, but the theory and study of the art of interpretation; it provides both a theoretical foundation for that art and a necessary critique for its various historical and contemporary manifestations. Regardless of school or approach, interpretation remains at the heart of literary studies because of the very nature of its subject matter. Besides focusing on epistemological and phenomenological critique and description, literary hermeneutics will have to assume the additional task of studying the "art of interpretation" in its discursive contexts. Nineteenth-century philologists like Schleiermacher or Boeckh interpreted their texts from within their own system of discourse and undertook the theoretical justification of their art from this same basis. The new literary *Hermeneutik* must concern itself with the contexts of different systems of discourse if it is to study successfully constitutive structures, modes, and methods of interpretation. Its work must be accompanied in turn by an awareness of its own discursive situation. Such an awareness was outside the horizon of classical hermeneutics. By focusing his attention upon it, the student of literary hermeneutics will be able to go beyond the purely verbal demand often raised by dialectical sociologists and the adherents of philosophical hermeneutics to reflect "critically" upon his economic, social, or ideological conditions. This abstract call for "reflexion" will thus be removed from its dogmatic pedestal and be transformed into a practicable hermeneutic directive.

The study of discourse and discursive structures in the human sciences, inspired largely by recent developments in structural and post-structural linguistics and semiotics, has drawn interest in some quarters.[50] Literary hermeneutics will have to assess the work that has been done from its own perspective and eventually advance its own theory and praxis of discursive analysis.

Notes

1. Thus in a widely read anthology of German intrinsic or *werkimmanente* criticism, the notion of interpretation is identified with the task of interpreting individual works of poetry and literature: H. Enders, ed., *Die Werkinterpretation*, Darmstadt, 1967, in particular, "Vorwort," p. vii. The reaction against this school in Germany has been equally ill-informed in its rejection of "interpretation." As was recently pointed out by Ingrid Strohschneider-Kohrs ("Textauslegung und hermeneutischer Zirkel. Zur Innovation des Interpretationsbegriffs von August Boeckh," *Philologie und Hermeneutik in 19. Jahrhundert*, ed. H. Flashar et al., Göttingen, 1979, p. 85f.), none of the lately published works on literary theory and methodology in Germany seem to be aware of the existence of the body of theories of interpretation from the nineteenth-century philological tradition. In this connection Strohschneider-Kohrs lists books by H. L. Arnold–A. V. Sinemus, V. Žmegač, J. Hermand, and N. Mecklenburg. In the same vein, in this country "interpretation" has been associated with the methodology of the New Criticism. Structuralist and post-structuralist criticism claims that interpretation should be replaced by other "methods." See J. Culler, *Structuralist Poetics—Structuralism, Linguistics, and the Study of Literature*, Ithaca, 1975, esp. p. 118ff.. In France, however, Tzvetan Todorov in one of his latest books (*Symbolism et interprétation*, Paris, 1978) attempts an evaluation and analysis of the hermeneutic theories of Wolf, Ast, and Boeckh from the point of view of what he calls "operational interpretation." Todorov does not discuss the concept of understanding, nor does he make an attempt to investigate the relationship between his own structuralist operationalism and the hermeneutic principles developed by the nineteenth-century philologists— without which their operational procedures cannot be properly understood.

2. For the relationship between philosophical hermeneutics and reception theory see the article by P. Rusterholz: "Hermeneutik" in *Gundzüge der Literatur-/und Sprachwissenschaft*, ed. H. L. Arnold and A. V. Sinemus, Göttingen, 1974, vol. I, pp. 89–114; and the criticism by Strohschneider-Kohrs, *op.cit.* Elsewhere I have given an analysis of the shortcomings of the concept of interpretation in reception theory and structuralist criticism and have tried to pinpoint some of the hidden interpretive assumptions made by these two schools: "Interpretation: Discourse or Discipline? a Phenomenological View," *Monatshefte*, vol. 71, no. 4, 1979, pp. 379–386; and "Zur Problematik des Interpretationsbegriffs in der Literaturwissenschaft," in *Deuten und Erkennen*, ed. *Gedenkschrift Edgar Lohner*, M. Woodmansee and W. F. Lohnes, Berlin, 1982.

3. Wilhelm Dilthey, "Die Entstehung der Hermeneutik," *Gesammelte Schriften*, vol. V, 2nd ed., Göttingen-Stuttgart, 1957, pp. 317–338. I am in complete agreement with Joseph Strelka, who states that "literary criticism until today has left the problem of elaborating a systematic hermeneutic theory to the discipline of philosophy": Joseph Strelka, *Methodologie der Literaturewissenschaft*, Tübingen, 1978, p. 17. My critical reflections are intended as a contribution towards preparing the ground for such a hermeneutic theory.

4. Alfred North Whitehead, *Modes of Thought*, New York, 1938.

5. Peter Winch, *The Idea of a Social Science and Its Relation to Philosophy*, London, 1958.

6. "Und eine Sprache verstehen, heisst, sich eine Lebensform vorstellen." *Philosophische Untersuchungen, Schriften*, Frankfurt am Main., 1960, p. 296.

7. Johann Gustav Droysen, *Historik: Vorlesungen über Enzyklopaädie und Methodologie der Geschichte*, ed. by R. Hübner, 4th ed., Munich, 1965.

8. Wilhelm Dilthey, *Der Aufbau der historischen Welt in den Geisteswissenschaften, Gesammelte Schriften*, vol. VII, 2nd ed., Stuttgart-Göttingen, 1958.

9. Only recently have the affinities between the new methodological concern and the older Continental hermeneutic traditions been noticed. Cf. Georg Henrik von Wright, *Explanation and Understanding*, Ithaca, 1971. See also: Maurice Roche, *Phenomenology, Language, and the Social Sciences*, London, 1973.

10. Rolf Wiggershaus, in his introduction to *Sprachanalyse und Soziologie*, Frankfurt am Main, 1975, p. 19. See also Maurice Roche, op. cit. (footnote 9), pp. 59ff.: "Action Theories."

11. A fact which was well known to Hegel, viz. his famous dictum of the "cunning of reason" (*List der Vernunft*).

12. Aaron Cicourel, *Cognitive Sociology. Language and Meaning in Social Interaction*, New York, 1974.

13. Alfred Schutz, *The Phenomenology of the Social World*, trans. G. Walsh and F. Lehnert, with an introduction by G. Walsh, Evanston, Ill., 1967.

14. Much of the subsequent discussion was derived from Heidegger's analysis of "understanding" as an existential category. See sections: "Being-there as Understanding" (#31), "Understanding and Interpretation" (#32), "Assertion as a Derivative Mode of Interpretation" (#33), and "Being-there and Discourse Language" (#34), in Martin Heidegger, *Being and Time*, trans. John Macquarrie and Edward Robinson, New York, 1962. First German edition, 1928.

15. Rüdiger Bubner, "Transzendentale Hermeneutik?" in *Wissenschaftstheorie der Geisteswissenschaften*, eds. Roland Simon-Schaefer and Walter Ch. Zimmerli, Hamburg, 1975, p. 64.

16. *Gesammelte Schriften*, vol. VII, p. 205: "Verstehen und Deuten ist die Methode, welche die Geisteswissenschaften erfüllt." ("The method pertaining to the human sciences consists of understanding and interpretation."—My translation.)

17. Bubner in Simon-Schaefer and Zimmerli, eds. *Wissenschaftstheorie*, op.cit., p. 64—my translation. In German the passage reads: "Für die Hermeneutik bedeutet Verstehen ein grundlegendes Erfassen von Wahrheit, das in intersubjektiven Verständigungsprozessen und in der Vermittlung mit Geschichte sich vollzieht. Die soziale und historische Basis des Verstehens liefert der kognitiven Leistung des Erkennens ein tieferes Fundament, wo Theorie gleichsam in Lebenspraxis eingebettet ist."

18. "Der Akt des Verstehens gilt deshalb als grundlegend, weil keine intellektuellen [sic!] Erkenntnisanstrengungen dahinter zurückzugehen vermögen." Ibid.

19. ". . . soll sich die methodisch geregelte und kontrollierte Sonderform der wissenschaftlichen Erkenntnis aus elementaren Verstehensakten ableiten lassen." Ibid.

20. Hans-Georg Gadamer, *Wahrheit und Methode*, Tübingen, 1960; 3rd edition, 1972. English edition: *Truth and Method*, trans. Garret Barden and William Glen Doerpe, New York, 1975. All quotations are taken from the first (1960) German edition. [My translations]

21. Ibid., p. 376.

22. David Couzens Hoy, *The Critical Circle. Literature, History, and Philosophical Hermeneutics*, Berkeley, 1978, p. 5f. Gadamer never makes such claims and credits Schleiermacher for having defined "understanding" as a linguistic phenomenon for the

first time. See Gadamer, "The Problem of Language in Schleiermacher's Hermeneutic" in *Schleiermacher as Contemporary*, New York, 1970, pp. 68–84.

23. Johann Martin Chladenius, *Einleitung zur richtigen Auslegung vernünftiger Reden und Schriften*. Photomechanischer Nachdruck der Ausgabe Leipzig, 1742. Mit einer Einleitung von Lutz Geldsetzer, Düsseldorf, 1969. Quotations translated by me from this edition.

24. Kant, Immanuel, "Logik" in *Kants Werke*. *Akademie-Textausgabe*, Berlin, 1968, p. 65: ". . . etwas verstehen (intellegere), d.h., durch den Verstand vermöge der Begriffe erkennen oder concipiren" (my translation).

25. As Kant points out in his "*Logik*," we may not be conscious of the rules which underlie our experience and our cognitions. A person may be able to speak without knowing any grammar. But if he speaks without an explicit knowledge of grammar, he is "really in possession of a grammar and is speaking according to rules of which he is not conscious" (my translation). For Kant, the task of the philosopher is therefore to analyze the rules which govern our thinking, i.e., our rational competence ("*Logik*," op. cit., p. 11.). It is not difficult to see how this Kantian model would find an application in hermeneutic theory.

26. Friedrich D. E. Schleiermacher, *Hermeneutics: The Handwritten [sic!] Manuscripts*, edited by H. Kimmerle, Heidelberg, 2nd edition, 1974; trans. J. Duke and J. Forstman, Missoula, Montana, 1977. Meanwhile a new edition of Schleiermacher's hermeneutics containing both the Schleiermacher manuscripts and the edition collated from student notebooks by Lücke (first published in 1838) has appeared: *Hermeneutik und Kritik*, edited and with an introduction by Manfred Frank, Frankfurt am Main, 1977. All quotations are from the Duke-Forstman translation with some minor adjustments to maintain uniformity in the use of terminology.

27. Schleiermacher: Frank, p. 76; Duke-Forstman, p. 97.

28. Schleiermacher: Frank, p. 79; Duke-Forstman, pp. 98–99.

29. A successful attempt was made by Manfred Frank to re-evaluate Schleiermacher's hermeneutics in relation to current trends in literary criticism in his book, *Das individuelle Allgemeine. Textstrukturierung und -interpretation nach Schleiermacher*, Frankfurt am Main, 1977.

30. Schleiermacher: Frank, p. 75; Duke-Forstman, p. 96.

31. Joachim Wach, *Das Verstehen. Grundzüge einer Geschichte der hermeneutischen Theorie im 19. Jahrhundert*, 3 vols., Tübingen, 1926–1933.

32. Droysen, *Historik*, *op. cit.*, p. 328. Part of this work (*Grundriss der Historik*), which Droysen had published during his lifetime, appeared in an English translation in Boston in 1897 under the title *Outline of the Principles of History*, trans. E. Benjamin Andrews, president of Brown University. The quotation is from p. 11 of this edition.

33. Droysen, *Historik*, p. 330; *Outline*, p. 12f.

34. Droysen, *Historik*, ibid.; *Outline*, ibid.

35. On Droysen see Wach, *Das Verstehen*, *op.cit.*, vol. II, and von Wright, *Explanation and Understanding*, *op. cit.*.

36. Droysen, *Historik*, pp. 22, 328; *Outline*, p. 12.

37. August Boeckh, *Enzyklopädie und Methodologie der philologischen Wissenschaften*, edited by E. Bratuscheck, 2nd edition, Leipzig, 1886. English edition (containing Parts I–III: The Idea of Philology, Theory of Hermeneutics, and Theory of Criticism): *On Interpretation and Criticism*, trans. and with an introduction by Paul Pritchard, Norman, Oklahoma, 1968.

38. Pritchard, p. 8; Bratuschek, p. 10.

39. Bratuschek, p. 75. Pritchard renders *Fertigkeit* (competence) incorrectly as "prepara-
    tion" (*Vorbereitung*), p. 43.
40. Bratuschek, p. 76; Pritchard, p. 44.
41. Bratuschek, p. 83 (my own translation). Pritchard has "the writing, the symbol of the
    thing signifying" for "das Zeichen des Bezeichneten, die Schrift."
42. Wilhelm Dilthey, *Leben Schleiermachers*, 2nd edition by H. Mulert, Berlin, 1922
    (first published in 1870). vol. II (parts 1 and 2) *Schleiermachers System als Philosophie
    und Theologie*, Berlin, 1966. Vol. II (part 2) contains: "Das hermeneutische System
    Schleiermachers," pp. 596–787. At one point Dilthey defines the principle of Schleier-
    macher's hermeneutics as "Theorie der Nachkonstruktion des Werkes aus der Sprache
    und der Individualität des Schriftstellers auf Grund des Verständnisses von Sprachen-
    und Gedankenproduktion in ihrer Einheit," p. 707.
43. *Gesammelte Schriften*, Vol. VII, especially pp. 196–204.
44. Dilthey, ibid., p. 216f. The Dilthey quotations have been taken from H. P. Rick-
    mann's translation: *Dilthey, Selected Writings*, Cambridge, 1976, with some adjust-
    ments to assure accuracy in rendering Dilthey's terminology.
45. Dilthey, ibid., p. 217. The passage concludes with a definition of hermeneutics: "This
    art [of interpretation] is the basis of philology. And the science of this art is hermeneu-
    tics."
46. Paul Ricoeur, *Interpretation Theory: Discourse and the Surplus of Meaning*, Fort
    Worth, 1976; and "Der Text als Modell: hermeneutisches Verstehen" in *Seminar: Die
    Hermeneutik und die Wissenschaften*, ed. H. G. Gadamer and G. Boehm, Frankfurt
    am Main, 1978, pp. 83–117.
47. "Der Text als Modell," p. 116: ". . . hat das Verstehen nichts zu tun mit einem
    unmittelbaren Begreifen fremdseelischen Lebens oder einer emotionalen Identifika-
    tion mit einem geistigen Gehalt. Das Verstehen ist durch und durch vermittelt durch
    den ganzen Komplex der explanatorischen Verfahren, die ihm vorausgehen und die es
    begleiten."
48. Roman Ingarden, *The Cognition of the Literary Work of Art*, trans. from the German
    by R. A. Crowley and K. Olson, Evanston, Ill., 1973.
49. Peter Szondi, *Einführung in die literarische Hermeneutik*, ed. J. Bollack and A. H.
    Stierlin, Frankfurt am Main, 1975. The "Introduction" to this *Introduction* appeared
    in *New Literary History*, vol. X, 1978, no. 1, pp. 17–29, trans. T. Bahti.
50. *Introduction á l'analyse du discours en sciences sociales*, Paris, 1979, with contribu-
    tions by, among others, Landowski, Greimas, Giroud, Geoltrain. Part III is entitled
    "Discours d'interpretation."

John Fizer

"ACTUALIZATION" AND "CONCRETIZATION" AS HEURISTIC DEVICES IN THE STUDY OF LITERARY ART

CONDITIONS UNDER WHICH A WORK OF LITERARY ART CAN BE REFLECTED UPON

Literary criticism, i.e., the conscious reflection on the work of literary art, in various degrees and forms, has continually been affected both by the psychological makeup of those who pursue it and by the ideological complexities of the time in which it is undertaken. Attempts to neutralize or at least minimize these effects, so that the object of one's reflection could be grasped *sine ira et studio*, have a long history.[1]

Today the question concerning the neutralization of such effects is as relevant as it has been in the past. Opinions as to whether such neutralization is indeed possible range from explicit denial to explicit affirmation. Edmund Husserl's theory of *époché* is perhaps the most rigorous attempt of our time to make the intellectual inquiry free from the psychological presuppositional interferences into our reflective cognition.[2] On the other hand, some of the structuralists, notably Lacan, Derrida, and particularly Foucault, postulate the impossibility of the cognitive transcendence of one's own structure and hence of comprehending the *interpretandum* on its own terms. Foucault observes: "Interpretation will henceforth always be an interpretation by the 'who.' One does not interpret that which is in a signified but in the last analysis the one 'who' has laid down the interpretation. The principle of interpretation is nothing but the interpreter himself."[3] To Derrida, the thing "out there" cannot be reached and interpreted as it is. In attempting to do this we always end up with creating an illusory depth beyond our words, in sedimenting our language upon someone else's.

The question whether we are or are not capable of comprehending something that is distinct from our own constitution is one of the most complex questions in the history of philosophical thought. All that can be said here is that, at least in the realm of practical knowledge, intersubjectively valid judgments, as representations that are intentionally related to the objects of our consciousness, are possible. Without such judgments, discernment between knowing and the known, between signifier and signified, would indeed become completely blurred. Therefore, the fundamental phenomenological claim that our consciousness can *cogitate* the *cogitatum* has to be posited at least as a matter of intellectual expediency.

In this article an attempt will be made to show how two theoretical concepts, or two heuristic devices, actualization and concretization, as they were conceived by a leading phenomenological theorist of literary art, Roman Ingarden, can facilitate our knowledge of the object of literary art, which is situated "out there," but which exists as a phenomenon of our consciousness.

Phenomenological analysis, as James E. Edie has aptly observed, "requires a consciousness which can achieve a complete awareness of its own acts and their objects within consciousness,"[4] or, one may say, requires an awareness of awareness. Unlike other methodologies that hope to locate and seize "these objects" outside consciousness, an aim that is either incredibly daring or absurd, phenomenological method attempts to "seize" them only as they are given in consciousness. The "seizure" of "this or that"[5] is predicated upon and constituted by the functioning intentionality of our consciousness. Without this intentionality, it would not be able to contain what already exists within its horizon, much less to create new possibilities for what will or might be.

The object of literary art, both in its phenomenological givenness and in its aesthetic potentiality, can be perceived and reflected upon provided, first, that our consciousness neutralizes within itself everything that might impede it from engaging freely in such acts and, second, that this object is also freed from all those contingencies that might prevent it from manifesting itself as "this or that." Specifically, as a linguistic construct, this object is to be freed from that extraliterary context that seeks to ascribe to it specific functions, values, qualities, and the like. It is to be disconnected from all this so that it can be constituted in our consciousness immediately rather than mediately. Further, it is to be discerned from its aesthetic potentiality, both as already attested at a specific time of its existence and as a pure readiness (*Parathaltung*) to take variant or even different semantic and poetic significations. In short, the object of literary art of the artistic datum is to be isolated as a schema, as "a completely static construct (*ein ganz starres Gebild*) which in this stasis secures its identity."[6] It is only upon this operation that we can ascertain this schema as an optimally organized lexical construct endowed with readiness to transcend itself aesthetically.

As a datum, the literary work of art is identical with itself, but as an aesthetic potentiality, it is transcendent to itself. The relationship between artistic datum (A) and its aesthetic potentiality (B) could then be expressed as $A = B$, $A \doteq B$, $A > B$, $A \leqq B$, A / B. Yet, it can never be $A \equiv B$ since such relationship would negate the readiness of A to become also B. In the $A \equiv B$ equation, the artistic datum would cease to be aesthetically productive, would become tautological with its aesthetic addendum. In historical time the readiness of the work of literary art manifests itself intermittently. Thus, at a .certain moment of its existence, it may or may not demonstrate this attribute. Hence the histories of artistic datum and its aesthetic addenda are not always coextensive.[7]

ARTISTIC DATUM AND AESTHETIC ADDENDUM OR TRANSFORMATION AND THEIR CRITICAL RENDITION

In view of the above it is expedient to distinguish between an inquiry into the artistic datum from an inquiry into aesthetic concretization or aesthetic addendum. To seize the former, first we are to bracket the work's historical context as well as our own aesthetic expectancies, i.e., we are to render it both ahistorical and apsychological and only then reflect upon it and describe it. Description of it, by necessity, must be transformational. However, even though nonproportional to the datum, it must be interchangeable with it. Like all descriptions of this kind, it is not to be disturbed by petitio principii.[8] Except the prejudgment that the artistic datum is telic rather than ecbatic, i.e. that it is a classified rather than a quantified construct, all other assumptions about it are to be placed into inaction.

Sharing Roman Ingarden's position on the structure of the artistic object, I shall say that it can be described in terms of its four organizational strata: language sound patterns, unified meanings, presented objectifications, schematized aspects.[9] Description of these four strata could be undertaken on two levels: on the level of material or coded discourse, and on the level of the model. Both can be rendered by different semiotic systems. However, nonverbal and particularly algorithmic and mathematical renditions of the model, *per se*, are likely to lose recognizable affinity with the work of art.[10] The material or coded discourse, either as metonymic chains or metaphoric equivalences, and which contain numerous places of indeterminacies,[11] are to be described both selectively and in their partial representation. Completed percepts of partially given objects that might emerge during our reading of the text are to be treated as aesthetic addenda, i.e. creative additions of our mind, since, as Ernst Cassirer aptly observed, our mind in every moment of its intentional acts tends to convert structural incompletions "into comprehensive totalities, into distinct groups and series."[12]

Aesthetic addenda, unlike artistic data, originate out of the specific encounter of our consciousness with the partially determined objects of the artistic work.[13] The nature and the magnitude of these addenda depend both upon the degree of the schematizations of all four strata of the artistic work as well as upon the creative capacity of the perceiving consciousness. Should, for example, the work's stratum of "unified meanings" be dense, then the valent aesthetic addenda will tend to approximate it rather closely. On the other hand, should it be minimal, they will tend to deviate from it. However, no work of art, irrespective of its minimally or optimally given strata, can exempt itself from aesthetic addenda since its actuality and potentiality are not coextensive. As Ingarden has observed, that which *is* in actuality might be perceived from "basically different positions," e.g. from the naive position of a simple consumer of literature, from the specifically aesthetic position, from the position pursuing political or religious interests . . . and finally from the research position, adhered to by the literary scholar. In each of these cases there will be different modes of completion of interminant places, . . . *But of all these we apprehend only one, i.e. an aesthetic position,* since only this type corresponds to the aim of *artistic* literature."[14]

Aesthetic addenda do not yield as easily to description and analysis as do artistic data. Here the mere selection presents a formidable problem. Description must be limited only to those addenda which have already been expressed through generally acceptable communicative systems, for example, the theatrical or cinematographic presentation of the dramatic text, the visual illustration of the novel's plot or protagonists, the critical amplifications of specific components of the poem, the creation of the poetic work as a response to a poetic work, etc. These are but very few examples that might contain aesthetic addenda to artistic datum. One should remember, however, that they always represent particular historicity rather than atemporal qualities of the work of art. In part, studies of these addenda might enable us to see to what extent particular concretizations reveal or conceal the work's aesthetic potentialities, how

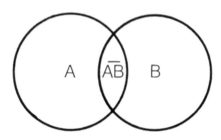

our own concretizations differ from those we study, and to what extent they are subjective or intersubjective.

The Extent of Comparative Inquiry

Actualization of what is given and reconstruction of what has been added to the work of literary art, as methodological or heuristic devices for the study of intentional objects, can also be applied to the comparative study of two or several literary works. Phenomenologically oriented scholarship has not yet explored this possibility fully. What follows here is by no means intended to be programmatic. Much would have to be done theoretically before a definite method could be offered. As a preliminary speculation this can be said: Having arrived separately at the intersubjectively invariant description of all four compositional strata of two artistic objects, we are then in a position to compare only several of these strata or only two of them. No comparative inquiry can describe affinities of all four strata of the two literary works since such affinities hardly exist unless, of course, one deals with explicit parody or close imitation. Consequently, such limited comparative study can describe, for example, affinities of protagonists, or quasi-statements, or language, or aspects, but hardly ever two works *in toto*.

Graphically one could represent such study as two intersecting sets $(A \cap B)$ in which $AiB \equiv AB \neq 0$. Two epistemic prejudgments are to be observed in such study: first, both structural and material or coded affinities between two or more works of literary art are to be asserted only after they have been "seized" and reflected upon separately, and, second, such affinities exist between only some components of the work of literary art.

As an example, let us take Dostoevsky's *The Brothers Karamazov* and Schiller's *Don Carlos*, two works that have already been studied comparatively.[15] But first, what is the initial impetus for undertaking such a study? First and foremost, in both works there are grand inquisitors who resemble each other a great deal. In *Don Carlos:* "Enter the Cardinal Grand Inquisitor, ninety years of age and blind, leaning on a staff, and led by two Dominicans. As he proceeds through their ranks, the grandees all cast themselves down before him . . . He accords his blessings." In *The Brothers Karamazov:* "He is an old man, almost ninety, tall and erect, with a withered face and sunken eyes . . . The crowd instantly bows down to the earth, like one man, before the old Inquisitor. He blesses the people in silence and passes on." Both Inquisitors, guardians of the ultimate order, are highly enigmatic and apodictic in their pronouncements. Both act from the position of ultimate power. Between two works of literary art, this is, then, the point of contiguity. Moreover, *The Brothers Karamazov* contains thirty-two references to Schiller. Using this as a point of departure, let us see whether the two works, as artistic data, are related and in what way.

First, let us look at their material, or coded aspects. *Don Carlos* is written in the iambic pentameter, blank verse, with numerous enjambments. Its vocabulary and syntax are highly rhetorical, exalted and often impassioned. It is a typical *Bühnensprache* of the *Sturm und Drang* type, at least to line 2940. Its semantic function visibly attempts to retrieve a pseudohistorical drama from the French prose romance of 1672 (*Don Carlos*, Nouvelle Historique, by César Vichard, Abbé de Saint-Réal). Its language, therefore, is not explicitly polysemous. Its protagonists, being *dramatis personae*, externally, are given *at once*, while internally, they are presented serially. Basically, the drama is constructed as a love triangle—father, stepmother, son—and treats all other themes, such as friendship, adultery, emotional agony, pride, and even death, as derivative of this triangle. Briefly, its aim is an artistic rendition of the tragic love with all the psychological and historical complexities thereof.

The Brothers Karamazov, on the other hand, is a romantic novel, written in prose, arranged into four parts, twelve "books," and the epilogue. Its vocabulary and syntax range from the simple colloquial to highly orchestrated philosophical discourse. It is Dostoevsky's most mature linguistic construct. Its semantic function is explicitly polysemous. Its protagonists, both externally and internally, are given serially. The novel, against the background of its convoluted love of father and son for Grushenka, explores the theological and moral complexities of God and Church, of man's existential choices and their tragic consequences. Here numerous themes exist as autonomous rather than hierarchically arranged phenomena. They seem to be coextensive with one another. Briefly, the novel aims at thematic multifunctionality.

Even within this highly schematic perception of the two literary works, the following observations seem to be plausible: on the level of their material aspects, they are explicitly disparate, but in terms of human relations, depicted in both works, there are some affinities. The King of *Don Carlos*, Philip II, and Fedor Karamazov both share in similar disposition toward their sons, Don Carlos and Dimitri respectively. Both are consumed by the crippling jealousy, both are adulterous, and both are hopelessly competing with their sons for the love of the considerably younger women. In *Don Carlos* the Cardinal Grand Inquisitor is juxtaposed with the submissive King, in *The Brothers* with the commanding figure of Christ.

Thus, in the former the awe-inspiring power of the Cardinal is left unchallenged, while in the latter it is translated into the apocalyptic opposition of good and evil. In other words, in Schiller's work it is a dramatic device, a denouement, while in Dostoevsky's, among other things, it is an intensely philosophical probing into the tragic dimensions of freedom and human will. In sum, the affinity between these two artistic data is partial. There is no reason, of course, why, after establishing this affinity, we should not proceed to describe their differences comparatively and thus perceive the two in their total givenness.

Aesthetic concretization of these two works of art, as a common denominator, cannot be studied, because it simply does not exist as such. *Don Carlos* is aesthetically concreticized per se, and so is *The Brothers*. The works do not *live* aesthetically as a unified configuration. However, what could be studied comparatively is the above common components as they are expressed aesthetically, for example, the aesthetic addenda to, or the aesthetic transformations of, the two Inquisitors, two fathers and sons, etc. Since such additions and transformations are always historical, the comparative study of them is to be confined to one and the same period. As is well known, the aesthetic perception of *Don Carlos*, since its artistic inception, has undergone a series of shifts. It has been perceived as a King Philip play, a Marquis of Posa play, a Don Carlos play, a family tragedy, etc. *The Brothers*, on the other hand, has not yet had as extensive a history as Schiller's drama, but it, too, has been variously experienced. The aesthetic "lives" of the two might have something in common, especially since father/son erotic rivalries are considered as literary topos.

In this restricted way, Dostoevsky's celebrated novel could also be compared with other literary texts, e.g. Voltaire's *Candide*, Hugo's *Les Misérables*, Goethe's *Faust*, etc., to which Dostoevsky refers both in the text and especially in his *Notebooks*.[16] Such multiple comparison could show the extent of the "intertextual" character of Dostoevsky's novel. Diagrammatically, this intertextuality will be the sum of the set A and

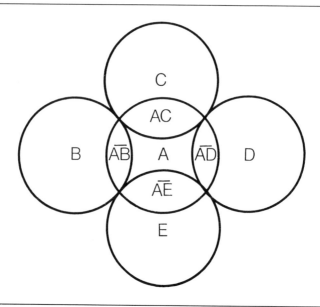

the complements of sets BCDE, i.e. A ∩ (AB ∪ AC AD ∪ AE). Separately, i.e. without the set A, these complements represents AB ∪ AC, etc. = ∅ or null set.

Actualization can, of course, be undertaken on the level of the modeling systems, i.e. on the level of the formal analogies. Inasmuch as the two systems are free of accidental features and thus are pure operational abstractions that exist prior to the coded discourse, they do not have to be subjected to the reductive process mentioned above.

The modeling system of Dostoevsky's novel can be compared with modeling systems of the works of Schiller, Hugo, Goethe, etc. Comparison of Dostoevsky's and Schiller's works reveals profound differences. Thus, while indeed some components of Schiller's and Dostoevsky's works display striking similarity in terms of their modeling systems, the two works share little in common.[17]

The question whether aesthetic concretizations can be studied at all is and still will remain open. For example, a reader of *The Brothers Karamazov*, or for that matter any other work of literary art, experiences at least two types of aesthetic concretizations, one while reading the novel and another upon completing it. These two may resemble each other or may be at variance, since in the unfolding of the text, its objects might be perceived differently. For example, during the initial chapters, Ivan Karamazov might be concretized as a person with an integrated personality, in the subsequent ones as a split personality. If one adds to this the fact that many aesthetic concretizations do not get verbalized and that those which do may be transformed by the prevalent linguistic code, then the question of the objective and comprehensive study of aesthetic concretizations, as such, might indeed appear very complicated.

True, one can argue that what does not exist as a linguistic or any other semiotic fact does not exist as a datum and therefore one need not speak of aesthetic concretizations which have not been expressed one way or the other.[18] And yet, as Jean Piaget has observed, between the recognition of sign and the conduct involving reconstitution and evocation, there are at least ten levels of transition which may be empirically ascertained.[19] Hence, aesthetic concretization might not necessarily occur only as a verbal completion. Nevertheless, it must be expressed somehow in order to be studied objectively.

Whether what is being expressed correlates exactly to what is intended to be expressed is a question that cannot be answered easily. This could be, however, said: aesthetic concretizations, in order to be studied, must be arrested or frozen in time by some system of verbal, cinematographic, choreographic, etc. communicative signs. Only such concretizations may yield to descriptive analysis. Most "book reviewing," "l'explication de textes," "découverte du poème," "paraphrase," "perspectival and depth interpretations," most academic and nonacademic lecturing on this or that work of literary art, etc., are such "frozen" concretizations. All of them attest to the multiple mode of the work's aesthetic existence.[20] Consequently, *The Brothers Karamazov* could be studied in terms of continuous temporal changes as attested by the aesthetic addenda ascribed to it. Specifically, one could study the perception of this novel in the span of its historical life in one or in several countries; one could study comparatively the Russian, German, French, and American perceptions of it; one could study its aesthetic concretization as part of the particular cultural syncretism or as part of the cult; and, finally, one could study it in conjunction with the aesthetic concretization of thematically or structurally similar works of literature.

Aesthetic concretizations, unlike reconstructuve actualizations, occur on the material and never on the formal level. And since our consciousness is organized as a process of categorization, i.e. as differentiation and discrimination, works of creative art are never concretized in their totality. In other words, in perceiving the work of literary art aesthetically, our consciousness amplifies, transforms, and changes only some of its components and circumvents others. In consequence of this fact, even the most attentive contact with the work of art cannot be aesthetically comprehensive.[21] Because of this fact, in order to acquire an inclusive knowledge of the aesthetic sensibility of a particular period, the historian of literature must not limit himself to only one aesthetic perception, no matter how "representative" or sophisticated it claims to be. He must study as wide a range of them as possible. Thus, to acquire a comprehensive view of aesthetic perception of *The Brothers Karamazov* in Russia in the eighteen eighties, one must read a number of often mutually exclusive "concretizations" of it, e.g. that of Solovëv, who considered Dostoevsky a "prophet of God" as well as that of Mikhailovsky, who thought of him as a "sadist." These and many other perceptions are simultaneous modes of this novel's "life" in the eighteen eighties. Comparative study of aesthetic concretizations, for example, could mean multiple possibilities: to name only a few, comparison of such concretizations within the same period as well as within different periods; comparison of aesthetic concretizations by different generations, by different nations, by ideologically different groups, by committed as well as by objective criticism, by those with extraliterary and those with purely literary interests. Would such a study contribute in any essential way to our knowledge of aesthetic sensibilities of a given historical period? Should we agree with Pichois and Rousseau that the comparative study of literature "est l'art méthodique, par la recherche de liens d'analogie, de parenté et d'influence, de rapprocher la littérature des autres domains de l'expression ou de la connaissance, ou bien les faits et les textes littéraires entre eux, distant ou non dans le temps ou dans l'espace, pourvu qu'ils appartiennent à plusieurs langues ou plusieurs cultures, fissent-elle partie d'une même tradition, afin de mieux les décrire, les comprendre et les goûter,"[22] then, such a study would in no way be devoid of intellectual significance.

SUMMARY AND CONCLUSION

Reconstructive actualization of the work of literary art, as an artistic datum and concretization of its aesthetic potentialities, as a creative addendum to it or transformation of it, have been proposed as two viable devices for such an inquiry by phenomenological aesthetics and particularly by its most prominent reprensentative, Roman Ingarden.

In this brief exposition of these two devices, an attempt has been made to assess their applicability to comparative approach to literary art. Adhering to Ingarden's ontology of intentional objects, it has been stated that (1) problems of formal and material structures of the work of literary art in their immediate givenness cannot be explored objectively unless, by a process known as *épaché*, we free our consciousness from all those presuppositions which will impede such exploration; (2) after having bracketed both the particular presuppositions of our consciousness which tend to subordinate the object of our perception to themselves as well as the contextual contingencies of this object, we are to discern between artistic datum and aesthetic addenda; (3) the discernment of the former, via reconstructive *actualization*, is to be strictly descriptive. The comparative study of two or more works of literary art, as artistic data, is not subject to historical delineation. Works produced in different historical and aesthetic periods can be brought into common focus; (4) the comparative study or aesthetic concretizations, on the other hand, is always historically bound. To be studied objectively, they must be rendered by some semiotically meaningful mode.

Notes

1. Aristotle's views on *methodos* mark perhaps the initial thrust of what subsequently became the perennial issue of practically every humanistic and scientific inquiry. In his *Psychology*, he wrote: "To arrive at any 'trustworthy connection' (*pistis*) about the soul is one of the hardest tasks with which we are ever confronted. As we are faced here with the same problem as in many other fields of investigation—the problem of discovering a thing's 'essential nature' (*ausia*) and 'what it really is' (*to esti*) it might be supposed that there is some single procedure (*methodos*) applicable to all the objects whose essential natures we may wish to ascertain, just as there is a single way of demonstrating each derivative property. If such were the case, it would be our task to discover the procedure in question. If, on the contrary, there is no universal procedure for finding a thing's 'real nature' (*to esti*), we are faced with an even harder task; for we shall then have to determine with respect to each particular subject what method (*tropos*) is to be pursued. Moreover, even if it is obvious that the method is to be a certain kind of demonstration (*apodeixis*) or 'logical division' (*diairesis*) or something equally familiar, we are still beset with difficulties and liable to error when we look for the proper starting point of our inquiry" (*Aristotle*, trans. Philip Wheelwright, [New York, 1951], p. 117).
2. Cf. Edmund Husserl, *Ideen zu einer reinen Phänomenologie und phänomenologischen Philosophie* (The Hague, 1950/52), vol. I, p. 6. Cf. also Roman Ingarden's discussion of *époché* in "Probleme der husserlischen Reduktion," *Analecta Husserliana*, ed. A. T. Tymieniecka (Dortrecht, 1976 pp. 1–73). On the other hand, Hans-Georg Gadamer, known for his views on hermeneutics, believes that the neutralization of one's prejudice is not only unnecessary, but even harmful. Such neutralization renders us sterile and incapable of effectively grasping the object. Hence, "it is not so much our judg-

ments as it is our prejudgments that constitute our being" (*Wahrheit und Methode* [Tübingen, 1960], p. 261). Merleau-Ponty believes that the containment of the thesis of the world, as it exists in our consciousness, is neither possible nor necessary since the subjects and objects achieve an accord prior to all reflection. What is necessary is that the subject prepares itself for the object, comes to be on a par with it. Such prepraration, through an intensive self-awareness, contains the perceiving consciousness to destroy the object (cf. *Phenomenology of Perception* [New York, 1922]).

3. Michel Foucault, "Nietzsche," *Philosophie* [Paris, 1967], no. 6, p. 189.

4. James M. Edie, "Transcendental Phenomenology and Existentialism," *Phenomenology: The Philosophy of Edmund Husserl and Its Interpretation*, ed. Joseph J. Kockelmans [New York, 1967], p. 243.

5. Cf. Joseph J. Kockelmans, *Phenomenology and Physical Science*, [Pittsburgh, 1966], p. 40–47.

6. Roman Ingarden, *Das literarische Kunstwerk*, 4th ed. [Tübingen, 1972], p. 389.

7. Roman Ingarden defines the work of literary art as an intentional object this way: "All their material determination, formal moments, and even their existential moments, which appear in their contents, are in some way only ascribed to purely intentional objects, but they are not embodied in them, in the strict meaning of this word. . . . In other words, a creative poetic act cannot create a self-existent object. It is 'impotently creative.' What it creates lives by its grace and its support, and cannot become something 'spontaneous, independent, autonomous.' If it may be so expressed, it cannot have any other properties in its contents, any other identity, arbitrarily chosen, *but those* which have been ascribed to it. It does not have its own existential foundation in itself. Its existential foundation is in the conscious act that produced it intentionally, or more exactly in the psychic subject who performed the act" (Roman Ingarden, *Times and Modes of Being* [Springfield, Ill., 1964], p. 64).

8. Cf. Roman Ingarden, "Über die Gefahr einer Petitio Principii in der Erkenntnistheorie," *Jahrbuch für Philosophie und phänomenologische Forschung* [Halle, 1921], Bd. 4, pp. 545–568.

9. Cf. my "The Concept of Strata and Phases in Roman Ingarden's Theory of Literary Structure," *The Personality of the Critic, Yearbook of Comparative Criticism*, ed. Joseph P. Strelka [University Park, 1973], pp. 10–39.

10. Mikel Dufrenne speaks about such renditions of the structure in this way: "(1) The mathematical formula discovered in the construction of a work is often only approximated. (2) No formula can be evoked to explain the beauty of a work. A schema, whether numerical or not, instructs us concerning the structure of a work and reveals to us the procedure of its fabrication, but tells us nothing of the total work, which can be considered only on the condition of relegating the results of our analysis to a second level. (3) We must not believe that this formula is indispensable to artistic creation. We could discover an order in a picture which is rigorous and subject to mathematics without that order's having been deliberately willed by the artist. Inspiration can lead to the same results as calculation and an artist can incorporate geometrical shapes into his work while having no thought of geometry as such" (*The Phenomenology of Aesthetic Experience* [Evanston, 1973], p. 294). Roman Ingarden stated his views on the quantitative analysis of the work of art in "Sprawa stosowania metod statystycznych do badania dzieła sztuki," *Studia z estetyki* [Warsaw, 1970], vol. III, pp. 56–94.

11. Cf. Roman Ingarden, *Das literarische Kunstwerk*, pp. 261–270. Also Henryk Markiewicz, "Places of Indeterminacy in a Literary Work," *Roman Ingarden and Contemporary Polish Aesthetics*, ed. P. Graff and S. Krzemien-Ojak [Warsaw 1975], pp. 159–171.

12. Ernst Cassirer, *The Philosophy of Symbolic Forms* [New Haven, 1957], vol. III, p. 115.

13. By specific encounter, I mean a perceptual posture through which the reader seeks no particular objective, e.g. knowledge, verification of his assumption, support for his ideology, etc. In this type of encounter he neither reconstructs nor adapts the artistic work to his expectations, but simply lets it unfold itself in its fullness. Hence the term concretization could have a variety of meanings. Actualization of the work's structure or the cognition of its sound system could also be regarded as concretization. In this article this term is applied only to the "aesthetic addenda" or aesthetic amplifications.

14. Roman Ingarden, *Issledovaniia po estetike* [Moscow, 1962], p. 85.

15. Cf., for example, E. I. Čyževskyj, "Schiller und die Brüder Karamazov," *Zeitschrift für slavische Philologie* [Leipzig, 1929], VI.

16. Cf. Edward Wasiolek, ed. and trans., *The Notebooks for The Brothers Karamazov* [Chicago, 1971].

17. Edward Wasiolek believes that Dostoevsky knew what he was writing about. Dostoevsky's notes for *The Brothers Karamazov* "are not those of germination, quest and discovery . . . The subject is firm, the identities of the chief characters are fixed, and the basic dramatic situation is clear . . . The differences between notes and novel are differences between schematic representation and dramatic embodiment, summary and amplification, between ideas and the dramatization of the ideas" (Edward Wasiolek, ibid., p. 12).

18. Some psychologists maintain that reality cannot be grasped independently of language once language has been acquired (cf. J. Church, *Language and the Discovery of Reality* [New York, 1961]. Psychoanalytic theories of consciousness are also predicated upon the notion that consciousness is identical with the ability to verbalize (cf. J. Dollard and N. Miller, *Personality and Psychotherapy* [New York, 1950].

19. Jean Piaget, *Main Trends in Psychology* [New York, 1970], p. 13.

20. This, of course, implies that ontologically artistic objects are ahistorical or synchronic, while aesthetic concretizations are historical or diachronic. Ingarden is rather explicit on this point. He writes: "For us the point of greatest importance is the fact that concretizations which occur in particular epochs are primarily exponents of a relation between the work and the literary atmosphere of this epoch rather than between the work and an individual of a reader. In its concretizations the work becomes typical of its epoch. Since the work lasts through various literary epochs and is perceived through its concretizations, it seemingly undergoes characteristic changes and, considered from this vantage point, it becomes a particular *historical, temporal object*, whereas considered as a work in itself, most faithfully reconstructed, it is a *timeless object*" (*Studia z estetyki* [Warsaw-Łodz, 1966], vol. I, p. 242).

21. Ingarden describes this process this way: "Of course, the ideal reading would be such in which the reader would face only those *strata which compositionally and artistically are most prominent* so that the work could express all its aesthetic qualities in concretization. But simultaneous exposure of the perceiver to all sides of the work can hardly take place, especially when there is an explicit presence of the point of view, a definite orientation of the work in its concretization, and hence the 'narrowing' of the perspective in concretization. All this results, on the one hand, from the multistratal nature of the literary work, and, on the other, from the fact that the reader must fulfill *many* different cognitive, reproductive, and creative functions and therefore is unable to fulfill them simultaneously and with equal attention, participation, and involved gratification of all aesthetic values appearing in the concretization in its different strata" (*Issledovaniia po estetike* [Moscow, 1062], p. 90–91).

22. *La littérature comparée* [Paris, 1967] p. 174.

Eugene H. Falk

INGARDEN'S CONCEPTION OF AESTHETIC VALUES IN LITERATURE

If we wish to comprehend literary aesthetic values—in the sense in which Roman Ingarden conceives of them—we need to understand how they are founded in the presented objects of the text. We must also recognize that these aesthetic values can be apprehended only if we assume an aesthetic attitude toward the literary work of art. Such an attitude requires that our attention be directed to the *presented world of objects* as they appear in our imagination, rather than to the *represented world*. Above all, it requires that we should focus on the *qualities* of these presented objects, rather than on their identifying characteristics.

In a literary text, sentences do present a world of things, characters, actions, emotions, places, etc., but not all sentences can render these objects imaginationally apprehensible. Sometimes words with special sound-formations are particularly suited to cause a presented object to vividly appear in our imagination.[1] The rhythm of sentences, their brevity, or their convolution may also affect the appearance of presented objects. Sometimes the perspective from which an object is projected may reveal some of its striking aspects and conceal or leave "opalescent" other aspects.[2] The selection of aspects through which an object is made to appear in our imagination determines some of the qualities with which that object is endowed. Moreover, such artistic devices as appropriate sound-formations, figurative word-meanings, complex syntactic structures provide the foundations of various qualitative characteristics with which the presented objects appear in our imagination. The very dynamics of the unfolding of the presented world endow its occurrences and thereby its characters themselves with a qualitative dimension that is founded in the manner in which the "structural order of sequence" is arranged.[3]

All of these *artistic* devices, derived from the layers of sound-formations, meaning-units, aspects, and from the structural order of sequence, contribute to the *aesthetic*—the intuitably qualitative—appearance of the objects of the presented world. Therefore, in a work of art the qualities of objects are not merely stated: they are "exhibited" through the presented materials which are the "carriers" of their aesthetic qualities. For instance, the aesthetic qualities of courage, self-control, self-indulgence, generosity, vanity, gentleness, pettiness, friendliness, wittiness, wisdom, intelligence, strength, joy, weakness, as well as all those experienced through sensation, are inaccessible to perceptional cognition. Only their carriers are perceptionally apprehensible, whereas aesthetic qualities must be intuited to be experienced.

The literary work of art provides the reader only with the skeletal structure, the schematic base, of all its presented objects. No object can ever be exhaustively presented through language, which means that all objects are projected only schematically: they all have their "points of indeterminateness." Because of their schematic nature, all presented objects are necessarily addressed first to our intellectual apprehension— to our understanding and our acts of objectification, which may sometimes involve acts of incipient imagination. However, we must be able to *imagine* the presented objects if we are also to intuit their qualities. This means that the objects must be not only *presented*, but also *exhibited* for our imaginational perception.[4] Our acts of imagination constitute the indispensable first phase of our aesthetic experience. These acts are, however, possible only when we "concretize" the schematically presented objects, i.e., when we "fill out" at least some of their points of indeterminateness, and thereby render them imaginationally perceptible. Our intuition of aesthetic qualities is always based on perception, be it direct (original) or imaginational. We call qualities "aesthetic" only when they are thus founded, when we do not need to deduce them from our intellectual apprehensions, in which some of them (though not those derived from sensations alone) are also founded.

In a literary work of art, artistic devices are selected with a view to the aesthetic qualities which the presented objects are meant to carry. The devices and the presented objects themselves must also be arranged in a manner conducive to the formation of a harmonious, cohesive configuration of aesthetic qualities, i.e., of an "aesthetic object" (or of several aesthetic objects that coexist harmoniously within the concretion of a single work). Only those aesthetic qualities which are congruous lend themselves to the constitution of an aesthetic object, and are therefore judged to be "relevant" and of aesthetic value.

It follows from what we have noted so far that a literary work is a work of art when all its artistic elements are selected and arranged to enable the reader to constitute an aesthetic object on the basis of an imaginational experience of the presented world. It also follows that: (1) all elements that perform this function have *artistic value;* and (2) all relevant aesthetic qualities have *aesthetic value*. The artistic value of a work as a whole is consequently subordinate to the aesthetic value of the aesthetic object, while every single artistic value depends on the aesthetically valent quality which it founds. This founding and dependence characterize the relation between artistic and aesthetic values, and we may therefore say that artistic values are "relational" to aesthetic values.

When we examine our responses to these very different kinds of value, we note first of all that each has its own "material quality" (*Wertqualität*), its particular material foundation. The artistic value of a work is founded in the exhibiting devices of its various layers and of its structural order of sequence. These devices constitute the material quality of that work's *artistic value*. Our response to this value is based on our aesthetic experience and on our subsequent reflection on the effectiveness of the artistic elements that found the relevant aesthetic qualities. Our response to artistic values is thus reflective and judgmental. On the other hand, when we respond to the aesthetic value of an aesthetic object, we do so with a spontaneous appreciative acknowledgment, with what we call an *aesthetic valuation*, elicited by the harmony of congruous aesthetic qualities capable of being constituted into a cohesive aesthetic object.

Moreover, the particular selection and arrangement of the aesthetic qualities assumes a form which has its own quality—unique in every literary work of art—and this *Gestalt* quality has its own value, to which we refer by vague designations such as "beauty," "gracefulness," "excellence," or "powerfulness." These values are grounded in the set of aesthetically congruous and relevant qualities that constitute their material foundation. Since the same designations may be ascribed to the *Gestalt* qualities of different literary works of art, the material foundations of such values may be constituted by various assortments of congruous aesthetic qualities. Therefore, there must be some as yet undetermined principle that governs the artist's selection and arrangement of those aesthetic qualities which can found the material quality of the value that we call, for instance, "beauty."

Because the qualities that can form the material foundation of "beauty," "gracefulness," or "powerfulness" must be a set of congruous qualities, the very *principle of congruity* of aesthetically valent qualities needs to be ascertained. Ingarden's suggested division of groups of such qualities into "primary" and "secondary" is a useful beginning.[5] However, the discipline of aesthetics needs a Cuvier, who, almost two centuries ago, established the principles of the subordination of organs and the correlation of forms, according to which some characteristics are in a necessary relation of mutual coexistence, whereas others are mutually exclusive.

The discovery of the principle of congruity of aesthetic qualities would not only solve the problem of the constitution of material qualities of various aesthetic values. It would also elucidate for the literary artist the principles that govern his or her selection, assortment, and arrangement of all artistic elements with a view to the reader's constitution of the aesthetic object. Obviously, such a discovery would guide the competent reader in his or her concretization and constitution of the work's aesthetic object. Moreover, in light of this principle of congruity, the critic could objectively assess the author's artistic accomplishment.

However, there are also other problems that pertain to the aesthetic value of a literary work of art.[6] For instance, how can we reconcile the differences in aesthetic valuations by various readers of the same work?

To be sure, not every valuation is based on a faithful concretization that observes the directives of the text, on an imaginational perception of the presented world, and on a proper regard for the work's artistic elements, aesthetically valent qualities, and aesthetic object. Yet all of these elements of an aesthetic experience are prerequisites for an aesthetic valuation of a work's aesthetic object. Since no two readings of the same work, even by the same individual, will ever yield identical aesthetic concretizations, no two aesthetic valuations can ever be quite the same. This is so because every difference that distinguishes any one concretization from any other necessarily affects the imaginational appearance of at least some of a work's presented objects, and, therefore, the aesthetic qualities which these objects carry. Consequently, each constituted aesthetic object of a given literary work of art must differ at least in some minor respect from each and every other aesthetic object of the same work.

Must we then conclude that the aesthetic value of a work is "relative"? According to Ingarden, every work of art has its own ideal aesthetic object, which corresponds to its perfectly faithful concretion carried out by an ideal reader with superhuman powers of perception, attention, memory, and language. The aesthetic value of a work's own aesthetic object does not depend on individual concretizations which are necessarily imperfect. This does not mean, however, that individual concretizations of a work must be invalid. In fact, Ingarden believed that a series of competent scholarly aesthetic-reflective cognitions of certain works may lead to their increasingly adequate concretions and aesthetic valuations. If the aesthetic value assigned to a work by a given reader results from a competent concretization and from a sensitively constituted aesthetic object, its validity should not be questioned only because that aesthetic object is bound to fall short of the work's own. If someone were to consider such an aesthetic value "relative," we would have to point out that it is relative only in the sense of being (1) imperfect "relative to" the value of the work's own aesthetic object, and (2) "relative to" an individual reader's competence and sensibility.

We know that an appropriate aesthetic valuation is based on an aesthetic concretion, which results from a faithful reconstruction of the work's schematic structure, and from sensitive responses to aesthetic qualities, which are functions of recognizable artistic elements. However, not all of a work's artistic devices are always recognized at the time of their first appearance. Once these devices enter the literary tradition, competent readers recognize them and respond to their aesthetic functions. It may then happen that their perhaps unintended presence is discovered even in works written long before those devices became the focus of reflective critical awareness. For instance, a type of coherence that links textually scattered but correlative motifs, and ultimately affects the *Gestalt* of the work's aesthetic object, has proved to be fairly prevalent in modern novels and recognized for its artistic efficacy.[7] The same artistic devices have now been noted in several works of the past, and our aesthetic valuations of these works can hence be the result of more incisive and more adequate aesthetic concretizations than previously.

When Ingarden spoke of the "life" of a literary work of art, a life that emerges through its various aesthetic concretizations and through receptions by "consumers" in different cultural environments and historical periods, he had in mind (1) different aesthetic valuations of the same work and (2) different evaluations of one work in relation to other works.[8] The life of a work, whose various artistic elements become increasingly manifest as the critical tradition evolves, reveals concretions that yield different but ever closer approximations to that work's own aesthetic object, concretions whose aggregate enhances the *validity* of our valuation. In the light of such new aesthetic valuations a work's aesthetic value may undergo revaluations which may sometimes favorably affect its place in the hierarchy of literary works of art. However, its hierarchical position may. be ultimately weakened—in spite of its transitory acclaim—when it is superseded by works of greater artistic sophistication and aesthetic richness.

These changes in valuative responses do not derive from the reader's taste but from the work's artistic and aesthetic values, which are merely brought to light by the reader's competence and sensitivity. We should note again that this circumstance does not render the aesthetic value of the work "relative," for the reader is not the source of this value; he merely discovers its existence. However, some individual valuations may be relatively more appropriate than others, depending on how closely the constituted aesthetic objects approximate the work's own aesthetic object.

Nor does the value of a work become "relative" only because in relation to other works it proves to be sometimes superior and sometimes inferior. The valence of a value—by virtue of which a value is a value—depends solely on the constant material quality of the value. What does change, and is therefore relative, is its hierarchical position which derives from readers' evaluations. Some of these evaluations are based on variable aesthetic valuations, whereas others may be the result of, for instance, ideological assessments or prevailing tastes which derive from shifting, socially approved trends.

If we do not assess the value of a work on the basis of an aesthetic valuation, but on that of its *reception* among various types of readers in different periods, its popularity and place in the hierarchy of works coexistent with it, and its successes and failures, we deal with its life within the literary traditions of sociocultural communities at different times and in different places. In this instance the value of the work is subject to fluctuations, for here we do not deal with the work's aesthetic value, as we have defined it, but with its sociocultural value. That is to say, we deal with the value it acquires as long as it fulfills certain socially desirable functions or satisfies certain tastes or appetites, regardless of its artistic and aesthetic merits. This value fluctuates because of changing norms within cultural communities, and it is "relative" because it depends on these norms rather than on its material quality.

Ingarden emphasized the difference between a work's artistic and aesthetic values. The material quality of the former consists of artistic elements, whereas the material quality of the latter consists of the congruous aesthetic qualities that form the work's aesthetic object. Because artistic elements are the carriers of aesthetic qualities, a work's artistic value is by its very nature subordinate to the work's aesthetic value. This means that the artistic value is *relational* with respect to the aesthetic value. We might compare the aesthetic value of a work with the nutritive value of a plant. The material quality of this nutritive value derives from the plant's constitutive nature. When this plant proves to be beneficial (or harmful) to an animal, it acquires an additional, positive (or negative) relational value with respect to this animal. We should emphasize, however, that the material quality that constitutes its nutritive value exists regardless of whether that value becomes *also* relational. We may conclude that the material quality of that nutritive value is in a sense absolute. The work's aesthetic value is also absolute, but it is differently structured: it is founded in the congruous qualities of the aesthetic object, and also grounded in the material quality of the work's artistic value. When a work's aesthetic value is recognized by a competent reader, it may become *also* relational, whereas a work's artistic value is always *only* relational.

Now that we have distinguished between (1) artistic and aesthetic values, and (2) individual aesthetic and sociocultural valuations, we should ask how the aesthetic valuation may be integrated into the historical stream of varying receptions. Collective taste most typically derives from philosophical, political, religious, and social normative sources, and focuses primarily on the presented objects—the characters, their environment, view of life, manners, and destiny. Such taste may at times also derive from artistic (presentational) considerations, i.e., from artistic norms that govern a movement or a period. Most literary works reflect the effects of both these types of norms. During a properly executed aesthetic concretization, leading to an aesthetic valuation, we are intent on the discovery of the artistic elements of the work's *formed content,* of its entire stratified structure, and of its structural order of sequence. Even though an aesthetic concretization ignores the presented world's referential function, it nevertheless does not neglect the work's historical *moment,* since its language and its presented objects constitute an implicit historical background. When the sociocultural norms of the collective taste determine the reception and evaluation of a work, however, the truly aesthetic value is frequently neglected.

From the point of view of literary scholarship, it would be a mistake to assume that these very different approaches to the value of a literary work of art are exclusive of each other. Once we understand the differences in their goals and procedures, we realize that these approaches should be complementary, and that aesthetic valuation must be integrated into the literary historical process. This valuation should precede the study of the work's reception, because the work's aesthetic value may form a point of reference with respect to which the varying receptions themselves can be evaluated. For instance, certain presented objects in a work of the past may no longer appeal to a modern public, but we should still recognize the work's artistic effectiveness, identify the artistic and the sociocultural norms to which it adhered, assess the advantages or disadvantages of deviations from them, and determine the turning points that mark the initial stages of new literary periods, those

crossroads at which the encounter between artistic innovation and reception occurs. The presented objects of a work of the past may seem
irrelevant to a subsequent generation of literary "consumers" who do
not take into account artistic means of presentation and their aesthetic
effects. However, from a distanced aesthetic point of view those same
characters, such as those drawn from Greek myths, may appear to be
especially appealing precisely because their particulars have lost relevance, and the universal significance of their views of life and of their
actions can appear all the more forcefully as we focus on their qualitative
determinations. Distanced as we are, we are in a better position to
constitute the aesthetic object of such a work, acknowledge its aesthetic
value, revive its favorable reception, and channel its reentry into the
cultural life of the present. That, for instance, was one of the glorious
achievements of the *Pléiade*.

Notes

1. Roman Ingarden, *Das literarische Kunstwerk*, 3rd rev. ed. (Tübingen, 1965), pp. 59–
   61. George G. Grabowicz, trans., *The Literary Work of Art* (Evanston, Ill., 1973), pp.
   60–61. Hereafter cited as *LK* and trans.
2. *LK*, p. 151; trans., p. 144.
3. *LK*, pp. 326–336; trans., pp. 305–313.
4. Exhibition is the function of effective artistic devices derived from the founding layers
   and the structural order of sequence.
5. See Ingarden's "Das Problem des Systems der ästhetischen Qualitäten," in *Erlebnis,
   Kunstwerk und Wert* (Tübingen, 1969), pp. 191–218.
6. The very complex problem of a work's aesthetic value, which derives from the relation
   between its aesthetic object and what Ingarden calls a "metaphysical quality," requires
   special investigation. I have briefly dealt with that relation in my recent book, *The
   Poetics of Roman Ingarden* (Chapel Hill, 1981), pp. 119–120, 198. That investigation
   would have to be based on the solution of a series of problems pertaining to assortments and configurations of aesthetic qualities appropriate for the emergence of individual metaphysical qualities.
7. See the discussion of "generic coherence" in my *Types of Thematic Structure* (Chicago, 1967).
8. *LK*, pp. 353–380; trans., pp. 331–355.

PHILOSOPHICAL CONCEPTS AND IMPLICATIONS IN
LITERARY CRITICISM

Jürgen Naeher

PHILOSOPHICAL CONCEPTS IN LITERARY CRITICISM

The very formulation of the question of the relationship of literary scholarship or criticism on the one hand and philosophy on the other already implies that there is a possible relationship between the two fields: one should not, however, consider such a relationship to be *eo ipso* a proven fact. Accepting the *possibility* of this relationship should not mean that we then unquestioningly assume, or even substitute for it, the existence of the *real* relationship as a definite concept: this is still something which would have to be developed. However, given that we accept the possibility, this then brings us to the question as to the *conditions* of this possibility (to put it in Kantian terms): that is, as to the conditions of the possibility of literary-theoretical knowledge. Incidentally, modifying the question in this way does not mean that we are already deciding in advance in favor of Kantian philosophy, e.g. of Kantian aesthetics.

What this essay *can*, of course, learn from Kantian philosophy is to conduct its inquiry into these conditions at a measured pace and to reflect historically upon them. This is all the more essential in a case where there may be a *relationship* (that is, the relationship between literary scholarship or criticism and philosophy) which is not merely conjecture but for which there is obviously historical evidence, and which also might be characterized by a fundamental *difference*. The formulation of our topic should not be taken to mean that we have already decided that this relationship exists. The topic is intended only to indicate our line of inquiry as to the exposition of the problem.

LITERARY SCHOLARSHIP, PHILOSOPHY,
PHILOSOPHICAL DISCIPLINES

If we have already spoken of the relationship between philosophy and literary scholarship or criticism in terms of a possible sourse of *literary-theoretical knowledge*[1] (and experience), the reason is that a widespread preconception equates philosophy heuristically with *epistemology*. The epistemological aspect cannot, however, be the only connection between philosophy and literary scholarship or criticism: after all, philosophy, for its part, is not solely epistemology or—in line with its historical development—theory of science.[2] While epistemolgy might be in a position to describe the phenomenon of literary-theoretical knowledge if applied to that particular aspect, the connections between literary scholarship and philosophy could turn out to be far more diverse.

The fact that we may come across many apparent contradictions in the course of our reflections on these connections need not be confusing, given that these contradictions can be comprehended as concepts, as specific differences, *differentia specifica*. In other words, the fact that there must be points where literary scholarship and philosophy differ is the hypothesis of the considerations that follow; indeed, these considerations may even make the relationship between the two more precise in that we do not claim that there is a pure identity between them, even in a disguised form. For philosophical tradition teaches us that definitions are essentially definitions of differences, of what distinguishes one thing from another.

What we *do* claim, however, is the possibility of a fruitful dialogue between the two fields, and some of the conditions of this dialogue will be described here.

PHILOSOPHICAL DISCIPLINES, SCIENTIFIC DISCIPLINES
(LITERARY SCHOLARSHIP): METHODS

Much as one would like to start right away by rejecting the reduction of philosophy to epistemology that we questioned above (and philosophy, in its tradition, continually makes this reduction itself), one can probably say the same of epistemology and of the other "disciplines" of philosophy as of literary scholarship: when one considers both their earlier and their most recent history, philosophy and literary scholarship have one central point in common—their discussion of methods (and this in spite of their great difference in age).

What in literary scholarship, as far as German literary scholarship is concerned, appears as a history of problems of method, is—with its (standardized) sequence of Romantic, historicist or positivist, humanistic-hermeneutic literary study—a tradition which has clearly been influenced by philosophy from the very beginning.

In addition we find at least a provisional analogy to the development within philosophy in the concentrated self-examination to which this tradition has once again been submitting itself during the recent discussion of methods which started, at the latest, in the 1960s.[3] The splitting away of the individual sciences from philosophy had—for both sides— obviously "settled" only superficially the problem of which field was responsible for what subject matter. In fact, the problem smouldered on, at least with regard to the sort of methods that should be used to treat these subjects, and broke out anew in the 1960s, although with a qualitative difference. In literary scholarship, the logical development was to take recourse to philosophy again.[4]

"Paradigms"[5] (positivistic, hermeneutic, and dialectical) were applied to the course of the development of early and modern literary scholarship in a manner analogous to the way they were applied to the history of philosophy—once again paradigmatically reflecting their partly common history. Although within the canon of these methods as paradigms (a canon which at the same time called itself into question), dialectics— both philosophical and aesthetic or literary-critical—claimed to be the mediator of all the others "in the no-man's land of ideas,"[6] this dispute still remains to be resolved. Beyond all the one-sided views that have been propounded, this may be an indication that there are indeed valid grounds for dispute. Indeed, the fact that in the meantime positions have often drawn as close together as is to be expected (thus in the final event only conceivable, after all, in dialectical terms) also speaks for the validity of the dispute.

The result of this latest development is, both in literary study and in philosophy, a pluralism of methods which has been regarded as the "conceptual reflection of a pluralistic society."[7]

In this pluralism, philosophical disciplines, by virtue of their common reference to method, have opened themselves up first to each other, and then to methods of the other individual sciences, which are once again opened up to each other in, for example, literary study: the methodic pluralism of literary study itself is probably evidence of this.

Thus the toto-genere division of (philosophical) truth and method adhered to by philosophy (still, for example, by Gadamer), which has also had important consequences for literary scholarship,[8] has been partly abandoned or has been registered as historically obsolete.

The brief outline of the problem which we have just given enables us to distinguish between at least two extremes of methodical procedure in order to further our reflections on the relationship between literary scholarship and philosophy:

1. To give a historical outline of the development and changes in the relationship as it has actually existed (hence inductively and descriptively).
2. To develop the relationship systematically, demonstrating how it would be methodologically possible to establish the relationship (hence deductively and normatively).

Both aspects are interconnected. The limited space allowed by an essay requires, however, that we select one facet to concentrate on. Since the history of literary-theoretical methods is too extensive for this essay and, moreover, is sufficiently familiar, we shall focus on the second point, although we shall, of course, also take the perspective of the history of methods into consideration as far as is possible.

In the light of our introductory remarks, it is also clear that, however "deductive" our approach to the topic, we shall not be setting out by giving priority to philosophy. Bearing this in mind, we shall discuss in what follows the relationship we outlined before (philosophy, philosophical disciplines, individual sciences (methods), literary scholarship) entirely from the angle of literary scholarship, so far as we feel that this is justified. It is equally obvious, however, that in the course of this discussion, indispensable metatheoretical reflections are bound to come close in method to philosophy. This is already one of our first hypotheses as to the connection and basic common relationship of principles of literary scholarship and philosophy. Furthermore, it should be evident that precisely this special perspective again implies a twofold perspective—inductively taking historical aspects into account.

In this way we shall go on to discuss:

—the relationship between literary scholarship and the associated disciplines,
—the question of whether and to what extent philosophy is an associated discipline with a special status,
—finally, the relationship between literary scholarship and philosophical disciplines, and
—especially the relationship with aesthetics.

For the literary scholar, this raises the question of the legitimacy of applying a genuinely philosophical concept of truth to art. The core of our argumentation will be a discussion of Rüdiger Bubner's essay "On Some Conditions of Contemporary Aesthetics" ("Über einige Bedingungen gegenwärtiger Ästhetik").[9] The paradigms of aesthetics (from Plato on) which are discussed by Bubner enable us first of all to outline a very broad frame of argumentation which is still in principle not indebted to any specific aesthetics. After that, Bubner's recourse to Kant's aesthetics as a possible model is discussed in the terms of this framework.

LITERARY SCHOLARSHIP: ITS RELATIONSHIP WITH ASSOCIATED DISCIPLINES

The pluralism of methods described above can turn into confusion of methods[10] if literary scholarship gives precedence, even if only covertly, to one or several of its associated disciplines, thus tending to lost sight of its real "object": literature. This remains a constant possibility so long as its relationship with the other associated disciplines is not reflected upon *systematically* and *historically*.

The Systematic Aspect

From the more systematic point of view, the fundamental question with regard to the problem of method in literary study concerns those central categories which are used to reflect upon the development of method in the associated sciences. In this connection, one first of all encounters the *concept of the symbol*. If this is understood as a category used continually by literary scholarship (in an almost philosophical way) to characterize the nature of its literary object,[11] we would suggest talking in this context of dimensionalization (*Dimensionisierung*)[12] rather than of category building.

The dimension of the symbolic is meant to denote that central layer in the (literary) work of art which is defined by a historically evolving variety of categories: they are in principle infinite but in practice kept finite. These categories do not refer subsumptively to "symbol" as a general term, that is, they do not disappear *into* that term, but are formed analogously both to a logical paradigm and to epistemological premises.

This model of literary-theoretical concept building, which should not simply follow a predetermined concept of philosophy, enables us for the first time to meaningfully incorporate concepts (categories) with interdisciplinary relevance. In addition, its orientation toward the logical paradigm helps it to keep the conceptual confusion associated with confusion of method within determinable limits. In this way, we should be able to give shape to the multivalency of a concept and a method of the symbolic (and also of the allegorical) already seen in the tradition of literary scholarship.

This diversity of meaning can be justified precisely because it refers to an object which is in itself multivalent and which ultimately allows of no *reduction*.

At the same time we can see analogous methods of concept building in the associated sciences: beyond mere logistic forming of analogies[13] based on the conceptually similar form (the letter), we must pay attention to synonyms where they still relate to the spirit of literature.

Thus, when one reflects upon the associated sciences of literary scholarship, especially when these reflections are based on definitions of literature as "symbolic," one encounters the concept or dimension of *myth*.[14] At the same time one also encounters those aspects which are included by these dimensions. It is logical that when literary scholars reflect on interdisciplinary relationships in the context of the dimension of the symbolic, they take these aspects—historical (cultural and philosophical), religious, sociological, psychological increasingly into account. Analogies have also formed (equally naturally for scientific logic) the basis for definitions which operate *ex negativo*.

In order to give further, brief clarification of the model of dimension building suggested here: the concept of the rite and also of the dream[15] have also been included in the same fundamental relationship. They refer to associated sciences—religion, philosophy of history,[16] sociology, and communication theory[17] (rite), and also, among others, to psychology (dream), as if they had developed out of an implicit dynamic of the concept and at the same time the very subject-matter of literature.[18]

The Historical Aspect

From the more historical angle, we see plausible evidence of the closeness, or perhaps even relationship, implied by the term "associated discipline" in the (relative) unity expressed by the definition and self-definition of these sciences as *humanities (Geisteswissenschaften)*.[19] Without being able to go into this connection in more detail here, we shall once again dwell briefly on the relationship between literary study and these disciplines from the perspective of literary study.

Particularly if one accepts as a definition of the humanities that all these disciplines are to some degree sciences which work with hermeneutic methods and procedures and thus rely on the understanding of *texts*,[20] then an approach based on literary study, on philology in the broadest sense, should be systematically and historically legitimate for more than just our present context. Legitimate, that is, in a methodological sense, in that it continually questions the authority, or at least the level, of this methodological legitimation, and thus brings philosophy, at least implicitly, into play.

The inevitable consequence of such a broad definition of "humanities" is that the range and definition of the text concept becomes extremely broad as well. A partial correlative of this is probably to be seen in the extension which has taken place in many areas, and particularly within recent literary scholarship.[21] The text concept has also been extended to include *situative contexts* (social, psychological, etc.), which were meant to be analyzed and interpreted analogously to the procedure of text interpretation, and which were then also related back to the texts in search of situative contexts within the texts themselves.

This paradigm demonstrates what we were able to ascertain from the paradigm of the symbolic when we considered the systematic and categorical aspect: that is, the at least heuristically valid relevance of the methods of the associated sciences. This was the reaction to a changing concept of the object of literary scholarship which recognized an increasingly diverse range of levels and perspectives: this was, in turn, a response to an object (i.e., literature) which is, both in reality and as a phenomenon, multivalent, and demonstrates the productive recognition of its essence in its historical development. At the same time, an essential part of this development is also the fact that, particularly from the philosphical point of view, it represents a history of increasing desubstantialization of substance (*Entsubstantialisierung der Substanz*).[22]

PHILOSOPHY: AN ASSOCIATED DISCIPLINE OF LITERARY SCHOLARSHIP WITH SPECIAL STATUS?

We are not entitled to deduce the existence of a special relationship between literary scholarship and philosophy merely from the historical fact that the individual sciences, like literary scholarship, ultimately developed (indirectly) out of philosophy. This is all the more true in that the element of autonomy in the process of splitting away as an individual science must be taken particularly seriously. On the other hand, from what has been developed before with regard to symbol, myth, and rite, we can assume that there is a particularly close, even if somewhat tense, relationship between philosophy and literary scholarship. This is true on the level of both content and form: on a very general level of definition, the symbol-myth-rite dimension might well characterize central aspects of both art (and thus of literature and literary scholarship) and philosophy.

Furthermore, if one considers that the history of modern literary scholarship, seen in the context of its relationship with the associated sciences, is essentially a history of (methodical) absolutizations—at least in the sense that influential methods (paradigms), including "fashions," have continually appeared in the form of such absolutizations[23]—then, hypothetically, it is conceivable that literary scholarship could best avoid the shortcomings of absolutization by engaging more intensely in dialogue with philosophy and by referring back, as it were, to philosophy in its capacity as a science whose very nature it is to reflect on abstractions.

This is contradicted by the fact that the recent development of philosophy is itself essentially characterized by hypostatization of methods. Within philosophy too, for example, there was a linguistic turn, clearly biased in part by fashion. But precisely the example of linguisticization (*Linguistisierung*) can show that this need not necessarily be the case, but that it runs especially counter to a concept of philosophy which defines itself, in the light of hermeneutic and dialectical methods, as theory building. Following the speech-act theory of "ordinary language" philosophy (Austin, Searle), Wittgenstein's theory of language games,[24] and finally (equally important but less well known) Humboldt's philosophy of language, Jürgen Habermas outlines the hermeneutic-dialectical framework of a "theory of communicative competence,"[25] and yet, in spite of all the linguistic theorems[26] he necessarily includes, this theory is directed toward a theory of truth, the basic problem of linguistic universals, i.e., philosophy. The fact that scholars (even within philosophy itself, particularly within some of the individual sciences, not least of all literary scholarship[27]) have responded to this sort of pluralistic theory, with its claim to philosophical validity, by ignoring, misunderstanding, or re-interpreting this claim (insofar as Habermas' conception of a theory of truth was related to other than "ideal speech situations") merely indicates a limitation of the *reception*. Particularly theories of "counterfactual" idealizations (Habermas), especially if dialectical in intention or conception, make reception difficult. They require a power of productive fantasy[28] which literary scholars attribute in the final instance to the writer and poet (artist), and at the same time, a power of reflection which not only respects the gradual sequence of stages in abstractions but also reconstructs them and more. (This is a reflective power which some modern aesthetics[29] also analogously but not identically attribute to the artist).

When scholars of philosophy turn their object into a paradigm or even a fashion, they particularly tend to cancel out any possible suspension of hypostatization or to project abstractions to another level (*metabasis eis allo genos*). Thus they contradict at least the spirit of such theories (*philosophemes*), if not the letter as well.

On the other hand, philosophy could obviously be in a position—as the example of the reception of linguistic categories (*Linguismen*) shows—to reflexively transform reductions in the light of the truth-claim.

Under certain conditions, even referring to a philosophy which is nonreductionist (in tendency) is not enough to enable literary scholarship to escape reductionism: precisely our example of the reception of Habermas can go a long way toward making this sort of limitation clear. To make this more concrete, we shall take from a large number of examples Erika Fischer-Lichte's typical method of interpretation (applied to Goethe's "Iphigenie"),[30] a method "which is based on speech-act theory"[31]: on Austin, Searle, and particularly on Habermas. ("In the following we will use Habermas' terminology." [!])[32] A detailed analysis is not possible here: an outline of some of the main features will have to suffice.[33]

In Fischer-Lichte's method, the *dramatis personae* in "Iphigenie" become "constellations of characters"[34] and at the same time constellations of "speakers" and their "utterances."[35] The characters are determined by their "roles as speaker/listener," according to which they "use sentences in their utterances in order to communicate about certain subjects."[36] At the same time, referring to speech-act theory (thus presumably following what she imagines to be Habermas' intention) is meant to clarify the socially mediated function/role of such a speaker/listener on a meta-level of communication with others. Literature and literary scholarship are seen as constituting this meta-level. Thus literature becomes the "anticipation of social possibilities."[37] Further, it should be able to assume a pedagogic function, as "school reading" to serve "emancipatory goals,"[38] and thus possess "relevance for action,"[39] that is, "relate to situations which are socially relevant for the student."[40]

Fischer-Lichte does attempt to give a (provisional) "structural analysis"[41] of the work "Iphigenie" for these "concretized" aims and purposes, but in the final event has to bring individual elements, "utterances," "speech-acts" of the drama, into the individual interpretation: thus she falls into the trap of the methodological copy realism:[42] work/social reality, which she criticizes in others, although she does this (with the help of the *philosophemes*) on a more *reflected* level than she imputes to her opponents. The Utopian elements are coordinated (in the end still rather directly) to the "real," the concrete, the empirical. Witness an example:

The King acts by giving orders, his subjects by carrying out orders:
"One word from you and it [the Greeks' ship, line 2021] will be in
flames." This state of affairs determines a specific distribution of the
different categories of speech-act between Thoas and Arkas. In the
only two dialogues in which both take part, only Thoas expresses
himself in the regulative speech-acts of command, to which Arkas,
however, clearly has no right; he uses only constative speech-acts to
Thoas: he reports to the King on the way things stand at any given
time. (Note: On the different forms of speech-act cf. John L.
Austin, . . . John R. Searle, . . . Jürgen Habermas, ... In the
following we will use Habermas' terminology).[43]

This example of applying speech-act theory (as formulated by Austin,
Searle, and Habermas) to literature (to Goethe's "Iphigenie," for example) shows in our opinion that it is impossible for literary study to
transfer theories with such an abstract claim to validity (theories of truth)
except in that *specific* abstractness.

When a philosophical theory is being constructed, a process of abstraction takes place which can be called "concrete" at best in, for example, the Hegelian sense of the *development* of the (abstract) concept,
or concrete at most in the sense of a "*materialistic* prius" (that is, in the
paradigm of Habermas' theory which we are concerned with here: in the
context of his philosophy).

When literary scholarship does not develop and reflect this process of
abstraction in the same way, and at the same time—from the perspective of the literary work of art—turns it back, as it were, on itself, it
abbreviates in the way we have described above the circle which has
come to be completed; it closes the circle too quickly, omitting precisely
the process of abstraction mentioned.

A theory such as, for example, that of linguistic universals has had to
distance itself much too far from empirical reality for this reality to
continue recognizable in such universals. Literary scholarship does not,
however, interpret its object exclusively, or even primarily, on an empirical level, precisely because this object, by virtue of its aesthetic
mediation of empirical experience, refers us to a meta-level where it can
be reflected upon. It is in this aspect that it differs from the other
(mainly empirical) sciences and comes particularly close to philosophy.
Consciously or unconsciously, it is for this very reason that literary
scholarship has all too often sought refuge with philosophy. All too often
this has happened in an extremely unreflected way, without adequate
consideration of the intermediate steps, that is, of the conditions for the
possibility of establishing such a relationship.

Thus Fischer-Lichte's relating literary scholarship to philosophy is, in
our opinion, half correct: correct, that is, where the totality of the liter-

ary work of art, its relationship to truth, suggests resorting to a philosophical theory of truth. It is also valid when (as is especially true in
Habermas' case) this truth theory is based precisely on the empirically
individual (speech-acts) in its counterfactual abstraction.

(With this line of argument we are following literary-theoretical and
aesthetic theories and will not be able to subject our assumption to a
more rigorous examination until later, in the context of our discussion of
the relationship literary scholarship/aesthetics/philosophy.)

The relationship which Fischer-Lichte establishes is incorrect in the
sense that it curtails the process of reflection and arrives too quickly at
the empirically individual, that is, at speech-acts, which she tends, at
least, to describe as analogous to empirical acts, as if deliberately ignoring their aesthetic mediation.

If it is the special position of its object with regard to empirical experience which brings literary study particularly close to philosophy and vice
versa, then it should also have become clear where we see the central, the
specific, difference between literary scholarship and philosophy.

The fact that, according to an insight in Hegel's aesthetics (which we
shall for the time being pursue only in this one point), art does not
simply turn the individual phenomenon into an example as science does
but rather lets "its object subsist freely and in independence,"[44] suggests
that literary scholarship should likewise let its object "subsist freely and
in independence," at least in its essentials. At the same time literary
study, as a science, cannot do this: this is because it is required, on the
other hand, to clarify basic structures (examples). This clarification
should go beyond mere reconstruction.[45] (Literary) science entirely
shares this requirement with philosophy and, in addition, can probably
most legitimately be related to philosophy in those cases where it tends
to a large extent to preserve the individual nature of its object. Where
this individual aspect is meant to be identified precisely as the most
general (in Fischer-Lichte's case, as the utopia of emancipation), interpretation of literature can be especially legitimately related to philosophy. In procedures like the one outlined here, however, this relationship does not satisfy the claim to philosophical validity when it brings
philosophical theory relatively directly into the *individual* interpretation
of the literary work of art, especially as an interpretation of *individual
elements*. This degrades philosophical theory to a mere theorem. The
methodologically reflected relationship must still, however, be legitimated even when, for whatever reasons (which should be stated), it has
to present these reflections in abridged form: it must be made clear
where the abbreviation is being made, for instance, where individual
elements are being taken in isolation out of the context of a philosophical

theory as a whole. Isolating elements in this way seems to be especially justified in cases where it is possible to demonstrate the influences of, or at least (underlying), analogies[46] to such elements (*philosophemes*). These elements then refer to content rather than to methods (i.e., procedures which are determined by form or determine form).

The answer to our initial question concerning the special status of philosophy can be summarized as follows: of the sciences associated with literary scholarship, philosophy has a special position in at least two respects:

1. Of the other allied sciences, philosophy is particularly close to literary scholarship and its object because of its relation to abstraction and truth (for instance, ideas, utopias, emancipation), which takes it beyond empirical experience.
2. Its special status with regard to all the individual sciences extends in part to its relationship with literary scholarship as well. Philosophy is more "abstract": this enables it, as a theory of science, to reflect upon the methodology of the other sciences, including literary scholarship. This involves a meta-level. The specially close relationship mentioned in (1) could be characterized by the particular adequacy, the particular validity of its methodological reflection.

Thus we have reached the meta-theoretical (methodological) level into which philosophy enables us to inquire, and we can now formulate our findings more precisely. Both on the level of our reflections on literary scholarship in the context of the associated sciences, and on the categorical level (the level of the construction of scientific categories or methods), it has already become evident that it is at the same time necessary to transcend this level to a level we called *dimensional* (the level of dimension building). In the same way, our reflections on the special status of philosophy have enabled us to establish more precisely that this transcending movement must take us in the direction of philosophy.

To express it in philosophical terms with reference to methodology as well: dimension building ought, in other words, to accommodate such a transcending movement. This does not happen when philosophy is applied to literature in a way that tends to be empirical in method, leveling out the intermediate stages of reflection which philosophy went through: such an application, that is, an application of philosophy to literature which curtails the circle of philosophical and (literary)-theoretical knowledge was rejected.

LITERARY SCHOLARSHIP: ITS RELATIONSHIP TO THE PHILOSOPHICAL DISCIPLINES; THE SPECIAL STATUS OF AESTHETICS

This raises the question—which becomes all the more acute when we consider Hegel's dictum—as to whether aesthetics is capable of definitely reflecting upon, completely formulating one of these essential intermediate stages: for only "philosophy of art," aesthetics, is conceivable as a "philosophy" which undertakes to reflect upon art in a responsible manner. In the following reflections upon aesthetics and *its* manner of reflection upon art, we shall, therefore, also reflect upon a reversal of the circle described above: philosophy will not just be considered in terms of the praxis of applying it to art in order to reflect upon art (in scientific terms, empirical in tendency), but also within the field of tension of the construction of a theory where closeness to philosophy is embodied in the extreme. It could, hypothetically, represent or put back what we complained of being lost in the process of abstraction.

If closeness and also *toto-genere* division characterize the relationship between literary study and philosophy, it is possible that there is a particularly close link with individual *disciplines* of philosophy. And within the canon of these disciplines (epistemology, philosophy of history, ethics, philosophy of religion, jurisprudence, etc.), aesthetics, understandably, has a special position. Since its object is art, relating aesthetics to literary scholarship is more legitimate than relating philosophy of history, philosophy of sociology, or ethics to literary scholarship would be, since their objects only correspond in part to fundamental aspects of the artistic object (literature).

Again and again writers/poets and literary critics have demonstrated this in practical terms: even before the Romantic period important poets reflected on the philosophy of art themselves. Literary scholars have always taken this particularly seriously. And at least since Hegel's "refutation of some objections to aesthetics,"[47] in which he tried to prove the *scientific nature* of aesthetics, this has been considered legitimated (at least in the sense that it has been approved from "above").

With regard to the problem as developed so far, we are less interested in the question of *whether* than of *how* aesthetics is positioned within the framework of the basic relationship of principles between literary scholarship and philosophy, that is, how it includes itself, or is included, or *can* legitimately be included.

In the scholarly *communis opinio* at least, there is an ever increasing pressure to legitimate the extent to which the inclusion of aesthetics in this relationship automatically, as it were, means or can mean the inclusion of other philosophical disciplines, such as the philosophy of history. This is probably only the case if one follows quite *specific* aesthetics which postulate and substantiate the existence of such connections.[48] Within the more general discussion of principles which is the object of this essay, this question can, and indeed must, be neglected.

It enters into the discussion only indirectly: that is, in the context of the last question broached ("aesthetics as a possible intermediate stage") it merely arises as the question concerning the special relationship of aesthetics to philosophy to literary scholarship *in toto*.

When important aesthetics, such as, for example, those of Hegel or of Kant, are located within a philosophical *system*, the problem of methodological pluralism vs. confusion can be seen as a problem to be settled in terms of general principles, that is, *systematically*. This means, however, as a common objection (against Hegel, for instance) has it, settling it at the expense of aesthetics and, in the final analysis, of art. Aesthetics comes under pressure to conform to a system, to the dictates of epistemology, and becomes a precondition of abstract knowledge, remote from art. This criticism must be re-investigated for each individual aesthetics. If it is examined here on a more general level, however, (on the basis of Rüdiger Bubner's essay), this is done bearing in mind that the provisional, heuristic reduction of philosophy to epistemology which this entails must be undertaken in a critical spirit, following Bubner's central objection that philosophy, *as* aesthetics, traditionally makes precisely this reduction itself.

AESTHETICS/LITERARY SCHOLARSHIP: THEIR RELATIONSHIP
TO PHILOSOPHY; TWO CONCEPTS OF TRUTH?

Rüdiger Bubner's essay "On Some Conditions of Contemporary Aesthetics,"[49] offers what is probably one of the most remarkable approaches for reflecting on the possibilities and limitations of aesthetics. Particularly indebted to Kant, Bubner discusses conditions of the possibility of aesthetics today. Using aesthetic theorems, he criticizes paradigmatic aesthetics (both traditional and modern) for being *heteronomous*: "critique *of aesthetic reason*" "which may appear as science:"[50]

"Considered soberly, the prevailing appeal of aesthetics to the truth concept, and thus to philosophy, must appear like an attempt to use philosophical terminology to subordinate the theory of art. For this reason I would describe all the aesthetics considered so far as heteronomous. It is typical of them that they do not construct theory of art autonomously but subject it from the very start to alien determination by a preliminary notion of philosophy, its objectives and its terminology."(60)

The object of this criticism is to protect art, the work of art, from being taken over by philosophy and from having a genuinely *philosophical* concept of truth imposed upon it.

"Philosophy does not say what art is; instead, art should show what philosophy is." (40)
"Philosophy interprets art [in heteronomous aesthetics—J.N.] in the light of its own problems. . . ."(41)

The negative circular relation of philosophy (truth theory) to art is also applied here, with a critical intention, in reverse: art is related to philosophy. Here Bubner's formulation of the problem comes close in intention to some of the central objections continually raised by literary scholars against certain aesthetic methods of interpretation, of reflection. Obviously motivated by the desire to *critically* avoid the circle we outlined above, Bubner goes beyond this dimension of criticism, with its literary-theoretical accentuation, in that his critique starts with the concept of the work (of art) as the categorical center of ("heteronomous") aesthetics. Thus, indirectly, he is also referring to a very large extent to the approach of that kind of traditional and contemporary literary scholarship which criticizes and questions methods based on philosophy of art in the sense described above: the work of art as a concept probably constitutes a common, both fundamental and minimal, consensus of aesthetics *and* literary study.[51]

By calling this central category of "work" more radically into question (especially in the light of developments in modern literature and art) than literary scholarship, to a large extent at any rate is willing to do, (for both justified and unjustified reasons), Bubner also furnishes from the "heteronomous" angle an unexpressed *"critique of literary-theoretical reason,"* a critique of the way in which literary scholarship constructs its methods. The validity of Bubner's critical definition, for its part, will be discussed in what follows.

With hermeneutic (especially Gadamer) and *"ideologiekritische"* (Benjamin Adorno) aesthetics in mind, [the Frankfurt school calls its basic approach of criticizing middle-class ideologies from another ideological viewpoint, based on leftist Hegelianism or Marxism, "ideologiekritisch" as it is called in German]*. Bubner suggests that this "enforced and controversial *canon building* represents the result of aesthetics working

*Translator's note

with concepts of truth with different emphases. These aesthetics can fulfill their various programs only by hypostatizing corresponding works." (62) Even when separated from the development of modern art and aesthetics, this aims right at the heart of the work concept, at the heart too of the very method of forming such canons and also of methods derived from that which have developed in the past in German-speaking countries in the form of Romantic positivist or humanistic-hermeneutic literary study, and still occur today.[52] The works of Goethe, for example, whether projected forward or backward (backward to Walther von der Vogelweide, for instance) have continually been a paradigm of this sort, i.e., that of the hypostatizing canonization of the "classic" work. This canon forming, in turn, is always the result of working with a concept of truth, even if, in the final instance, with concepts of truth with "different emphases," as Bubner interprets it in the case of paradigmatic aesthetics. Working in an analogous way, literary scholarship has always tried to legitimate this by referring to *philosophemes* for support (especially in the case of hermeneutic literary scholarship).[53] This would only be a negative circular conclusion if the canonization of the works, in the end of the work concept, as canonization in the name of philosophically specific truth, were already discovered to be such a circular argument— or a *metabasis eis allo genos*—on the level of aesthetic theory which Bubner describes.

It must of course be understood (as a necessary condition of the criticism) that literary scholarship must in any case respect the aspect of *toto-genere* division, the differentness of precisely this level of aesthetic theory and thus of philosophy, and not get involved in a bad circular argument in this respect: just as philosophy, in turn, must respect the differentness of literary scholarship if it wishes to furnish literary study with supporting arguments, methods, and ideas.

Although Bubner throws doubt on the *work* concept as the "ontological vehicle" (49) of a (philosophical) concept of truth, and thus on the generally accepted vehicle of the autonomy of art, yet, at the same time, he insists in a *second* sense of autonomy, that is, on an understanding of the "arts" (38) which tries to do justice to their *intrinsic value* as an "autonomous development" (*ibid.*), even if that means autonomous *against* philosophy.

Much seems to indicate that ultimately this insistence implicitly (or inescapably) points in the direction of the individual sciences: to literary scholarship, for instance, as a potential custodian of this very intrinsic value, so long as it sees its relationship to philosophy as one of dialectical autonomy—and not of hermetic seclusion—and as long as this is in fact the case. The intrinsic value can then manifest itself as the autonomy of the *work of art* after all: as that "poetic truth of a work" (Emrich)[54] which would be respected if autonomy were neither merely the result of the hypostatization of the individual (individual works, for instance) nor of the application of a philosophical concept of truth.[55] Yet this seems to me to be a rather minor strand in Bubner's argumentation which—possibly going against the main thread of his line of argument—I have already linked in advance with this main thread. It now remains to clarify this main line of argument somewhat more.

It is in this context, within the framework of our original argumentation from the perspective of literary scholarship, that we have raised as an urgent question the problem of heteronomous vs. autonomous aesthetics (*vis-à-vis* philosophy), that is, the question concerning the negative circle, where it is perhaps not solely the relationship between literary scholarship and philosophy that is curtailed, but where the short-circuit, concerning the relationship between aesthetics and philosophy, might already have occurred prior to that on a mediating level between the two. This last problem can now, *pars pro toto*, be discussed using some of Bubner's central arguments and following his main line of argumentation.

A paradigm of aesthetics which has for good reason been restricted, or shown its limits, or even rejected in the light of this problem will probably not prevail unquestioned either in literary-theoretical theory building or in methodologically oriented interpretation.

CONCLUSION

According to Bubner, for all their disagreements, both hermeneutic (Heidegger, Gadamer, and their followers) and *ideologiekritische* aesthetics (Benjamin, Adorno) see "art as the locus of truth," "which takes on, especially for philosophy, a paradigmatic significance." (40) "Inasmuch as they essentially relate art to truth, both the hermeneutic doctrine of understanding and radical criticism (i.e., Benjamin, Adorno—J.N.) argue in the same direction, albeit with opposite results." (42) What according to Heidegger's and Gadamer's aesthetics aims primarily at effect, that is, as "original presencing and making clear of truth so that it has an immediate and direct impact by itself [*Wirkenlassen*]" (ibid.), transcends this level systematically in Bubner's aesthetics to become part of the problematic of understanding in the *humanities*. Literary scholarship, as one of these humanities, has responded to this logically and, at the same time, by developing a still unfinished methodological dispute, has criticized this sort of methodological regulation of knowledge.[56]

We cannot discuss here the extent to which Bubner's reconstruction of the analogies which actually exist between hermeneutic and *ideologiekritische* aesthetics ultimately flattens out the *differentia specifica* of both—despite all the differentiation that he also undertakes.[57]

Adorno did indeed perceive the understanding and understandability of art analogously to the "hermeneutic circle" (as Heidegger named it) which Dilthey gave a primarily epistemological dimension.[58] He differed more clearly, however, from the philological-historical method inasmuch as he maintains that we should be able to gain, from the present situation of art, retrospective insights not only into art in the past, but into art in general.

This is a perspective to which Bubner in particular is indebted. This means, however, that it is not just the *"result"* of hermeneutic and *ideologiekritische* aesthetics which is "reversed," as Bubner analyzes it, but even their methodological *approach*. For all the criticism which Gadamer, for instance, made of historicism, the ontologization of the work of art which is rooted in historicism links Gadamer with historicism as its epistemological explication. Bubner has again and again intimated in different formulations such relationships of genesis and effect (or result). For the problem we are concerned with, however, an especially important question on the level of genesis is whether one does not have to reverse Bubner's argumentation, which would logically require the rejection of *any* recourse by literary study to aesthetics as a legitimate discipline. We must ask ourselves to what extent the philosophy which is indeed genuinely developed in individual aesthetics (especially, for instance, in those of Benjamin and Adorno) is a philosophy which has, from the very beginning, been thought through and reflected upon from the perspective of art and, furthermore, whether philosophy can gain access to a (hermeneutically) circular process of understanding only in the form of this kind of *dialectically* developed prejudgment of art: this understanding process takes place for art's sake, but without art being that authority which subordinates philosophy. (Then "a preconception of philosophy" [60] no longer corresponds to a definition of art using a "foreign definition" [*ibid.*] inasmuch as a preconceived idea of art corresponded to it in the definition of philosophy.)

That such reflections arrive at a concept of aesthetic *experience* is (in many ways) logical; both the hermeneutically conceived problematic of *effect* and also the hermeneutically and, in a different way, dialectically conceived problematic of *understanding* refer to a *work* concept which can no longer posit itself as something being in itself without being called into question. Bubner states here, in what is an interpretation of Hegel: "In the wake of conscious thought, the ontological role of the work as vehicle disappears" (49): before this background later ontologies—where there has really been no progress beyond them—must be seen as marking a regression to *before* Hegel. Bubner himself suggests (ultimately more for systematic than historical reasons) going back to before Hegel, i.e., to Kant's *critique of judgment*. In this he sees the only remaining "possibility of a heteronomous aesthetics." (60)

In his main line of argument, Bubner, with this recourse to Kant, disregards at least those problematizations which arose, precisely in literary study, in connection with the overimportance attached to the problems of *effect*,[59] without simply neglecting, for instance, the special construction of an *a priori* preceding all aesthetic experience.

On the contrary, Bubner's recourse to precisely the transcendental nature of the aesthetic-subjective does not take into account the fact that, in its construction, Kant's conception of the genius, his idea of the artist who *freely* creates the work of art (i.e., of subjectivity) falls short of the *critique of pure reason*. Such analysis is, on the other hand, possible for aesthetics only if—on a meta-theoretical plane—it paradigmatically reflects upon *epistemology*, for instance, on the possibility that Kant's *a priori* could be "in any case merely an *epistemological* concept."[60] Here aesthetics requires epistemology—literary scholarship must recognize this—as is made clear by the tradition of philosophical "systems" leading from Plato and Aristotle to Kant, Hegel, Schopenhauer, Nietzsche, and Heidegger, and on through to antisystems like that of Adorno.

Bubner's return to the "critique of judgment" starts with his intensified criticism of the work concept. He finds the work concept heteronomous even in Aristotle's *Poetics* which, in his opinion, makes an "ontological preliminary decision" (61) in the thesis of.the technical imitation of nature which has far-reaching consequences for the later "use of the work concept" (*ibid.*).

If one submits this line of argumentation to philosophical criticism (again from the perspective of literary scholarship), then it is indeed beyond doubt that Aristotle's *Poetics* is dependent on the *technical* (i.e., *techne*, artistical) and also on the empirical—"psychological" aspects. Aristotle's concept of appearance, however (unlike Plato's concept of appearance[61] which Bubner finds more convincing), indicates a central problem which both aesthetics and literary scholarship, if they do not want to be "heteronomous" (in Bubner's sense), ought to reflect upon, particularly if they do not wish to follow Bubner's line of argument to the point of totally rejecting the work concept: in contrast to Hegel, aesthetic appearance is for Aristotle not appearance as the form in which the absolute (the essence) appears. Such an aesthetic is excluded from mere heteronomy by a special construction, the postulate that, although this absolute (essence) *may* in fact appear, this does not necessarily prove the truth-content of the work of art. Aristotle's ontology does not finally posit the work of art as the ontological locus of the truth of the essence. Thus the *Poetics* shapes laws which reflect precisely upon their own intrinsic value, and do not reduce subsumptively to the idea of beauty. In the *Poetics* Aristotle set aside the subsumptive logic of "logic," thus probably first providing the necessary condition for his legitimate reception not only in later poetics, particularly in those that are oriented toward literary scholarship, but also in artistic praxis: the principle of contradiction, which is fundamental to Aristotle's logic, is, for such literary study, not applicable to its object.[62]

The question posed at the beginning of this essay concerning the concept of philosophy appropriate for art, and thus for literary scholarship, must be answered anew from this angle. It must be seen from a historical perspective and go beyond Bubner's reduction to the paradigm of Kantian "reflecting judgment." This philosophy would be one that takes into account that the character of art is inherently contradictory. Dialectical *philosophemes* ranging from Hegel to Kierkegaard through to Sartre's existentialism and Adorno's "negative dialectics" ought to be considered first for heuristic reasons. What must be clarified by scholarly theoretical discussion on that meta-level of which we have given a (provisional) description, with arguments which justify relating art and literary scholarship to philosophy, is whether and to what extent such *philosophemes* do not dissolve in a reductionist manner the basic structure of the contradictory, rather than accommodating and pursuing it.

(Translated from German by
Penelope Willard and Keith Hoeller)

Notes

1. See, for example: P. Szondi, "Über philologische Erkentnis," in Szondi, *Hölder-lin-Studien*, Frankfurt am Main 2, 1970. Szondi, "Einführung in die literarische Hermeneutik," *Studienausgabe der Vorlesungen*, vol. 5, ed. J. Bollack and H. Stierlin, Frankfurt am Main, 1975. J. Strelka, *Vom literarischen Kunstwerk und seinem Erken-*

nen, recently reprinted in *Werk, Werkverständnis, Wertung. Grundprobleme verglei-chender Literaturkritik*, Bern-München, 1978. See also references to literature on hermeneutics given in the following; paradigmatically we would mention E. Staiger, *Die Kunst der Interpretation. Studien zur deutschen Literaturgeschichte*, Zürich, 1955, and the ensuing debate.

2. Cf., for example, J. Habermas, *Erkenntnis und Interesse*, Frankfurt am Main, 1968 ff. (referring particularly to Hegel, Marx, Comte, Mach, Peirce, Dilthey, Freud, Nietzsche).

3. Inevitable abbreviations cannot be discussed here.

4. Because of their historical development both philosophy and literary study felt—and in my opinion still feel today—the need to catch up on a methodological discussion which relates philosophy more strongly to the individual disciplines, and (*vice versa*) the individual disciplines to philosophy.

5. Cf. Th. Kuhn, *Die Struktur wissenschaftlicher Revolutionen*, 1962, Frankfurt am Main, 1967. I. Lakatos, "Die Geschichte der Wissenschaft und ihre rationalen Rekon-struktionen," in W. Diederich, ed., *Theorien der Wissenschaftsgeschichte*, Frankfurt am Main, 1974. Cf. also H. Schnädelbach, who talks of changes in paradigm as "qualitative leaps": *Geschichtsphilosophie nach Hegel. Die Probleme des Historismus*, Freiburg-München, 1974, p. 164 f.

6. Th. W. Adorno, in Adorno et al., *Der Positivismusstreit in der deutschen Soziologie*, Neuwied/Berlin, 1969, p. 10. With regard to the claim of aesthetics and literary theory to dialectical mediation, cf., for example, J. Naeher, *Walter Benjamins Allegorie-Begriff als Modell: Zur Konstitution philosophischer Literaturwissenschaft*, Stuttgart, 1977.

7. K. Wuchterl, *Methoden der Gegenwartsphilosophie*, Bern, 1977, p. 5.

8. Cf., for example, H. R. Jauss, *Literaturgeschichte als Provokation der Literaturwis-senschaft*, Frankfurt am Main 2, 1970.

9. In *Neue Hefte zur Philosophie* 5, 1973.

10. Cf. Strelka, p. 19 (note 1 above).

11. Here we are thinking of a tradition which started at the latest with Goethe's coinage of the term. As examples in modern literary scholarship, cf. W. Emrich, K. Burke, N. Frye, and J. Strelka; for a more philosophical treatment, W. Benjamin.

12. An analogy to this can be found in methodologies like those connected with "content analysis," a research model which has developed closely along the lines of literary-theoretical methods for the purpose of research in communication theory. Cf., for example, G. Wersig, "Inhaltsanalyse. Einführung in ihre Systematik und Literatur," *Schriftenreihe zur Publizistikwissenschaft* 5, Berlin, 1968. Further developments in this type of more quantiative methodology toward qualitative methodology have logi-cally allied themselves even more definitely with literary-theoretical or aesthetic the-ories. Cf. J. Ritsert, *Inhaltsanalyse und Ideologiekritik*, Frankfurt am Main 1972 (Rit-sert follows especially S. Kracauer and Th. W. Adorno).

13. On criticism of *analogy* cf. H. Gallas, Enzyklopädisches Stichwort, "Strukturalismus," in G. Schiwy, *Der französische Strukturalismus*, Reinbek, 1969, p. 230. The (structur-alist) analogy concept comes in for particular criticism when it neglects causality—a motif which probably already occurred in its tradition in the dispute about universe and in the rationalism/empiricism dispute.

14. Following, for instance, N. Frye, but also working from the very different approach of W. Benjamin (his work on Goethe's "*Wahlverwandschaften*" for example).

15. Cf. again, Frye.

16. Such varying approaches as, for example, that of O. Spengler on the one hand and M.

Horkheimer and Th. W. Adorno on the other, bear this out. In both approaches, incidentally, there are analogies to Freud's rite concept.

17. Example: E. Goffman, *Interaktionsrituale*. *Über Verhalten in direkter Kommunikation*, Frankfurt am Main, 1967. (*Interaction Ritual: Essays on Face-to-Face Behavior*, New York, 1967.) The potential significance of such theories for literary theory (and *vice versa*), which cannot, of course, develop any kind of reduction of one discipline to the other, seems to have been nowhere near fully exploited.

18. Again, not establishing analogies with undue haste (cf. note 13). Within the framework of a theory to which such a critical understanding of analogy building is fundamental, a concept of action like that of K. Burke should be given further critical attention, as should the symbol concept in the individual disciplines associated with literary theory, among others P. Bourdieu and A. Lorenzer.

19. Following W. Dilthey.

20. Cf.: M. Riedel, *Verstehen oder Erklären? Zur Theorie und Geschichten der hermeneutischen Wissenschaften*, Stuttgart, 1978, especially pp. 9 ff., 49–54, 65–69, 88–112. U. Japp, *Hermeneutik. Der theoretische Diskurs, die Literatur und die Konstruktion ihres Zusammenhanges in den philologischen Wissenschaften*, München, 1977.

21. The debate among, for example West German literary scholars, has shown the limitations of such an extension, too.

22. Here a divine or at least metaphysical substance is meant.

23. Linguisticization (*Linguistisierung*), sociologization (*Soziologisierung*), didacticization (*Didaktisierung*), among others, as the absolutization of the linguistic form, of the social viability of production and reception, and of the (content) information/"message."

24. On the reception of Wittgenstein's theory of language games in literary scholarship, cf. P. Sloterdijk, "Die Ökonomie der Sprachspiele. Zur Kritik der linguistischen Gegenstandskonstitutionen," in J. Kolbe, ed., *Neue Ansichten einer künftigen Germanistik. Probleme einer Sozial- und Rezeptionsgeschichte der Literatur, Kritik der Linguistik, Literatur- und Kommunikationswissenschaft*, München, 1973. For our context, also see T. Schroyer, *Die dialektischen Grundlagen der kirtischen Theorie*, in W. Dallmayr, ed., *Materialien zu Habermas' "Erkenntnis und Interesse*," Frankfurt am Main 1974, especially p. 60 ff.

25. J. Habermas, "Vorbereitende Bemerkungen zu einer Theorie der kommunikativen Kompetenz," in J. Habermas and N. Luhmann, *Theorie der Gesellschaft oder Sozialtechnologie*, Frankfurt am Main, 1971. J. Habermas, *Erkenntnis und Interesse*, op. cit., especially the chapters on Dilthey and Freud and the epilogue to the 1973 edition. J. Habermas, "Was heisst Universalpragmatik?" in K.O. Apel, ed., *Sprachpragmatik und Philosophie*, Frankfurt am Main, 1976.

26. Apart from those already mentioned: N. Chomsky and D. Wunderlich (who has also received critical attention in literary didactics and scholarhip).

27. Apart from literary scholarship, also in pedagogics.

28. Cf. Goethe's definition of phantasy as the "fourth imaginative faculty," an extension of Kant's triad.

29. This is referring especially to approaches by what W. Benjamin called "artist-philosophers": From Sartre and Valery through to Adorno.

30. E. Fischer-Lichte, "Goethes 'Iphigenie'—Reflexion auf die Grundwidersprüche der bürgerlichen Gesellschaft. Zur Kontroverse Ivo/Lorenz," in *Diskussion Deutsch, Zeitschrift für Deutschlehrer aller Schulformen Ausbildung und Praxis*, eds. H. Ivo, V. Merkelbach, R. Rigol, H. Thiel, 6, no. 21 (1975).

31. Fischer-Lichte, p. 5

32. Fischer-Lichte, p. 6, note 30.

33. Elsewhere I shall give at least an outline of such an analysis.
34. Fischer-Lichte, p. 4
35. Ibid.
36. Ibid.
37. Ibid., with reference to Fischer-Lichte, p. 2.
38. Ibid.
39. Ibid.
40. Ibid.
41. Fischer-Lichte, p. 2.
42. Cf. ibid.
43. Fischer-Lichte, p. 6.
44. G. W. F. Hegel, *Ästhetik*, vol. I, Frankfurt am Main, 1967, p. 48.
45. The element of truth in the "reconstruction" probably reaches its limits when radical subjectivity in the end actually prevents the "completion" of a "hermeneutic circle" (as, potentially, in Staiger's case, loc. cit.) (note 1 above).
46. On this sort of process of drawing analogies cf., for example, the method of K. -H. Bohrer, *Die Ästhetik des Schreckens. Die pessimistische Romantik und Ernst Jüngers Frühwerk*, München, 1978.
47. Hegel, p. 15 ff. (note 44 above).
48. The aesthetics of Kant, Hegel, Schopenhauer, Nietzsche, and Marx, through to the aesthetics of the diverse representatives of Critical Theory. Cf. in this connection: J. Naeher, p. 234 ff., *et passim* (note 6 above). M. Zenck, *Kunst als begriffslose Erkenntnis. Zum Kunstbegriff der ästhetischen Theorie Th. W. Adornos*, München, 1977 (especially Chapter 1 and part of Chapter 4).
49. Cf. note 9 above. Cf. the recently published R. Bubner, "Kann Theorie ästhetisch werden? Zum Hauptmotiv der Philosophie Adornos," in *Materialien zur ästhetischen Theorie Th. W. Adornos. Konstruktion der Moderne*, eds. B. Lindner and W. M. Lüdke, Frankfurt am Main, 1980. In this context I can restrict my remarks to the earlier essay, since this presents the problem I am interested in especially cogently—and at the same time, as far as the approaches of *recent* aesthetics are concerned, goes even further beyond the emphasis on Adorno's approach. In addition there is evidence of the 1973 essay having been acknowledged in both literary scholarship and philosophy.
50. As I should like to characterize Bubner's program in analogy to Kant's *Critique of Pure Reason* and its prolegomena, its equally programmatic subtitle. In the same way, I later speak of the critique of literary-theoretical reason.
51. W. Kayser's definition of a "linguistic work of art" gave literary scholars an especially succinct expression for this, which also had great influence (for aesthetics too, to a degree). (*Das sprachliche Kunstwerk: Eine Einführung in die Literaturwissenschaft*, Bern, 1948.)
52. As, for example, in the famous (and much used) histories of literature by H. de Boor (*Geschichte der deutschen Literatur von den Anfängen bis zur Gegenwart*, vol. 1 ff., 1959 ff.) and G. Ehrismann (*Geschichte der deutschen Literatur bis zum Ausgang des Mittelalters*, vol. 1 ff., 1918).
53. Cf. especially notes 1 and 8, above. H. -R. Jauss, "Negativität und Identifikation. Versuch zur Theorie der ästhetischen Erfahrung," in H. Weinrich, ed., *Positionen zur Negativität*, München,, 1975 (*Poetik und Hermeneutik VI*). Jauss, *Ästhetische Erfahrung und literarische Hermeneutik*, vol. 1, *Versuche im Feld der "ästhetischen Erfahrung"*, München, 1977.
54. W. Emrich, *Protest und Verheissung. Studien zur klassischen und modernen Dichtung*, Frankfurt am Main 2, 1963, p. 56.

55. This is then discussing on a methodological level which is at the same time related to literary scholarship something which, when based on the concept of the symbol in an equally methodological sense, is at times too hastily applied to a philosophical (metaphysical) truth concept.

56. Cf. Bubner, *ibid.*, p. 42. Cf. note 53 above, etc.

57. Cf. F. Grenz' critique of Bubner ("Zur architektonischen Stellung der Ästhetik in der Philosophie Adornos," in *Text und Kritik, Sonderband Theodor W. Adorno*, ed. H. L. Arnold, München, 1977 p. 121 ff.), a critique with which I do not entirely agree.

58. Here I am following the lecture "Ästhetik II." J. W. Goethe Universität, Frankfurt am Main, 24 October 1967 (from my own notes).

59. Cf. for example: W. Weidlé, *Die Sterblichkeit der Musen*, Stuttgart, 1958, especially p. 181 ff. Jauss, on the other hand (quoted by Bubner), refers expressly back to Kant, "Negativität und Identifikation," loc. cit. (note 53 above).

60. K. -O. Apel, contribution to a discussion, in W. Oelmüller, ed., *Transzendentalphilosophische Normenbegründungen*, Paderborn, 1978, p. 176.

61. Cf. Bubner, p. 59 f. (note 9 above).

62. Cf. J. Strelka, p. 39 f. (note 1 above). On the possible combining of theses from Aristotelian poetics with a theory of aesthetic experience based on literary theory, cf. Jauss, loc. cit. (note 53 above). This connection is also mentioned by Bubner, but without, in the end, any consequences for his critical approach.

Robert Magliola

EIGENTLICHKEIT AND *EINFALL:* THE HEIDEGGERIAN RETURN "TO THINGS THEMSELVES"

What are the structural conditions for the valid reading of a text, as revealed by a phenomenology of interpretative experience? How does interlocutory "common ground" pertain to the description of structural validity (that is, to the "mapping out," the "laying out"—*die Auslegung*—of the hermeneutic act)? How does interlocutory "common ground" pertain to the adjudication of material validity (that is, to whatever *thematization* is at issue)? My adaptation of Heideggerian thought—an adaptation technically analogous to what exegetes call recension and redaction, and which may very well be a "neo-Heideggerian hermeneutics" of some kind—does much to resolve the above questions.[1] The key to the argument is Section 32 of *Being and Time*,[2] adjusted here, of course, so that its more universal applications apply to literature as such.

The start of the hermeneutical process, begins Heidegger, is the projection of *Dasein* (the human person) toward the possibilities or "aspects"[3] "laid open" by a text to the sight of the interpreter; to the extent that the interpreter goes on to "meet" it appropriately, each of these aspects has the *potential* to participate in meaning. Significantly, "these possibilities, as disclosed, exert their own counterthrust [*Rückschlag*] upon *Dasein*" (188). This counterthrust collaborates in the mutual implication of interpreter and literary work, so that both belong to the same ontological field (in that they share the same being).[4] Thus, in the first stage of hermeneutical activity, the critic is *at-one-with* a text. (We shall treat the words "a text" and "a work" synonymously and mean by them a composite of verbal signs,[5] and of relations among verbal signs, identified by a society as a literary entity distinguishable from other literary entities and all other entities.)

Next Heidegger says that the "development of the understanding

[*Verstehen*]" is "interpretation [*Auslegung*]" proper. Though he will shortly describe the development more clearly, it suffices now to point out that by "understanding" he means the unitary ensemble wherein critic and text are one, and that by "interpretation" he means a phenomenological description[6] of this understanding. Heidegger attaches an admonition: "Nor is interpretation the acquiring of information about what is understood; it is rather the working-out of possibilities projected in understanding" (188, 189). By all of this, he intends to place the origin (of what becomes hermeneutical activity) at the level of understanding (which is the level of Being[7]) and not at the level of "assertion" (*Aussage*) or, even, interpretation (*Auslegung*). To rephrase it, Heidegger maintains that philosophy should become meditative "Thought about Being"—philosophy should take as its main concern how entities are the same, not how they are different. Indeed, all entities are ultimately alike in one respect: all are "grounded" in a "one and the same." This "one and the same" bears none of the triviality associated with a term such as "lowest common denominator": rather, it is a *vis primitiva activa*,[8] an "active primoridal power," a dynamic. This dynamic is the origin[9] of individualities or particularities. Interpretation (*Auslegung*), what we call "phenomenological description," is literally a "laying-out" of *Deutung* so the latter is apparent. Assertion (*Aussage*), in and of itself, is propositional thinking: it deals with "information," and therefore with individual Things-in-being (*Seienden*) instead of Being (*Sein*).

For Heidegger, hermeneutics is ontology (description of Being, the matrix of all beings) and not just ontic study (description of individual entities that particularize themselves within the matrix). Assertion, as we shall see, divides the holistic configuration which is interpretation into mutually distinct and isolable "subject" and "object," and then utters "truth-statements" which are measured by how well they "match" subject and object.[10] Heidegger laments the epistemological tradition which insists that philosophizing, from beginning through end, must operate on the level of assertion. Assertion is often necessary, says Heidegger, but it should be at the service of interpretation and understanding. Otherwise, thinking becomes effectively detached from the source of meaning.

Heidegger next attempts to ascertain what is common to all interpretation. The second level of hermeneutical activity, interpretation is descriptive (thus, phenomenological) rather than propositional (assertional):

> In interpreting, we do not, so to speak, throw a "signification" over some naked thing which is present-at-hand, we do not stick a value

on it; but when something within-the-world is encountered as such, the thing in question already has an involvement which is disclosed in our understanding of the world, and this involvement is one which gets laid out by the interpretation. (190, 191)

In his section 32, Heidegger's greatest contribution is a phenomenology of a phenomenology (i.e., a concrete description of the second level, which is itself a description of understanding). He finds that interpretative activity manifests three functions: the "As-question" (what we may call the "interpretative question"), the "As-which" (or "textual aspect"), and the "As-structure" (or "interpretation" proper, which—as we shall see—is equivalent to "meaning").[11] Regarding the "interpretative question," Heidegger simply means that an interpreter, never neutral, always approaches a text with an implicit or explicit question. The answer given is shaped by the question asked, "a point of view, which fixes that with regard to which what is understood is to be interpreted" (191).

The next function of interpretative operation raised by Heidegger is the "textual aspect" which the text proffers in answer to the question:

> That which is disclosed in understanding—that which is understood—is always accessible in such a way that its "as which" can be made to stand out explicitly. (189)

Any given interpretative question should select and illuminate its affiliated textual aspect (if one exists),[12] an aspect which is "there" in the text and which is appropriate to the question.[13] In a short story, for example, the plot and its mythemes, the images, prose rhythm, phonemes (including even their interstitial silences), and so on, all constitute aspects.

The third function of hermeneutical knowing is the "As-structure," the taking of "something-as-something" (189). The as-structure is the Articulation (*Artikulation:* literally, "exercising of the joints"), or description, of the "joining together" of interpretative question and textual aspect. The as-structure is the interpretation (or Articulation) proper:

> That which is understood gets Articulated when the entity to be understood is brought close interpretatively by taking as our clue the "something-as-something"; and this Articulation lies before [*liegt vor*] our making any thematic assertion about it (190). An understanding of this third function, in practice, may be helpful.

The Christian reader may ask religious questions of an ambiguous text (e.g., Flannery O'Connor's "The River"), and if the story displays affiliated aspects, an As-structure or interpretation solidifies the text *as* a

Christian document. The secularist may ask "humanistic" questions, and if appropriate textual aspects present themselves, the text appears *as* a secular document. If there are aspects relevant to each set of questions, they are real aspects—parts of the real text. But what about the case of equivocal verbal signs, for example, signs that contain two or more denotative or connotative significations? A case in point is the name "Bevel" in "The River." The noun "bevel" is lexically defined as a "slant" or "incline." While these two denotations may be more or less the same, their connotations are very different. Since, in the story, the name Bevel involves both the preacher and the little boy, and since the value-systems of both characters are "in question," the secularist interpreter can choose the signification "slant" (negative qualities); the Christian interpreter the signification "incline" (positive qualities). My point here is that the verbal sign "bevel" has two real aspects (as well as many more, of course, with which we are not now concerned), and both of these are part of the text: one aspect is the "typical phonic form" of "bevel" plus the signification "slant" (with its negative qualities); another aspect is the "typical phonic form" of "bevel" plus the signification "incline" (with its positive qualities).

To recapitulate, then: understanding is a prereflective at-oneness of critics and text; interpretation is the phenomenological description of understanding, and consists of an As-structure which is the articulated "hold" an interpretative question has on a textual aspect, and *vice versa*[14]; and finally, assertion is the logical language which abstracts from interpretation, and classifies interpretation into concepts (thereby breaking interpretation all the way down into subject and object).

We can proceed now to Heidegger's next observation, that of "fore-structure" (*Vor-Struktur*). When using the word "fore," he means (1) that a kind of structure[15] antedates encounter with text, and in part determines how the text will be understood; and (2) that the structure meshes with a text before the interpreter even knows this is the case.[16] Fore-structure is characterized by three kinds of fore-awareness, namely: (1) fore-having (*Vorhabe*), (2) fore-sight (*Vorsicht*), and (3) fore-conception (*Vorgriff*). Fore-having equates to the first grasp a critic has on a problem at the level of understanding (i.e., be-fore he consciously knows it has). Recalling that interpretation is grounded in understanding, Heidegger tells us "interpretation is grounded in something we have in advance—in a fore-having" (191). Fore-seeing adequates to the first interpretative grasp that the second level has on the first, so that "This fore-sight 'takes the first cut' out of what has been taken into fore-having, and it does so with a view to a definite way in which this [the understanding] can be interpeted" (191). Fore-sight occurs before the interpreter knows he has seen anything, and is shaped by the way of seeing his environment has encouraged. (As you will notice, Heidegger's earlier treatment of the interpretative question anticipated much of what he says about fore-sight.) Finally, there occurs in some instances a fore-conception, which is a set of prereflexive ideas that eventually become reflexive and assume logical form. Fore-conception works upon the material of interpretation, and transmutes it into concepts. Heidegger says "Anything understood which is held in our fore-having and toward which we set our sights 'fore-sightedly' becomes conceptualizable through the interpretation" (191). To rephrase it, fore-conception begins the process whereby the level of assertion conceptualizes the descriptive level.

Heidegger next takes up the question of "meaning" (*Sinn*), and the related percept of the hermeneutical circle. Keeping in mind that Articulation for Heidegger refers to the activity of the second stratum of awareness, we can conclude from the following that meaning is precisely that dimension of understood Being which can be "described":

> Meaning is that wherein the intelligibility [*Verständlichkeit*] of something maintains itself. That which can be Articulated in a disclosure by which we understand, we call "meaning." The concept of meaning embraces the formal existential framework of what necessarily belongs to that which an understanding interpretation Articulates. (193)

Meaning, in other words, is an as-structure—and this *aperçu* functions as the pivot for the whole of section 32. Whereas meaning for the early Husserl is appropriated from a pool of ideal significations and is incorporated into the *intending act*[17], and whereas meaning for Mikel Dufrenne (whose theory of meaning is the opposite of Husserl's) is situated squarely in the *intended object*[18], for Heidegger, meaning is the *holistic formation* constituted together by interpretative question and proper textual aspect. When Natanson cites Alfred Schutz's *mot d'ordre*, ". . . it is the meaning of our experiences and not the ontological structure of the objects which constitutes reality" (*Collected Papers*, p. xlii), Natanson singles out a motif in Schutz's thought which is very adaptable to Heidegger's "case," as it were. For hermeneutical meaning is "not the ontological structure" of the text taken-as-object, but rather the "meaning of our experiences"—experiences which behave according to the function of as-structures.

Heidegger concludes section 32 with a very important discussion of "authentic" (*eigentliche*—implies "taken as my own") interpretation, and he of course takes great care to distinguish the latter from mere "fancy"

(*Einfall*—"falling down/in"). Heidegger's treatment of "authenticity" comprises much the same range of issues subsumed under the notion of "validity" in English, although he eschews the literal German work for "validity" (namely, *Geltung*) because the term *Geltung* conjures up for him the antiquated methodology of positivism (I, however, shall use the English words "validity" and "authenticity" interchangeably). To understand the Heideggerian norms of validity, one must begin again with the notion of fore-structure. Recall that according to the first sense of this term, fore-structure is the psychological apparatus the individual brings to the text: for example, he may think in terms of English language syntax, he may be a Freudian, he may be an Archetypalist. Heidegger argues that without fore-structure, interpretation of any kind is impossible. That is, unless a person has the wherewithal to understand a phenomenon, it can make no sense to him whatsoever. Wittgenstein says as much, when he remarks, "If you went to Mars and men were spheres with sticks coming out, you wouldn't know what to look for."[19]

To use an analogy, unless a person has a vantage-point, he cannot look at something else (because he is simply un-situated, or "not there"). The vantage-point is at once enabling and blinding. It enables him to see profiles of the something else, but not other profiles. The vantage-point helps to "structure" the character of his "view," and, chances are, people standing next to him and looking in the same direction will have much the same experience of the something else. But those on the other side of the something else may "see" profiles that are very different, or even contrary. Ethics, linguistics, philosophy, and other elements of fore-structure are, as it were, psychological vantage-points.

So fore-structure is essential to interpretation. But if fore-structures which illuminate a text differ from one another, how can interpretations ever be "invalid"? *Da capo*, let it be said that Heidegger most emphatically does not deny the possibility of invalid interpretations. Again, the crucial stratum is the interpretative stratum, which falls midway between the pre-objective awareness of the first stratum and the objective awareness of the third. The second stratum, in other words, does not dichotomize experience into subject and object as the assertive level does, but neither is it as unitary a phenomenon as the level of understanding. After all, as soon as one talks of an as-question issuing from the interpreter, and an as-which offered by the text, one is talking in terms of a dichotomy. But the second level, in its *essential* construct, does *remain true* to the experiential unity found in understanding: the interpretation strictly defined—that is, the as-structure— is precisely the mutual engagement of critic and text (and by engagement, we do not mean just the interface of critic and text, but also the holistic formation which includes the relevant elements of critical fore-structure and the text). The interpretation is constituted simultaneously by an interpretative question and a textual aspect, and thereby bridges the dichotomy of subject and object. The as-structure, in short, is a unitary phenomenon.

Regarding authenticity, Heidegger says the following:

> To be sure, we genuinely take hold of this possibility [primordial knowing] only when, in our interpretation, we have understood that our first, last, and constant task is never to allow our fore-having, fore-sight, and fore-conception to be presented to us by fancies and popular conceptions, but rather to make the scientific theme secure by working out these fore-structures in terms of the things themselves. (195)

Notice, this structure applies not only to the interpretative level, but also to contact between all three strata of fore-structure on the one hand and texts on the other. In fact, earlier, Heidegger spoke of the same requirement in regard to conceptualization (fore-conception), warning the thinker not to "force the entity into concepts to which it is opposed in its manner of Being." Heidegger is saying that the particular As-questions appropriate to the phenomena at hand (and not inappropriate As-questions, "fancies and popular conceptions" which do not suit the phenomena) are essential for validity. Or, to approach the matter from the other direction, Heidegger is saying that as-questions must grasp textual aspects that are *really there* in the phenomena. When such contact occurs, a *valid* interpretation, and a *correct* interpretation, materializes. Otherwise, there remains a merely fanciful or pseudo interpretation. Since Being exhibits itself precisely in and through meaning, and meaning (as we have seen) is interpretation, a valid interpretation is by necessity *true*. To have several valid interpretations of a text, then, is to have several true interpretations—each of them determinate and self-identical (that is to say, each exegesis discloses a different aspect of a literary work which by nature has many aspects, and each combination of question and relevant aspect is a "truth").

The issue that next surfaces for us, of course, concerns criteriology. How does one determine what are apposite as-questions? How does one demonstrate that the textual aspects alleged are "really there"? Clearly, a literary critic must convince his peers of the appropriateness of his interrogation; clearly he must "show" the presence of the textual aspects he claims; and clearly he must demonstrate how his interpretative questions engage the aspects. I shall address the conditions which characterize the "making of a case" for an interpretation. And I shall defend

Heidegger from accusations of relativism. First, though, some remarks on "authorial intent" are in order.

Throughout section 32, Heidegger ignores the relevance of authorial intentionality, that is, the significations[20] the author related to a text when he created it.[21] Since, in his practical exegesis of literary writers and others,[22] Heidegger often does involve the author's "willed significations" for a word or passage, it seems safe to conclude that Heidegger's position is more inclusive than, for example, Hans-Georg Gadamer's. Heidegger's arbitration seems to be that a critic may ask an "authorial" As-question, but he *need not*. Much depends on the critic's purpose. A critic may try to approximate (through biographical or other means) the author's fore-structure, and a textual aspect that accommodates it, so that the meaning that arises is similar to the author's meaning. Or a critic may investigate the medieval significations available to a medieval poet, say, and encounter the poem in that light. But again, the attached provision is that such a maneuver is by no means requisite. *In nuce*, biographical and historical critics incorporate their researched data into fore-structures and bring these structures to bear on aspects of a work. Christian, Jungian, and other critics execise their own distinctive options, dependent on other values and other kinds of research.

At this juncture I call to the reader's attention that the way I have "laid out" (*ausgelegt*) the above issues—the structure of hermeneutical activity, and so on—is itself Heideggerian and phenomenological. Obviously I have not tried to argue in the way a "logical atomist" does, or a "logical positivist" does. Rather, with the aid of Heideggerian As-questions, I have described what one "sees" if one collates the practical criticism of many reputable critics identified with many critical schools. One invariably sees fore-structures and textual aspects in collusion or attempted collusion. What we have called the authorial As-question—or an attempt to read a text in terms of the author's fore-structure—is a variable: sometimes it plays a role in a given critique and sometimes it does not.

As I have already indicated, I shall treat anon the functions of verification used by literary critics. Concerning my own principle of verification, in advancing a whole phenomenology of the hermeneutic act, I turn consistently to a traditional maxim of phenomenology: "Corroborative description is the only verification." In other words, phenomenology is ultimately a communal activity: we check our own concrete experiences of what is common to the subject at hand—in this case, critical practice. With many other phenomenologists over a long period of time, I have experienced and then described interpretative activity. *Sic feliciter evenit!* The reader is invited to do likewise.

The reader may further ask what is the status of this very essay of mine? First, I call to your attention that my essay manifests the "aspects" of an "assertive" paper (as Heidegger would say). It operates primarily on the level of assertion, so it is not just *Auslegung* (in this case, description of hermeneutical activity) but *Aussagen* ("explaining," or "the making of a case" for the embedded description). And I usually choose to "make my case" by the phenomenological means—I provide examples of representative critical activity, and explain them.[23] I ask the reader to consult the examples, and any others he pleases. Expository assertion, the kind of *Aussagen* of which my essay purports to be a kind, is by nature concerned with authorial intent—in this case, the significations Heidegger attached to section 32 of *Sein und Zeit*. So I consistently ask the authorial As-question. But, for that matter, my essay is far from true philosophizing—the deep "meditation on Being"; instead, it just hopes to perform a humbler, ancillary service.

Now let us face the issue of validity. If one reviews the panoramic history of literary criticism (i.e., does a "phenomenology" of the situation, seeking out the concrete essential structures), what follows becomes readily apparent. Privately, the critic adjudicates for himself the validity of his own interpretation (his norms may resemble or differ markedly from those of his contemporaries). Publicly, if he wants to convince others his interpretation is valid, the critic must accept the norms of his audience and try to show his interpretation suits their norms or he must convert his audience to new norms, and demonstrate that his interpretation suits the latter. Even if a critic maintains that the "author's meaning" is the only valid meaning, the critic must obviously convince his peers that such a norm is justified, and indeed, that his interpretation really coincides with the author's meaning. The role of critical audience leads at once, of course, to the concomitant issue of intersubjectivity—that is, publicly operable norms shared among a community of subjects (eighteenth-century neoclassicists, for example, were a body of subjects who agreed on many hermeneutical norms; so are American "New Critics" today, or Marxists, or Freudians, and so on).

A further description of literary history reveals that the meanings which various groups accept as valid can differ because of two different reasons. One reason is that the "work" or "text," which we have already defined as a literary composite of verbal signs and relations among verbal signs, is in fact a different work to different audiences. Recall that the meanings of a work are engagements of interpretative questions and textual aspects. If we suspend for the moment the factor of variable interpretative questions and deal only with textual aspects, we find the following. Textual aspects are appearances of verbal signs and relations among verbal signs, and these appearances are really "in and of the text" (see note 19). Now if the verbal signs of a "work" change, it follows that the work itself changes. And some of the aspects or appearances of the work, since they are "in and of the work," likewise change. If we recall that meanings are engagements of interpretative questions and textual aspects, the conclusion is inescapable: meanings can differ because textual aspects have changed. Sometimes these changes are synchronic—for example, different dialectical groups attach different significations (lexic values) to a given word sound.

Most changes, however, are diachronic. A famous instance is provided by René Wellek in his *Theory of Literature*.[24] In the seventeenth century, Andrew Marvell's phrase "vegetable love" signified what today could be called "vegetative love"—i.e., according to the scholar Louis Teeter (quoted by Wellek), "life-giving principle." But in the twentieth century, "vegetable" signifies "edible plant," and this signification opens the way to a new qualitative value: "vegetable love" connotes "torpidity," or "slow and stifled love" (love as an "erotic cabbage," as Teeter says). In short, the word sound "vegetable" has taken on a new signification, so that we can indeed have a new verbal sign (and, to that extent, a new "work" or "text").

Perhaps at some future time, the significations of "bevel" in the story "The River" will change, and with these mutations, the qualitative values contingent upon "bevel"; thereby, these permutations of aspect will change the literary work *per se*. In any case, it is crucial to recognize that changes in verbal sign are effected by the language-group which constitutes a work's audience at any given time. Signification, and qualitative values dependent on signification, are conferred by the language-community; individual interpreters and even whole "schools" of criticism naturally accept the lexic values, multiple as they may be, which a *langue* confers on word sounds so that verbal signs can occur. In this sense, and to this extent, the reader is merely a mechanism whereby *langue* vivifies word sounds—Freudian, Marxist, Christian, one and all will normally accept that the word sound indicated by "triangle" bears the lexic value attributed to it by the *language* which is English.

We can even submit the notion of *langue* to further examination by putting our conclusions to the test of the "extreme case." Here we can assume the original significations of a text have been lost completely. In other words, the *langue* has been lost. In terms of the twentieth-century interpreters and their culture, the text may then make no sense or perhaps some sense—the latter through chance alone. The marks on the page happen to make sense in a language known by the interpreters, even though their language is different from the language of the author (and the author's culture). Let us turn the screw another spiral. Through a fortuitous happening, the text makes complete sense in the second language. Surely one cannot appeal to the author's sense now! Yet, by chance, perhaps an exquisite poem has arisen. Whence come the significations? They can only come from the language of the *interpreter's* culture.

An entirely different matter is change in meaning which arises because interpretative questions differ. In this case, the work and its aspects remain constant—that is, a given language culture at a given time makes available one or several significations for a word sound. Since a literary work is the totality of verbal signs (word sounds plus significations) made possible by the circumambient culture, different As-questions can contact different aspects of the one work. Such changes are initiated on the side of the individual interrogator, but the meaning as a whole changes since meaning is the mutual engagement of As-question and relevant textual aspect. Notice that in such cases the literary work itself has not changed— only meanings have changed. In sum, the meanings which various groups accept as valid can differ because of two reasons: the work itself can change, so it is indeed a different work; or, while the work remains the same, the interpretative questions—assuming they are valid—can differ (the latter is often a synchronic phenomenon).

In his famous work *Validity in Interpretation*,[25] E. D. Hirsch argues that formulations of the above kind are relativistic. Although Hirsch has modified his position somewhat in a second book, The *Aims of Interpretation*,[26] Hirsch's arguments in that first book are still upheld by many theorists, and they remain the classic attack on Heideggerian thought as relativist. So I turn to what can be, I think, a Heideggerian *riposte*. In *Validity in Interpretation*, Hirsch discusses Wellek's example out of Marvell (see above). (Before we begin, however, I interject a provisional statement. In that the significations of "vegetable" have changed, historically, a Heideggerian can say that to such an extent the work has changed. So a comparison of "valid meanings" is here in a way inappropriate. It is really a matter of two different literary passages, each participating in several possible meanings.) However, since "To His Coy Mistress" has not changed (i.e., most of its words retain the same significations they had in the seventeenth century), we can make the practical choice of considering it the one and the same work which existed in the seventeenth century. (Actually, a more suitable ground on which to argue all this would be a modern text that bears contradicting significations, with each signification alive in the *langue* today. But the example out of Marvell has been sanctified by usage—Wellek's,

Hirsch's, and mine—so I shall stay with it.) We proceed to hear Hirsch's case. Hirsch advances the following argument. Wellek's very thesis, that the modern interpretation is also valid, assumes the distinction between the author's "sense" (what we have called "signification") and subsequent "senses" (significations, again). In order to avoid a relativism, a chaotic flux of meanings, it is absolutely essential to distinguish between an author's "willed" significations and other possible significations, thus the necessary distinctions, says Hirsch, between "meaning" (which is Hirsch's term for the author's willed signification) and "significance"[27] (Hirsch's term for the relation of authorial meaning to the reader's other meanings, emotions, etc.).

Heidegger would answer that he, too, sees distinctions among significations (how could he not?). However, he refuses to attribute an exclusivity to the author's willed significations. When one does a concrete phenomenology of any hermeneutical experience, one plainly sees that what Hirsch calls "meaning" and what Hirsch calls "significance" both arise from a live contact of an As-question and textual aspect. *In situ*, there is absolutely no difference in their functional nexus. Thus the same validity obtains for both. Hirsch's As-question can be: Did the author intend such and such a qualitative value for this verbal sign? A critic identified with the New Hermeneutics may ask: Can an Archetypalist, say, intend such and such a qualitative value for this verbal sign? Much excitement in exegesis, I might add, arises from the dazzling interplays of As-questions and textual aspects, as various combinations complement and contradict each other, converge upon and tug away from each other.

Remember that although Heidegger proposes plural aspects in texts, each of these aspects is determinate and self-identical (whether the author "willed" them there or not). To invert Hirsch, the work—in the grasp of various As-questions—means *many things* in particular. Hirsch's perception of a text is remarkably flat: a text cannot have more than one facet (our analogy for "aspect"). The author's chosen signification excludes all others. Thus *Validity in Interpretation* announces categorically: "it may be asserted as a general rule that whenever a reader confronts two interpretations which impose different emphases on similar meaning components, at least one of the interpretations must be wrong."[28] But why must this be the case? The often-used analogy with a diamond is appropriate here. Our interpretative glance at the diamond can contact one or more facets (aspects), each of which is really part of the diamond. But let's take a verbal example—the word *cleave*, which has two opposing definitions: *to separate* or *to adhere*.[29] Let us say a given text describes a God who descends in blinding theophany and utters to his hushed disciples, "Men and women, cleave!" Let us assume furthermore that the verbal context is of no help. But, and this is of utmost importance, let us take it as given that all authorial evidence points to one interpretation as the author's own—that he willed, let's say, "cleave" to mean "separate." Does this authorial data make the alternative interpretation, that to "cleave" is to "adhere," less determinate and self-identical? Both significations are held firm by the syntax and lexic of the *langue*, which gives them shareability and particularity. What further determinacy is needed? For a Heideggerian, Hirsch's argument remains ineffectual.

That many interpretative questions can be axiologically sound does not by any means deny the importance of historical criticism (the reactions of some past interlocutors of mine seem to require of me an addendum of this kind.) Heidegger, especially in his revelation of the past history of metaphysics, has repeatedly asked "the historical question"— to put it another way, he has asked what significations were attached to verbal signs by given historical periods. And he has also asked "authorial questions"—what significations a given author intended for given word sounds. Heidegger has often stressed the importance of "sedimentation," whereby word sounds accumulate significances historically.[30] And much depends, as I've previously suggested, on the kind of language under study—be it *Aussage*, for example, which involves interlocution of several kinds between authors and listeners; or *Dichtung*, which in a deeper and richer sense communicates Being without regard for the historical author.[31] But my point here is that, in the case of *Dichtung*, or literary language, modern interpretative questions, and modern significations, can be just as valid, and indeed fruitful, as historical and authorial readings. Hirsch's rejoinder is that such a propostion reduces to pure relativism. In answer, I postulate there is a constancy adduced by Heideggerian theory—the constancy imparted by intersubjectism. (The reader will notice, I think, that Alfred Schutz's treatment of intersubjectivity, especially in the *Collected Papers*, pp. 347–356, runs very effective interference for Heidegger here.)

We can begin with an example. In Henry James' novella *The Turn of the Screw*, a governess struggles to protect her two young charges against diabolical ghosts. It so happens that nineteenth-century critics brought a traditional Christian fore-structure to the text and saw the governess *as* an integrated and wholesome personality, fighting the war of a Christian heroine against Satan. Freudian critics of the twentieth century have seen the governess *as* a neurotic personality, perverting the children through her malign fantasies. If we were to perform a phenomenology of critical dialogue, we would find each critic trying to

"make a case" for his own interpretation (of course, this does not pre-
clude learning from others as well). Each critic would try to "convince"
the others. But "convincing" can take place only to the extent that the
critics share values in common. In the above example, Freudians could
convince both those already sympathetic to Freudianism, and those con-
verted to Freudian insights by the vigor of the Freudian argument in
this case. Of course, the "making of the case" would require much more
than beliefs-held-in-common. The Freudian interpreter would have to
show that, in terms of Freudianism, the precise questions they asked are
appropriate. The interpreter would also have to show that the textual
aspects he espies are "really there."

The interpreter would be obliged to demonstrate, for example, that in
"The River," Bevel exhibits the behavior of a young child who is rejected by his parents, and who, rebounding from this hurt, is subconsciously driven to suicide—a motive he must consciously disguise as holy
and beneficent, viz., as self-baptism. In this case, the Freudian critic
would be showing an engagement of As-question and textual aspect:
Bevel-as-delusive-and-suicidal. Obviously, the traits of repression, self-
delusion, and so on are seen as "really there" in the events of the story
only by readers who believe repression and self-delusion of this kind can
possibly occur, either in reality or in fiction. I add that important second
phrase "in fiction" because a reader may accept repression and self-delusion as possible ways of presenting behavior in fiction—even if they are
not (for the reader) a correct way of explaining behavior in the real
world.

But another reader—say a devout Fundamentalist Christian—may
pose other questions of "The River" and "see" other textual aspects
"really there" in the work. Because of the fore-structure this interpreter
brings to the text, he does not see repression and self-delusion. Yet he
can "make a case" for his Christian audience that the meaning (or As-
structure) he advances is appropriate: As-questions meet textual aspects
according to norms intersubjective among his peers. Even if he is told
the historical author of "The River" intended a Freudian interpretation
(which, incidentally, is probably not the case, but for our purposes
makes no difference), he can with perfect legitimacy answer that consul-
tation of authorial intent is unnatural and inappropriate for poetic writing, or *Dichtung*. After all, the Christian critic, from a formal perspective, is doing here no more and no less than other critics, including
critics asking the "authorial question." For example, the critic asking the
authorial question attaches a Freudian qualitative value to a verbal sign
because the author did. The Christian critic attaches a Christian qualitative value to the same verbal sign because the Bible does.

The Christian critic is asking questions vital to his group; he is show-ing to this group's satisfaction that textual aspects answer to these ques-tions. Surely, on the side of the work and its aspects, he must adhere to couplings of signification and word sound permitted by the language-community's *langue*. (If he and his group do not, they are bespeaking a new and different work.) But at any given time in history, several signifi-cations and even more qualitative values are available through culture and its *langue* to a given word sound, and *a fortiori*, to the work as a whole. The literary work, as we have said, is an organon comprising all of these synchronic significations and qualitative values. Practically speaking, all interpretations contact only some facets of a multifaceted work. The Christian critic in the above case is "finding" in the work significations and qualitative values the Freudian is not finding. The Freudian is finding other significations and qualitative values. But the collective language of our culture (which includes, indeed, many subcul-tures) comprises both sets of lexic and qualitative values, the Freudian, the Christian (and many, many more).

Relativism is the absence of truth conditions. But in the Heideggerian system, the collective *langue* vouches for the presence of determinate significations and qualitative values in the work. Each critical school accepts as a prerequisite the engagement of As-questions and textual aspects and establishes norms-held-in-common to "test" whether the engagement is achieved. Thus Heidegger establishes a universal truth condition for the function of validity (namely, the *agencement* of mutual implication, as already described) and upholds as a truth condition the necessity of group norms whereby this function can be evaluated (al-though he obviously affirms a plurality of norms, and leaves the determi-nation of these various sets of norms to the various critical subcultures which appoint them).

What Heidegger has accomplished, in other words, is a phenomenol-ogy of the structure of valid textual reading. By this time it should be clear that even the acceptance of this structure depends on interlocutory "common ground"—and can be denied by those who do not wish to pursue Heidegger's line of description "all the way" but choose to "bring him up short" at one point or another. If, on the other hand, one accepts the structure (that of "mutual implication," as we have seen), then one proceeds to find new interlocutory "common grounds" which enable interlocutors to agree, for example, on "assumptions toward" and "ques-tions for" a text, on the one hand, or on grounds which share specific correlations between "qualitative values" and significations, on the other. It is crucial to maintain here that each individual or group should be in pursuit of *real* common grounds, not personally subjective "ground" (because by definition such ground would then be noncommon), nor even—and here I insist on being quite Heideggerian—collectively subjective ground (some sort of "subjective universal"). Rather, each person and group should engage in "realistic" debate. For Heidegger, the interpreter does not argue that it is *as if* a verbal sign had such-and-such an aspect (David Bleich's *as if* theory is too relativistic, I think); instead, one argues whether a verbal sign really functions *as* such-and-such an aspect.

But needless to say, even when contending schools agree that common ground should be "real," or relate to the "real," it will often be the case that each school regards the rival school as collectively subjective rather than "true to reality." It seems to me that Alfred Schutz, as Natanson presents him, makes a point corroborative of mine: "Insisting as common sense does, if questioned, that there is an objective reality which is the 'same' for all normal observers is not to be confused with demonstrating that this is indeed so or even understanding what is implied in such a claim" (*Collected Papers*, p. xxxvii). In other words (if one adapts his passage to our immediate concerns), it is crucial that the reality of the Life-World be granted, that literary language be somehow true in relation to the Life-World, and that our as-questions be true to the real literary work, but that such "agreement on principle" has not, does not, and probably will not abrogate argument over *what* and *how* is the real.

But the further objection can be raised: perhaps Heidegger's formulation is not solipsistic relativism, yet it does suggest a kind of peer-group relativism (similar to Dilthey's, and others). My answer is that neither is this the case. Group relativism would "found" its truths on the beliefs of the group pure and simple. But, Heidegger says, "That which is 'shared' is our *Being-towards* what has been pointed out—a Being in which we see it in common. One must keep in mind that this Being-towards is Being-in-the-world, and that from out of this very world what has been pointed out gets encountered."[32] The validity of a meaning requires implication of As-question and As-which, but whenever this implication really occurs, Being is manifested. Validity, and the truth that consecrates validity, is at bottom founded not on subcultures or "critical schools" but on Being; truth is only mediated through subcultures and critical schools. Different critical schools can reflect different facets of Being. Remember that, for Heidegger, Being is not *tiefsinnig* (deep); in other words, Being is not "underneath" or "above" phenomena, nor is it the *telos* of speculation. Being is the real (both actualities and possibilities); Being is the "common-sense" world (not the superficial world of *das Man*, but the Life-World of the "peasant's shoes"). Being is *only* revealed in phenomena, and *uniquely* revealed in each phenomenon.

Nor does Heidegger imply that one must accept every critical school that emerges in history. One may be convinced that a given school, with its own distinguishing norms and so on, does not reflect Being. It may just produce *Einfälle*, or fancies. And what about a perverted author who produces textual aspects which bespeak hatred? A reader may (and indeed, for my part, I think should) decide that the proper As-questions for such aspects would be questions displaying the plot, qualitative values, and so on of the work *as* evil and perverted. Then the As-structure or meaning of the work appears properly—Being ultimately is "the way things really are," and the interpretation here would show evil to be evil. So again, Heidegger is not advocating an "anything goes" criticism. Rather, he is saying that if we wish we can simultaneously affirm some contradictory schools and interpretations and that we can do so without ontological embarassment.

Notes

1. The critical "feedback" from my first book on these issues, *Phenomenology and Literature*, has enabled me, I believe, to elaborate and clarify my position.
2. Heidegger, *Being and Time*, trans. John Macquarrie and Edward Robinson (New York, 1962), pp. 188–195. Page references to this English edition are enclosed parenthetically within my text. The translation is from the seventh German edition.
3. A definition of "aspect," and various insights into its functioning, will appear in several places in my presentation.
4. For definitions of "mutual implication," sees Magliola, *Phenomenology and Literature*, 2nd printing (Lafayette, Indiana, 1977), pp. 14, 61, 69, 70, 72, 76, and *passim*. "Implication" here bears the signification of "enfoldment," the signification of its Latin etymological root.
5. By verbal sign, we mean (and in my opinion Heidegger can concur) what Roman Ingarden calls a "word sound" or "typical phonic form," plus the significations (lexic values) available to this form by way of a culture's *langue*. Typical phonic form is to be distinguished, of course, from written or phonic material, such as quality of voice or shape of print, which can be individually new and different with each implementation. Thus, to use an example cited by Husserl, the word sound *Hund* transcends any individual articulation of it, and the primary German significations available to this

word sound are "a dog" and "a truck used in mining." See Roman Ingarden, *The Literary Work of Art*, trans. George C. Grabowicz (Evanston, 1973), pp. 34–35, for a discussion of word sound.

6. For Heidegger, the word "phenomenology" means "that which shows itself in itself." Phenomenological description delineates what shows forth concretely, *in* experience.

7. I implore the reader's patience: indications of what Heidegger means by the elusive term "Being" are forthcoming later in my paper.

8. The phrases "the one and the same" and *vis primitiva activa* are applied to Being by Heidegger himself. See Heidegger, "Hölderlin and the Essence of Poetry," in his *Existence and Being*, trans. and introd. by Werner Brock (4th printing, Chicago, 1965), p. 278; and Heidegger, "What Are Poets For?" in his *Poetry, Language, Thought*, trans. and introd. by Albert Hofstadter (New York and London, 1971), p. 100.

9. Jacques Derrida, the brilliant and chilling contemporary French philosopher, would decry Heidegger's quest for ontological origin, and even Heidegger's "logocentricism." Though there is no space to treat the matter here, my next book (now under way, and entitled *Beyond Derrida: The Recovery of Poetic Presence*) will argue at length that Heidegger, in his own way, "deconstructs" metaphysical language, but does so in order to suggest a *via negativa* similar to that of mysticism. Heidegger's *Dif-ferenz* provides fullness where Derrida's *Différance* "closes" ontology.

10. For a comparison of "correspondence theory," which "matches," and "commemorative truth," which "brings forth," see *Phenomenology and Literature*, pp. 65, 66 (note 4 above).

11. In order to avoid what may seem to be the jargonistic timbre of the actual Heideggerian terms, all of which feature the prepositional "as," I offer the alternate terms provided within the parentheses. Hereinafter, where possible I will substitute the alternate terminology. But it is important to recognize that Heidegger features the prepositional "as" for the sake of precision and emphasis: we shall see that the interpretative question takes the text *as* something; the textual aspect, for its part, is taken *as* something; and the interpretation proper is textual aspect *as* something. Heidegger, like Derrida after him, invents new terms because conventional terminology reflects a world-view he repudiates. Moreover, Heideggerian terms are no more "jargonistic" than the phraseology of American "New Criticism," for example, or even "Analytic" philosophy—they are just less familiar to an Anglo-American audience.

12. As we shall see, if a relevant aspect is lacking, the interpretation is invalid.

13. I do not use Husserlian nomenclature—*noema* instead of "As-which" or "textual aspect"—because Husserl's *noema* (at least in his later philosophy) may "be distinguished from the real object" (see Aron Gurwitsch, the great Husserlian specialist, "On the Intentionality of Consciouness," in *Phenomenology*, ed. J. Kockelmans [Garden City, N.Y., 1967], p. 128). Heidegger's As-which, on the other hand, is a facet of the real object, the text. Nor is my surrogate term for the Heideggerian As-which, namely "textual aspect," to be confounded with Husserlian "aspect": the latter is usually adjudicated unreal (see R. Ingarden, *The Literary Work of Art*, sections 40 and 42, where Ingarden speaks as a faithful Husserlian). As for Husserlian noesis, it is unlike Heideggerian "As-question," since Husserl's noesis bestows meaning (see *Phenomenology and Literature*, pp. 98–101; note 4 above) and Heidegger's As-question does not.

14. Heidegger's As-structure reminds one of Husserl's old maxim: intentionality is at one and the same time the grasp and the grip which grasps it.

15. Take care not to confuse the terms "fore-structure" and "As-structure."

16. Perhaps not enough Heideggerian phenomenologists have realized that Husserl, with his notion of *habitus*, approximates some of what Heidegger means by fore-structure. For example, Husserl says that each experience causes a *habitus*, or "new abiding property," which further determines the ego; thus habituated, the ego goes on to its next experience in a different (i.e., proportionately modified) way. See Edmund Husserl, *Cartesian Meditations*, trans. Dorian Cairns (The Hague, 1960), pp. 66, 67, for his discussion of *habitus*. However, when dealing with formal interpretative activity, Heidegger would validate some fore-structures that Husserl would consider "presuppositions" in the technical sense, and thus "bracket out." Closer than Husserl to Heidegger's fore-structure is Alfred Schutz's concept of "knowledge at hand" (see Schutz, *Collected Papers*, vol. I, ed. Maurice Natanson (The Hague, 1967, p. 208).

17. See *Phenomenology and Literature*, pp. 97–104.

18. See *Phenomenology and Literature*, pp. 146, 148, 151, 156, 157, 160, 161, and *passim*.

19. Ludwig Wittgenstein, "Lectures on Aesthetics," in *Philosophy of Art and Aesthetics from Plato to Wittgenstein*, eds. Frank Tillman and Steven Cahn (New York, 1969), p. 517.

20. In my essay, I use the term "signification" in lieu of the more common term "sense" because of what has been a knotty problem for translators. Husserl's and Ingarden's word *Sinn* has been customarily translated "sense," but Heidegger's word *Sinn* is translated "meaning," and Heideggerian "meaning" is very different from the Husserlian or Ingardenian notion of "sense." When I mean an idea and/or image operative in a culture's *langue*, I resort to the word "signification."

21. Contrast Roman Ingarden, who speaks of the "bestowal of meaning" by the author's "sense-giving acts." See *Phenomenology and Literature*, pp. 110, 115, 116 (note 4 above).

22. See *Phenomenology and Literature*, pp. 73–78. Notice, however, that Heidegger uses As-questions even when involving the author's "willed significations." Heidegger is by no means "objective" in his own practical literary criticism.

23. Consult also *Phenomenology and Literature*, pp. 185, 186, for the examples I provide from Nathaniel Hawthorne's short story, "My Kinsman, Major Molineux."

24. René Wellek and Austin Warren, *Theory of Literature*, 3rd ed., paperback (New York, 1956), pp. 177, 178.

25. E. D. Hirsch, *Validity in Interpretation* (New Haven and London, 1967).

26. Hirsch, *The Aims of Interpretation* (Chicago and London, 1976).

27. Take care not to confuse "signification" and Hirsch's term "significance."

28. Hirsch, *Validity in Interpretation*, p. 230 (note 25 above).

29. *Webster's Seventh New Collegiate Dictionary* (Springfield, Mass., 1963), p. 154.

30. See Heidegger, *Being and Time*, pp. 377–380; and Heidegger, *On the Way to Language*, p. 34.

31. But see my discussion of an inconsistency in Heidegger's practical criticism of literary works, *Phenomenology and Literature* (note 4 above), pp. 77, 78.

32. Heidegger, *Being and Time*, p. 197.

Edward Wasiolek

IN SEARCH OF THE PURE RELATIONAL CONTEXT

New Criticism began with chasing philosophy out of the critical enterprise. I. A. Richards in *Science and Poetry* and in *Practical Criticism* carries on a spirited argument against the type of reading—it has been going on for a long time—that receives literature by way of philosophic validation. In its most ingenuous form, it takes statements from poems and assumes that they have "truth" value. In *Practical Criticism* Richards say that the statement "Beauty is truth, truth beauty" has no truth value, but is an expression of a certain blend of feelings. To attempt to guide one's life by way of philosophic statements that one abstracts from literature is to misread the function of such statements and to misconceive the function of poetry. The argument takes on a formal character in Richards' distinction between two kinds of propositions: those that point to the world and are verifiable and those that do not point to the world and are not verifiable because they point to the author's feelings. That is, there are philosophical propositions and poetic propositions. Indeed, what may look like philosophical propositions—generalizations about the world—are poetic propositions, set and specified by the context in which they appear, and determined by the intention of the author and the language he uses. In other words, philosophical propositions, even if they may look like such, are not to be found in literature and are not to be read as such. If they look like philosophical propositions, or if they once were, they have become "poeticized" by their context and function. Croce said something of the same thing considerably earlier; and although Richards does not mention him, he was aware of Croce's work. According to Croce's circle of moments, philosophical propositions descend from the theoretical moment into the aesthetic moment, and once there, the propositions are no longer philosophical but aesthetic.

Richards' war against philosophical truth, as he conceived of it, was one of the commonplaces of the various New Critics that followed him, and in the mature years of New Criticism in the late forties and fifties, theoretical arguments about the status of poetry tended to concern themselves with the defense of textual autonomy and the threat of the "intellectualist disciplines," among which the threat of philosophical thinking loomed largest. What is striking about the critical scene today is that philosophy has come back to invade the critical enterprise with a vengeance. Geoffrey Hartman chides his American colleagues for their lack of sympathy and attention to continental philosophy; there is hardly a theoretical argument that is not buttressed by references to Sartre, Husserl, Nietzsche. If Richards reacted against philosophical validation for poetic language, the contemporary critics seem to seek philosophical validation. The leading critics are often philosophers or act as such, the arguments are relentlessly abstract, and the locus of argument is often lifted above the individual text and onto fundamental questions. Questions such as how to read literature, what it is to be fictive, or what it means to narrate have become problematical. The New Critics concerned themselves with the examination of individual poems and the defense of what they conceived to be specific contexts; contemporary critics seem to be concerned with individual texts largely as illustrative of philosophical principles about literature. Jakobson's and Lévi-Strauss' reading of Baudelaire's "Les Chats" and Riffaterre's attack on the reading[1] had more to do with the adequacy of linguistics to reading than with the reading of the poem.

The absorption of specific literary contexts into the widened context of philosophic discussion may seem like a departure from the mole-like burrowing of New Critics in specific texts. But I am persuaded that the philosophizing of criticism is what New Criticism was reaching for, and that such current critical trends are a further development of what was in germination in the New Critical era. I am persuaded also that the "philosophizing of criticism" is not a flight from the individual text, but a return to it, in a special way. That special way is the way of this inquiry.

It is hard to catch the contours of the land while moving through it, but there are some things about criticism today that foreground themselves by repetition and insistence. Among these are: that literature is about literature and not about social, psychological, and experiential matters; that the literary order is autonomous; that every reading is a misreading; that interpretations deconstruct themselves and that there are no final interpretations. Some of this is provocative and some of it is questionable. Nikolai Gogol was a tormented man who found the most ordinary acts of life terrifying, who was in perpetual flight from himself, and who found some relief in objectifying his monstrous neuroses in literature. A recent study of his work insists that Gogol was not writing at all about his agonizing personal conflicts, but was writing about literature.[2] His life and writing, whatever the overt subject matter, was a search for a literary vocation. Perhaps, but inevitable today. That literature is about literature was already a strongly held view in the New Critical period. What has changed is the use of the linguistic model to confirm and expand this view.

The use of Saussurean linguistics, with its emphasis on language as a simultaneous and self-regulating system with no direct correspondence to a pre-existing validating reality, has been an almost indispensable model for criticism today. It has given to criticism a quasi-scientific character in its search for autonomy and self-referentiality and liberation from a correspondence with a pre-existing reality. The model has also permitted criticism to welcome back into its folds those so-called referential or intellectualist disciplines that were chased out of the halls of criticism in the New Critical period. Roland Barthes has had no trouble in including Marxism and Freudianism and existentialism into the folds of structuralism. Lacan has semioticized Freud's biology and Williams has problematized Marx's relations between base and superstructure. One could say that it was not only Gogol who was in search of a literary vocation, but also Freud, Marx, and almost everyone else. The absorption of the so-called content-oriented disciplines into the folds of structuralism would seem, at first, to be seriously at odds with New Criticism and the reach for autonomy and self-reflexibility. But only apparently. The linguistic model has permitted criticism to broaden its self-referential net. It was not only literature that was constituted by differences, but also "other" kinds of writing. During the New Critical period philosophy, religion, and psychology were commenting on life; by way of the linguistic model, they are commenting on themselves.

In the New Critical period self-referentiality was the defining difference between literature and "intellectualist disciplines"; today these disciplines have been "aestheticised" by way of their assumed self-referentiality and by assuming that self-referentiality is a property of literature. Stephen Marcus has shown brilliantly that everything that we consider to be literary method may be found in Freud's psychoanalytic method, that it is difficult if not impossible to distinguish the literary text from the psychoanalytic text. But if that is true, one can say with equal persuasiveness that the literary text is as much psychoanalytic text as psychoanalytic text is literary text. What seems to have changed from the New Critical period is that texts of different orders, philosophy and literature for example, implicate each other and do not exclude each other. And what is equally important, the linguistic model has permitted us to withdraw literature and other kinds of texts more and more from control of a corresponding or validating reality. I. A. Richards did not question that there was a pre-existing reality, nor did he question that there was such a thing as truth and correspondence between statement and reality. But such statements were not poetic statements. Philosophy made statements about the world; poetry made experiences. Poetry was withdrawn from acts of communication about the world; today poetry and the intellectualist disciplines are withdrawn from comments on the world. They have become self-referential or semioticized also.

The denial of a pre-existing validating reality, which has been a repeated and important corollary of the semioticizing of literary criticism, has important implications as to how we conceive of the literary fact. It has taken us a long time to realize that we don't know empirical facts in some direct, immediate, and sensuous way, but as Louis Althusser says, only by way of the cognitive categories we have of them. So, too, we don't know texts in some immediate and direct way but only by way of the knowledge we have of them. If we know objects and texts only by way of the concepts we frame of them, then our conceptions are not validated by a pre-existing reality—at least not by way of an atomistic correspondence—but by way of the concepts themselves. This leads to an elaboration and systematization of the conceptions, and truth becomes the wholeness and logical consistency of the system.

Such validation of facts by way of reference to a closed system of hypothetical relations is not an unfamiliar procedure in philosophy, and to the extent that literary criticism moves toward such relational, hypothetical, and self-regulating thinking, it begins to philosophize itself. This would seem to be at odds with the view we have had traditionally of literature as a way back from abstraction to immediate reality. The aesthetic intuition, we will remember, was for Croce particular, induplicable, and concrete image; for Viktor Shklovsky poetry was a way in which we came to feel again a rock as a rock; and for us, I would hazard, poetry and literature has always been our most sensitive and direct touch with the particularities of reality. Such immediate contact with reality may be an impossible nostalgia, or even an outright duplicity, but that apart, there seems no doubt that our conceptions of literature—at least since New Criticism—have been increasingly philosophical in the sense that there is in them a reach for more and more relational thinking, and in the latest conceptions the reach and assertion that literary criticism is "pure relational thinking." We do not give up easily or readily the view that reality in a direct and specific way is knowable, and New Criticism was such an attempt to hold on to a static, fixed, and immediate view of empirical and literary facts, while at the same time already reaching for that hypothetical, relational, and self-regulating thinking that has come to dominate our view of the literary fact today.

It was not long ago that Matthew Arnold could wrench individual lines and words from works of art and offer the discrete and finished form as models for what was literary and not literary. So, too, Croce could state that individual words and lines and even words could constitute complete intuitions in themselves, that is, perfect and finished works of art. Context, which has been for more than a generation of use one of our compulsive and honorific words, was less important for Arnold, because he was in the grip of a different view of the empirical fact and his conception of the literary fact followed from that. But context is everything for us today, and has been at least since the New Critical period; and I suspect this is so because it signals or is a symptom of a different view of empirical reality. Context for the New Critics was a way of "specifying" the literary fact, and defending it against the generality that philosophical and propositional statements threatened it with. But though much was made of "specification," not much was made of the fact that contextual meaning was a way of emptying the word of specific meaning. That is, the discrete and fixed meaning of the word was qualified by its immediate verbal environment. What it was was partly what it wasn't. Its substance was constituted by its relations, but such relational substantiation was limited, sometimes to the immediate environment and almost always to the confines of the individual poem. New Criticism may have broken down the literary fact as a separate and discrete entity, but it persisted in seeing the individual work as a separate and discrete literary entity. The word was relational, but the work was not.

What has happened since then—Northrop Frye was the conductor and the French movements the provocators—has been a broadening of a certain relational kind of thinking. What Frye did was create a bigger whole: the autonomy of the poem became the autonomy of the literary order, and the parts of that order were relational in a special and fixed way. Frye gave us a literary universe with a big bang, with central and genetic myth, which engendered displacements of itself. His thinking was conservative and retrogressive and the displacements of his "Biblical" and classic myths became attenuated in quality and vitality as they distanced themselves from the center of creation. Frye had broadened relations and fixed them; he broke down the arbitrary and fixed contexts of individual poems and placed them in an arbitrary and fixed context of an outlandish literary order.

Frye attempted to do what seems to be one of the central thrusts of the recent criticism, whether we call it structuralism, semiotics, or revisionism in Hartman's unhelpful term: that is, to reach more and more to what one can call a purely relational world, one which has been progressively liberated from a view of the world as consisting of discrete and fixed particles, succeeding each other in fixed order. The view of empirical facts as finished and fixed, impervious to the categories we frame to understand them, is possible, I suspect, when there is faith in a mind broader than man's to fix and finish the facts. Only God can see things in themselves and only he can see the beginning and end of history, and once we began to lose faith in a divine mind of that sort, we began to lose faith in knowing facts directly and exhaustively. We were left only with man's mind and his ability to frame lesser wholes in which the facts take on their hypothetical substance. The reach for a purely relational world is a reach for a world in which there is no beginning and end, no prime mover, or a world in which everything moves everything else and is moved by everything else. It is a view of the world that regulates and reads itself.

Whether such a pure relational world is possible, however, is problematical. The attempt to formulate such a world has been repeatedly undermined by subtler and subtler forms of substantializing residues. Insinuated fixed and validating elements are present in Frye's criticism in a fairly arbitrary and dictatorial way. They are there, too, in the work of the Russian Formalists and the Prague Structuralists, primarily in their insistence that though nothing has a fixed and determinate meaning in itself, every literary fact has a fixed and determinate meaning at some point in literary history. Everything depends for them on the system in which the literary fact functions and everything depends on the nest of relations the fact finds itself in. This was true of the literary fact within the poem, the literary fact as poem, and the literary fact as movement and as literary order. Iurri Tynianov came close to a purely relational form of thinking because there seemed to be no "fixed" and finished point in his thinking. Everything defined itself by relationships to other elements; even the literary order as a whole defined itself by way of relationships with such orders as psychology, philosophy, and sociology. But the fact that the changing nature of literary facts occurred in a strict succession of time and what was literary and what was not fixed and determinate at each point in history remained as a constraint on pure relational thinking.

The semioticizing of literary criticism owes much to Russian Formalism, as does deconstructionism and other germinations of contemporary criticism. The semioticizing is in part a further attempt to eliminate all residues of substantialist thinking and move literary criticism toward the pure relational thinking that has been promised, for more than a generation now, by the use of such terms as self-referentiality and autonomy. But the insinuation of residues of substantialist thinking leads one to question whether the reach for purely relational thinking is a reality or a form of self-deception that is practiced with ever increasing refinement. In essence a purely relational literary world would regulate itself and would constitute itself, and in literary criticism the text would read itself. Something of this kind was already implied in the practice of New Criticism, especially in the work of R. P. Blackmur, and much more is implied in the work of Paul DeMan, Geoffrey Hartman, and J. Hillis Miller, where the claims of self-regulation have now been extended to the act of reading and critical response.

Such claims lean heavily on the linguistic model of a system of communication that constitutes meaning internally, and only distantly, if at all, by way of correspondence to a pre-existing empirical reality. If we can persuade ourselves that the linguistic model is self-regulating, it is very doubtful that literature and literary criticism are. However we see language as constituting meaning, once such meaning is constituted, it is governed largely by an unspoken and inflexible consensus and is impervious to further "reconstitutions." "Bed" may be constituted by its relationship to "led" and "red," but once constituted, it does not change or else changes at a geological pace. But a purely relational world would be one in which the relationships are not fixed, but open. One can make a case for the fact that the relationship between bed and the object in reality is arbitrary—indeed one must—but one cannot question that the relationship exists. And it exists because it is arbitrary, that is, because it has been chosen. That is, the so-called purely relational model, the constitution of facts by way of self-regulating differences is, there, but only by way of choice, even though the choice has been made by social consensus. The so-called peculiarity of language as constituted by differences does not "save" it from regulation by social choice.

Each so-called self-regulating system has its privileged starting point, and to overlook that intervention in the self-regulating system is to indulge in a self-deception. A system is not self-regulating if the "mover" is outside the system. The choice in language may be obscured by time and collective will, but the choice in literary criticism is direct and clear. The literary system, for example, does not tell us what signifier "signifies." We do. Often, the system does not tell us what is "signifier" and "signified." One can take the outrageous moralizing of Gogol's *Selected Passages* as signifier of another chapter in his "literary" odyssey. Boris Eikhenbaum took the moral agonies of the young Tolstoy and made them not agonies but literary experimentations. So be it. But if

Gogol's moral terrors were a search for a literary vocation, why wasn't the search for the literary vocation an attempt to handle his moral terrors? Which is the privileged point? In a purely relational world, self-regulated and self-constituted, as the model of linguistics for literary purposes pretends, there can be no privileged point. But in literary criticism there always is, and an attempt to pretend there is not—as in the Gogol example—is to substantialize one view and to pretend that the text has to read itself. Texts don't read themselves and they don't regulate themselves, and literary texts are not only about literature. The point is that the proponents of the self-regulating world do not accept the implications of this autonomy, which is that in a purely relational world, there is no way to determine what determines what, what is signifier and what is signified, what is symbol and what is symbolized. No way except by intervention, by positing a privileged point, by accepting the reality and inevitability of choices. This is what Frye did, and although his choice was grotesque, it was clear.

Because there is no way in which the text will tell you what is signifier or signified or tell you too when a chosen chain of "signifieds" has exhausted itslf, the problem of "pluralism" has resurfaced with a vengeance recently.[3] The problem was vigorously debated in the early fifties between the New Critics and the Chicago Critics. According to the Chicago Critics the New Critics were "Platonic" because they tended to look for universal attributes of poetry and as such to blur differences of kinds between poems. The Chicago pluralism, however, with its emphasis on different questions and methods for different tasks, was different from the kind of pluralism that seems to be the consequence of the premises of Jacques Derrida and Miller. No one, I suspect, would take issue with the belief, espoused by M. H. Abrams, Wayne Booth, and Miller, that meanings are plural, that meaning is often or perhaps always partial, that even the best of readings are an approximation of the core meaning of the text, no matter how rich and equivocal. But Abrams insists that meaning, no matter how plural and equivocal, is determinate, and Miller insists that Abrams' determinate meaning is a demand for univocal meaning, which the history of criticism has demonstrated to be an impossible nostalgia. Miller is right, I think, no matter how offensive the word univocal may be to Abrams, that his demand for determinate meaning is a demand for univocal meaning, in the sense I take it that Miller means it: that Abrams believes that there is a defined meaning, no matter how complex, rich, and many-sided that meaning may be. For Abrams this "determination" is largely that of history and author, and our task as critics is largely one of excavation.

But there is an unclarity about "determinate" that neither Abrams or

Miller brings into the open. Miller understood Abrams' determinate meaning to be "final" determinate meaning, and Miller demonstrated over and over again that there was no final meaning. On the other hand, Miller refused to come to terms with the fact that meaning was always determinate, no matter how relational and "unfinal," because we choose the system the meaning constitutes itself in. I take it that this is what Abrams had in mind when he averred that Miller understood Abrams and Abrams Miller, and that the audience understood both, a fact that seemed to him to be impossible if there was no determinate meaning. Miller assumes that the text is anything that we want to make it. And he is right, but we never make it everything, but always make it something, and that something is always something determinate but never anything final. Pouring the history of words through the web of the work, somewhat in the manner of William Empson in the thirties, is to indulge again in the myth of duplicity that the text constitutes itself. The text is everything but not at the same time; final meaning is always deferred, but determinate meaning is not.

But if Miller was refusing to take responsibility for his choices, and pretended to believe that everything was relevant to everything, Abrams, too, was indulging in the myth that he could fix and constrict determinate meaning, that there was a point at which it could no longer be deferred. He was prepared to be, as was Booth, gracious and flexible about different points of view and accretions of meaning, but he was also fixed in his view that there was a final determinate meaning, on the logic, I suppose, that there must be a determinate meaning, if we can tell what is inadequate and adequate, right and wrong, rich and poor, distortion and fulfillment. This is so because there is a text that, though unknown, is known in some way and the evidence that it is known is that we can know when we are right and we are wrong.

In some respects the argument resembled the "affaire Picard," in which Roland Barthes and Raymond Picard tussled over the Racinian text, and in which Picard insisted that the text was determined by history and the task of the critic was to engage in a careful excavation of that text, and Barthes insisting that the text did not exist in itself but only in our "constructions." To be sure, Abrams is a great deal more sophisticated, gracious, and flexible than was Picard, but one suspects that in the final analysis he would subscribe to the premises of Picard. And if so he subscribes to an impossibility and Miller is right that he subscribes to an impossible nostalgia. Nor need he, to have his determinate meaning. He can, if he wants, choose the author to be his "determiner" of determinate meaning, but it will be a choice and binding on no one except those who would make a similar choice. His assertion that he understands what Shakespeare meant when Lear said "pray you undo this button" proves nothing except that the meaning he understands is part of an arbitrary system of sounds and concepts, meaningless and unconstitutable in endless other linguistic systems.

Georg Lukács has said that "facts" are never finished, meaning by that that our knowledge of facts is never finished, and that the same empirical fact is reconceived and recreated with the accretions of history. I don't see how we can restrict the meaning of a fact or a text to the mind that created it or the age that it was created in, without assuming at the same time that history is irrelevant to the constitution of the fact. In a curious way both Abrams and Miller have denied history: Abrams because meaning, no matter how equivocal and rich, is finished and unmodifiable by history, and Miller because all of history is present and simultaneous. If meaning constitutes itself in history, then it can never be finished, because history will never finish itself; we have to assume an end that is constantly denied.

Although one can hold to the view—and perhaps one must—that there are no fixed and finished literary facts, that *The Iliad* can be a commentary on *The Great Gatsby*, and *The Great Gatsy* on *Don Quixote*, nevertheless, what we say and what we conceive is determinate and finished at a particular time. The facts are not finished, but what we say about them is. The conceptions that arise in subsequent periods reconceive the fact, and as such the facticity changes. But even though all of history is reconceivable and reconstitutable, this is so only in potentiality and not in actuality. In actuality what we say is finished; it may be misreading, but it is finished and fixed. Even endless play with the traces of meaning is fixed once Derrida or Miller engage in the play, for others will play in another way.

I don't know what "pray you undo this button" means "precisely" or "finally," but I know what others in history have said "pray you undo this button" means. I don't know what is literary fact and what is literary unfact, but I know what has been literary fact in the past and what has not been. It is true that anything in human life and human conception may become literary fact. There is no way we can say that only these experiences are literary and these are not. Everything is and is not literary fact. But not in actuality, only in potentiality. It is a fact that certain kinds of languages, themes, forms establish themselves at certain points in history and not in others, and are succeeded by others in a fairly orderly fashion. Everything is not alway possible. All those deep chasms, daffodils, charming abbeys, and that special worship of the child in Romanticism are not possible today. Only certain potentialities of reality are actualized and not others. In the first decades of the century

factories, job hunting, something of the grim and souless grime of capi-
talism, of the industrial world, surfaced in the work of Sinclair and
Dreiser. The factories are still there in reality, or if you want, in other
semiotic orders, but they are not there in American literature, at least
not in the same way.

History is inevitable, but the kind of history is not. Barthes' influential
essay "History or Literature" misposes the problem: what he had in
mind was the determined and finished history of Picard versus a univer-
salized and simultaneous literature. There are no determinations without determiners, and no systems without posers of systems, and no
autonomous literary worlds without their privileged factors. It is not
facts that succeed themselves in time, not at least since we lost faith in a
being that determined those facts and validated their specific weight and
character; rather it is the reconstitutions of facts that succeed themselves. But such facts reconstitute themselves in a net of relations, not
the whole net of relations of all of history, but a chosen net of relations
at a particular point in history. That is, facts constitute and reconstitute
themselves in systems, and once chosen the systems are more or less
self-referential. But the systems are chosen and they are something
determinate, though hypothetical. One can be whimsical about the re-
conception of a literary fact, one can be confused, and one can certainly
be unsystematic. But none of that will alter the fact that what we see is
seen in a particular net of relations, which we can acknowledge as present and chosen.

The perception, acknowledgment, and especially the elaboration of
such a system of relations is what I would call the philosophizing of
criticism, because it has taken criticism from the mystifications of direct
contact with reality and from the unmediated touch of specific, concrete,
static, and discrete facts. I. A. Richards was in the grip of that mystification, and his work and that of New Criticism was a desperate attempt to
preserve a "primitive" mode of thinking, or at least a mode of thinking
based on a cosmology that we no longer subscribe to: that history is the
succession of discrete and autonomous empirical facts. Richards felt that
philosophical statements kept one from the specific contexts of the poet's
experience, and it is my contention that it is by way of the philosophizing of criticism that we come back to the specification and determination
of meaning. Our so-called direct contact with reality has almost surely
been by way of unacknowledged systems. Hartman and some of the
other "deconstructionists" as well as many of the French school have
gone out of their way to declare the death of the "I" or self in the
literary act. Some of this has been said, I assume, for shock value. It is
one thing to say that the self is traversed by codes, and another to say

that it is unnecessary. But the view of the "I" as something unmeshed in relations, a still point acting on but not acted on is part of that primitive view of reality that sees phenomena as discrete, fixed in character and in time. But to grant this is not to grant that the "I" is acted on without acting. The "I" cannot determine how they are seen or how they function. And in fact it cannot do this, but it can choose the system the fact functions in, and even that choice is not unmediated, but mediated by the systems that are available and those that have not worn out. It is, if you will, "condemned" to choose a system, and its freedom lies in its consciousness of such a choice.

If we turn to a work like *The Great Gatsby*, we have a set of determinate relations: the words are set down in a certain order, it is Gatsby that has the magnificent yellow car and not Nick, it is Gatsby that loves Daisy with a boundless and inflexible love and not Tom, and it is Tom that loves Myrtle and not Gatsby. But there is no way that one can restrict what the yellow car means, for example, and no way that one can determine with finality what the love of Gatsby for Daisy means. Nor is there any way that one can with finality say what signifies what. There is the text, of course, but as soon as we admit that the text exists in relation to other texts—and we must—and that Gatsby's yellow car has a relationship not only to Tom's blue car and Wilson's dusty Ford, but to other cars in American literature, and not only to cars but to all qualities of motion and power, then we can say it signifies almost everything. Gatsby's car has an infinitude of potential relationships. But this universal text does not exist, except as potential validation of specific texts that one constructs with the determinations of a determinate system. I can drop my *Great Gatsby* in any number of philosophical chemicals and the potential negatives will come out as fixed, historical, and determinate prints, but I can't limit the number of prints.

We can choose to confine ourselves within the system of what the author intended, but it will be a choice. But there is no way that we can make it the only text or at least no way that we can demonstrate that it is the only text. We know, for example, that Fitzgerald makes Nick honorific and Tom repugnant in the novel, and we know—and criticism has acknowledged—that Tom's love of Myrtle is dirty and Gatsby's love for Daisy is exalted and beautiful in its single-minded dedication. But Fitzgerald's and Nick's view of the literary facts are constituted in a humanistic, ethical, and Christian net, where a love pursued by sacrifice and dedication is exalted and fine, whatever the object of the love. But the same love constituted in a psychoanalytic philosophical system becomes something different: Gatsby's faithful loves becomes Gatsby's compulsive love; his pure love, his sick love; his worship of Daisy, his disregard of Daisy. The love for a Marxist system is the desire to possess and make solid and real what Gatsby had pursued from his obscure beginnings to his pathetic ending: the power and fixed identity that only a certain class and power can give him.

There is no way that one can say which system and which "constitution" of the facts is correct. That is another nostalgia: that we can play God and say once and for all what the end of meaning is. The philosophizing of criticism has led us to a relational world in which literary facts take on different bodies, but it has also led us to what is the most specific and most intimate of acts: choice and the responsibility of what we want the text to mean for us. That is not to say that we make the meaning anything we want. We make it what it can be; and we make it for ourselves, but only with a system that is not ourselves. We choose the philosophical system, and it forms and elaborates our choice. Jonathan Culler spoke of our cultivating a literary competence, somewhat along the lines of Chomsky's linguistic competence. But that literary competence cannot avoid becoming a philosophical competence. If we can know literary facts only by way of the systems that constitute them, then we must know the systems. I suspect, too, that if literary criticism has become and is becoming increasingly philosophized, that philosophy is becoming more and more poeticized. Nor is there any doubt of it.

Notes

1. Roman Jakobson and Claude Lévi-Strauss, " 'Les Chats' de Charles Baudelaire," *L'Homme*, II, janvier-avril, 1962, pp. 5–21. Also, Michel Riffaterre, "Describing Poetic Structure: Two Approaches to Baudelaire's *Les Chats*," in *Structuralism*, ed. Jacques Ehrmann (Garden City, N.Y., 1970), pp. 188–229.
2. Donald Fanger, *The Creation of Nikolai Gogol* (Cambridge, Mass., 1979).
3. The remarks that follow have to do with the controversy published in *Critical Inquiry* 3(Spring, 1977):407–448, among Wayne Booth, Meyer Abrams, and J. Hillis Miller.

Meir Sternberg

MIMESIS AND MOTIVATION: THE TWO FACES OF FICTIONAL COHERENCE

Fiction finds itself caught between the contending demands of what is traditionally (though not always unambiguously) designated as life and art. From one it derives its very capability of representation, from the other its distinctive logic and internal coherence; one provides the basis and the other the terms of reference. It is precisely this uneasy co-exis-tence (with its tensions, duplicities, imbalances, and compromises) that the concept of *motivation* embraces. It moves between the world and the teleology of art, explaining facts, effects, and choices in relation to the fictive reality that objectifies them (in the form of action, spatiotem-poral contiguity, narrative viewpoint) and/or to the aesthetic strategy that underlies or transcends such objectification.

What must first be got out of the way is the inessential though nonthe-less troublesome part of the problem, regarding the old sense and the new doctrinal associations of the key term. As in its more customary use, "motivation" here still denotes an explanatory procedure, but one ac-counting for the artist's rather than the characters' activity and for com-positional rather than psychological features. Figural psychology then turns from primary object into means of explanation, becoming one of many motivational resources—as when the villain's motiveless malignity makes sense in relation not (or not only) to some conception of character but also to the generic need for catastrophe.

In a sense akin to this, at least in the negative respect of detachment from psychological integration *per se*, the term was applied to literary study by the Russian Formalists, shortly after having made its controver-sial appearance in Saussurean linguistics. But the notion itself has a history almost as long, eventful, and discordant as that of its protean relative, mimesis. The wider one's net is cast, the more time-honored and variegated the catch: Poe's "Philosophy of Composition," the tradition of romantic irony that has bequeathed its anti-dissimulatory bias to the Formalists and their progeny, Sheridan's *The Critic*, Dryden's *Essay of Dramatic Poesy*, the traffic between nature and convention in French Neo-Classicism, and not least Longinus's *On the Sublime* with its insistence on the need for art to conceal its artfulness.

The conceptual twists and turns of the issue, like its normative ups and downs, make a story well worth telling—and not for antiquarian reasons alone. But since historical evolution is only incidental to the present argument, it needs to be stressed in advance that my choice to refer to the twofold intelligibility of fictive structure as "motivation" implies no commitment to the doctrine(s) with which that term has recently come to be associated. Indeed, the term is much happier than its (narrow and at that conflicting) uses at the hands of the Formalists and their more recent followers. It is applicable to both author and reader as patterning agents (unlike "dissimulation"), to both mimetic or referential and nonmimetic elements (unlike "illusion"), and to both operation and result (unlike "coherence"); it is also normatively neutral and semantically open, yet (unlike "integration") suggestive of a reasoning and reason-giving activity. Still, though logomachy has its allurements, my quarrel with various other uses of "motivation" will be far less concerned with establishing the proper meaning of the word than with distinguishing the ill-assorted approaches to literary structure and coherence that are bundled into it and, above all, with exploring the nexus of fiction and function in the literary text. As with terminological, so with expository choice. If the argument starts by juxtaposing philosophies of composition located at opposite ends of the historical continuum, with some emphasis on modern developments, it largely derives from the need to disentangle and articulate an explanatory tool of great power and relevance.[1]

REALITY AND MOTIVATION: DOCTRINAL BIASES, VARIABLE PRODUCTS, UNIVERSAL MODES

One line of motivational reasoning can be traced back to Aristotle's *Poetics*, where it first links up with a whole philosophical system and informs the very distinction between Art and Nature. Its earliest is also its most remarkable occurrence there, coinciding not just with a notorious crux but with what looks like a curious piece of self-contradiction and turns out to be a distinctive, if to many unpalatable, feature of narrative art.

No sooner has Aristotle established the vital role played by the element of character in determining action,

> Tragedy is the imitation of an action; and an action implies personal agents, who necessarily possess certain distinctive qualities both of character and thought. . . . These—character and thought—are the two natural causes from which actions spring, and on actions again all success or failure depends,

than he as emphatically demotes it in favor of plot:

> For Tragedy is an imitation, not of men, but of an action and of life, and life consists in action, and its end is a mode of action, not a quality. Now character determines men's qualities, but it is by their actions that they are happy or the reverse. Dramatic action, therefore, is not with a view to the representation of character: character comes in as subsidiary to the actions. Hence the incidents and the plot are the end of a tragedy; and the end is the chief thing of all. Again, without action there cannot be a tragedy; there may be without character. (Chapter 6; trans. S. H. Butcher)

If the agents necessarily possess character and if, moreover, character operates as the natural cause of doing, how can it be divorced or even altogether eliminated from action? Thus posed, the question is hardly answered by the common charge that Aristotle conceives of action in terms of external incidents to the exclusion of the secret of the self.[2] Such a view might at best account for the slighting of character, but it would not warrant character's sudden fall from necessary to dispensable status. The point is surely that the two excerpts do not relate to the same context but draw a basic distinction between life and art.[3] The qualifier *natural* in "natural causes" does not mean anything like "common" or "ordinary." Rather, it appears in its strict Aristotelian sense— retaining its reference to the physical world, where things move and develop according to inherent (as opposed to fabricated or imitative) principles of motion.

In life, the agent's character, itself the product and legacy of past actions, determines his action and accordingly produces happiness or unhappiness. From an observer's standpoint, making sense of a "real-life" success or failure thus consists in placing it as effect within a causal chain where the agent's character figures as pre-existent cause. Given such-and-such a character, we reason, no wonder that such-and-such a development should ensue.

But plot, the counterpart in literature to action in life, is regulated by quite a different logic—the logic of imitation. Being not an instance but a mimesis of an action, literary plot's fundamental obligation is to the quasi-natural principle which makes it a mimesis (and hence an artifact) in the first place: the principle of motion, whose artistic embodiment is the change of fortune from happiness to unhappiness or the reverse. The process of change inherent in nature must be fabricated in art. This leads ineluctably to an inversion of priorities and dependences. For while the artist cannot escape the need to initiate and sustain what may be called the actional dynamics of his plot, he enjoys a freedom of choice as regards the measures by which the dynamics may be actualized and justified ("motivated") in lifelike terms, including character. To motivate an unhappy change of fortune, for example, the artist can suddenly crush his protagonist under a falling statue; confront him with an invasion or a civil war; or turning from outer to inner propulsion, invest him with such character traits (hybris, blindness, jealousy, ambition) as must sooner or later get him into trouble.

Character thus comes in as subsidiary to the plot because, qua static element within the Aristotelian world-view, it ultimately forms no more than a means to the dynamic end—and not the only or perforce the central means at that. No longer the pre-existent cause of real actions, it is logically demoted to the position of an effect issuing from the distinctive and overriding artistic cause. In contrast to the natural reasoning "Given such-and-such a character, such-and-such an action ensures," the poetic reasoning goes, "Given such-and-such an action (as functional exigency), such-and-such a character (as representational motivation) ensues or may ensue." Of course, leaving aside the accidents of genesis, the contrast between these two lines of determinative reasoning is radicalized in the theoretical model of production rather than in the finished product. On the contrary, here we find the breach dissimulated, the inverted structure of determination more or less plausibly reinverted. The integration of character into the plot gives developments not just unity but also the appearance of a real flow, inviting the reader to perform the kind of causal reconstructions and inferential operations to which he is accustomed in the daily business of living. And the closer we get to the artifact itself—as we move from literary plot as such to generic plot and from generalized argument to concrete sequence—the tighter the ostensible synthesis.[4] But this precisely reflects the motivational two-facedness of mimesis as a bridge between art and nature. Psychological motive does not so much replace as overlie and substantiate artistic motivation.

Partly due to the Aristotelian philosophy of man, nature, and science that is so clearly at work here, all this doubtless offers ample ground for such objections as, among others, that it is inapplicable to referentially static literature (like descriptive poetry) on the one hand and dynamic character on the other; that it imposes a fixed ranking on components; and that it fails to distinguish necessary condition from contextual dominant. But whatever its problems, Aristotle's implicit view of motivation shows a consistency that is sadly lacking in most of its modern counterparts. A notable exception is the poetics of Henry James, whose harping on indirection and authorial distancing exerted a tremendous influence on the modern novel's motivational procedures—from the crusade against artificial "telling" to the Ford-Conrad "impressionistic" method. And yet, in spite of many differences, it ultimately proves too Aristotelian in spirit to afford the alternative we now require. Another exception—the early Formalist doctrine of motivation as originally adumbrated in Viktor Shklovsky's *Theory of Prose* and other writings—better serves our purpose. Its sharpness renders it easily definable while its extremism invites a comparison with Aristotle's opposed bias.

Although Shklovsky's closest approach to a definition, "By motivation I mean the explanation of artistic structure in terms of circumstances,"[5] is still too elliptical, it can be supplemented from Shklovsky's applications of it in specific analyses. Descriptively speaking, his "motivation" indicates the fictive (actional, social, psychological) facade which the text may put up to hide or justify the working of its devices and artistic laws. To cite a few examples from the well-known essay on *Tristram Shandy*: the convention of the discovered manuscript makes it possible to incorporate Yorick's sermon into the novel; Bobby Shandy's death, like deafness in Russian folk drama, serves to put the characters at cross-purposes; euphemistic dialogue promotes erotic defamiliarization. Since the camouflage here is taken to consist in hardly more than the tacking of some element onto the fictive world, the same device may appear either with or without that extra: "The interruption of the introduced manuscript [in *The Sentimental Journey*] is motivated by the fact that its conclusion has been lost. On the other hand, nothing motivates the conclusion of *Tristram Shandy*, which ends with a simple cutting off of the narrative."[6] But what is descriptively a plus is normatively a minus. The two variants are by no means co-equal, the recourse to "motivation" being deemed at best a necessary pretext and at worst a surrender to nonartistic pressures, but never a virtue. For motivation, according to Shklovsky, by nature attenuates what art (and Sterne as a great artist) always strives to sharpen and maximize—the perceptibility of form, device, and artfulness. However dubious this tenet, it at any rate firmly establishes motivated and unmotivated procedures as a contrasting pair, of which the first is (perceptually and hence typologically) the unmarked term.

Some of the reasons for my choice to start by collocating these historically removed philosophies of composition will now begin to suggest themselves. It is not just that each postulates a different relationship (imitative *vs*. perceptual) between the fictive and the real world: a difference all the more instructive in view of the common insistence on the primacy of this opposition and on the representational autonomy of the fictive analogue. Nor is it just that the underlying theories of literary structure are incompatible (Aristotle's holistic search for synthesis presenting a sharp contrast to Shklovsky's atomistic conception of the work as an aggregate of devices, with a smaller or larger residue of unformalized if not antiformal matter). Each extreme is also characterized by a doctrinal bias which severely limits the range (and understanding) of motivational factors and combinations.

On the one hand, Shklovsky's weaknesses mostly concentrate in what he would call the "motivated" area. Three of them are of immediate concern to us. First, his categorical prejudgment hardly accords with the facts of literary history, which reveal a constant clash and interplay between two traditions, often even within a single work: the tradition of Romantic Irony (from Petronius to John Fowles) with its flaunting of artifice and defiance of "motivation" as against the Illusionist tradition (whether of the Longinian or the Jamesian variety) with its *ars est celare artem*. From the generic viewpoint, the same tensions manifest themselves between parodic and straight art. So even the pursuit of convincing motivation, just like its exposure or abandonment, may itself form a "device" (function, end), let alone a central means to others.

Second, to equate the motivated with the unmotivated variety as something of a special case—restricted to a certain number of otherwise effective devices, avoided in good writing, almost wholly excluded from the cinema—is to miss the point of aesthetic representation. Unless one goes so far as to deny not simply a properly artistic effect but any role whatsoever to all mimetic elements and referential patterns—and that way madness lies—"motivation" cannot but be a *sine qua non* in all representational art: which is to say in all literature, with the possible exception of some concrete or indeed "transrational" poetry and the like. For what matters here is neither Illusionism nor verisimilitude but reference. However tendentious or unlifelike or attenuated the representation and however partial or perforated the mimetic camouflage, to postulate and refer to an imagined world is to motivate artistic ends (e.g., unity, variety, ambiguity) in other terms (e.g., causal sequence, hero's wanderings, observer's ignorance) than their own functionality.

This brings us straight to the third point, regarding the prevalent Fig-Leaf Approach to such motivation. The references to disguise, illu-

sion, pretext, etc.—though useful enough for shorthand notation or affective emphasis—prove misleading unless properly delimited and
translated into objective structural terms. That fictive "motivation"
forms the basis of representational art, no matter what its dissimulatory
power or perceptibility in relation to the devices it serves, is undreamt
of in Shklovsky's philosophy. That motivational factors may be elevated
into ends, as always in realistic and otherwise world-oriented art, or into
binding architectonic principles, like causality in Aristotelian and perspectival consistency in Jamesian poetics, is of course alien to its spirit.
Still more so is the fact that camouflage may assume the form of spurious
or mystifying *artistic* explanations as well. In *The Brothers Karamazov*,
for example, the narrator's contemptuous dismissal of Smerdyakov as
unworthy of thorough presentation ("I should really say something more
about him, but I am ashamed to keep my reader's attention occupied
with common servants too long" [III, 3]) serves the detective line of
interest no less than do the twists of the plot itself: the dissimulated-
undissimulated again cuts across the motivated-unmotivated antithesis.

But even such covers and pretexts as Shklovsky does consider reveal
the inadequacy of his overall notion of structure. For the dissimulation
of a device consists not just in superadding a fictive element but in
superimposing and foregrounding (or at least suggesting) a pattern
whose logic of combination differs from that of the dissimulated effect:
psychological determination overlies generic predetermination, the monologist's associative meandering conceals his creator's artful ordering,
figural repetitousness veils the authorial art of repetition. The perceptual tactics of art—like its semantic density or dynamics of surprise—
rests on its amenability to multiple frames of coherence.

This holds true in principle for any motivation, however transparent
or even parodied, that is anchored in the fictive world. Since in each
case we have to do with alternative and variously interacting organizations of the text, Shklovsky's atomistic model must be rejected along
with his normatve bias. Since fictively anchored motivations, moreover,
vary not only in plausibility but in their "coverage" of the device—
informational gapping and temporal displacement being, for example,
far more "justifiable" all round in restricted (*The Sacred Fount, Chance*)
than in freely omniscient (*The Bostonians, Nostromo*) narration—his dichotomy of motivated *vs.* unmotivated devices must also give place to
one of motivating principles. As I argued elsewhere, far from showing
the either/or choice suggested by the former dichotomy, devices more
often than not partly cohere in lifelike terms. Thus, the work's chronological manipulations may to some extent be passed off as the adherence
to the narrator's tortuous order of discovery, though the narrating self is

already well aware of the truth; the diary form by nature justifies such manipulations to a greater extent than standard retrospective telling; and it is not even quite true that "nothing motivates the [abrupt] conclusion of *Tristram Shandy*," which may be assimilated to Tristram's waywardness as distinct from Sterne's (largely overlapping) strategy.

But whatever varies in these instances of mixed and partial motivation, the two principles that inform them remain constant and properly polarized. Such a shift from textual units to the synthesizing logics that produce and cut across them gives us a basic opposition to operate with while allowing for all possible interplays of specific factors: this notably includes variations in representational coverage and also explanatory tensions within a single unit. And finally, since of the two organizing principles that co-exist in the "motivated" device, only one opposes whereas the other corresponds to that monopolizing the "unmotivated" variety, Shklovsky's primary contrast turns out less than happy even from the terminological standpoint. Apart from implying a positive feature ("motivated") where he sees a perceptual negative and a lack ("unmotivated") where he sees a superiority, this contrasting pair fails to suggest the complexity of integrative relations within one of its members and between the two.

Instead of motivated *vs.* unmotivated *devices*, therefore, I speak of two motivational *modes*, the quasi-mimetic or referential and the aesthetic or rhetorical: the latter omnipresent, because identical with the teleology of art, and the former either actually or potentially coupled with it, as a fictive image of life.

Shklovsky's assorted (and representative) omissions and commissions with regard to quasi-mimetically motivated art have their counterpart in Aristotle's attitude to aesthetically motivated artifice. Unlike Longinus or the Jamesians, he does not so much condemn outright such obtrusion of artifice as ignore it; but this is not wholly attributable to its infrequency within his literary corpus. That his silence reflects a theoretical preconception as well as an historical accident is suggested by the very definition of art as mimesis and further reinforced by several particular indicators. I refer for instance to the studied neglect of Aristophanes; to the objection to the *deus ex machina*, where the probabilistic grounds easily translate into a warning against bending the mimetic to the generic and functional demands of plot; and above all to another statement that has long troubled readers of the *Poetics:* "The poet should speak as little as possible in his own person, for it is not this that makes him an imitator. Other poets appear themselves upon the scene throughout, and imitate but little and rarely. Homer, after a few prefatory words, at once brings in a man, or woman, or other personage" (Chapter 24). This passage indeed makes little sense as long as Aristotelian "imitation" is interpreted as "idealization" and the like. But once grasped in motivational terms, as outlined above, mimesis at once links up with the showing-telling contrast. Entailing a mutual determination of artistic function and fictive reality, mimesis is at odds with any direct (as opposed to world-mediated) contact between the poet as producer and the reader as receiver of effects. Hence the general superiority of drama to epic.

It is not, then, that Aristotle is any less aware of "aesthetic" than of "referential" motivation. Rather, the two principles combine within his conception of mimesis and that is for him their proper, not as with Shklovsky their improper, mode of existence. To formalize art means to fictionalize and counterbalance it in terms of the world, not to bare its artfulness. If therefore Aristotle frowns on imbalances dictated by the exigencies of the plot and resulting in the exposure of the aesthetic logic—as in the *deus ex machina*—it is easy to imagine how he would regard its flaunting and explicit revelation as an independent force or pattern. This is exactly what happens when Trollope adduces the necessity of drawing out the plot as the reason for preventing an early *éclaircissement* between the hero and the heroine of *Barchester Towers*. How easily, he says, could Eleanor be made to burst into tears and Arabin to relent and declare his love: "But then where would have been my novel? She did not cry, and Mr. Arabin did not melt" (Chapter 30). But Trollope's display of artifice is still coupled with a quasi-mimetic justification on psychological and situational grounds—after all, it *is* a fact that she did not cry nor he melt. Elsewhere, this conjunctive form gives way to the monopoly of the aesthetic principle, with the denuded device as the only justification for compositional choices. Fielding thus motivates the delayed disclosure of Joseph's love for Fanny, and by implication the burlesque of the previous chapters where Joseph defends his virtue against Lady Booby's attacks, in relation to his doctrine of opening by small degrees: "For this reason, we have not hitherto hinted a matter which now seems necessary to be explained" (*Joseph Andrews*, I, 11).

The demands of length, recognition scenes, informational withholding: these are all problems that Aristotle has more than a nodding acquaintance with. In fact, the mechanism of his complex plot meets them as effectively as the modern systems of perspectival refraction. But that very fact suggests that he would subscribe not only to the recurrent Jamesian injunction "Dramatise it, dramatise it!" but also to the protest against "the baseness of the *arbitrary* stroke, the touch without its reason"[7]—the arbitrary being equated with the frankly artificial and the missing "reason" standing to the "reason" overtly provided by Fielding in the same relation as quasi-mimetic to aesthetic logic. What emerges beyond doubt, at any rate, is that Aristotle fails to consider purely aesthetic motivation and James to recognize its legitimacy. And given the prominence of the anti-illusionist and nonillusionist traditions, above all in narrative, these failures are no less radical than Shklovsky's: they even betray much the same concern with variable complexes or products of motivation rather than with the two universal modes that produce them.

Besides its other expository and admonitory uses, then, the juxtaposition of the two extremes brings out three minimal requirements for any viable theory of motivation:

A Functional Model of Literary Structure

Motivation is inextricably bound with purposive structuring and the interplay of its modes presupposes a means-end relationship between the organization of the text as a simulacrum of reality (a chain of events, a mental state, a milieu, a dialogue) and as a functional whole (a formal design, a thematic pattern, a sequence of effects). By definition, therefore, it is incompatible with nonteleological views of art and artistic coherence, notably those of the genetic variety: whether doctrinal, like the Romantic approach to poetry as an expression and index of the poet's personality, or *ad hoc*, like the explanation of a work's referential features and incongruities (e.g., what T. S. Eliot sees as Hamlet's pathological condition) in terms of the writer's creative process. Such approaches and interpretive procedures may be equally concerned to make sense of the t ext, but never the purposive sense yielded by the idea of authorial control. They may account for difficulties by establishing relations and referring textual parts to some whole (say, Shakespeare's psychology), but never to a whole consisting in the hierarchial ordering of elements according to their determinative power *vis-à-vis* one another.

Still, even the hierarchies extractable from Aristotle (with plot at the top, diction at the bottom, and character and thought in between) and Shklovsky (headed by devices and ending in motivating pretexts and similar dead weight) are both marked by static, preconceived ranking. What is indicated instead is a flexible means-end model, relating means to hypothesized functions placed above them and motivating them all in terms of the topmost, dominant pattern, but allowing for free (and freely reversible) hierarchical structuring in response to motivational variations between (and within) works. In the classical detective story, for instance, the construction of the fictive world (as regards

time, space, dramatis personae, interpersonal relations, normative attitudes, the progress of the hunt, Watson's obtuseness) is determined by
the generic necessity of retardatory structure; whereas within the detective framework of *Oedipus Rex* or *The Ambassadors* the retardatory
structure largely serves to unfold a vision of the world. Without going
into further details at the moment, I want to emphasize that such a
variable ordering of elements easily accommodates, among other
things, two-way motivations, developmental views of character as well
as plot, and functional disparities in the status of the represented
world.

Mimesis as the Mediating Term bewteen World and Artifice, Referential and Functional Structure

Whatever the causal or spatiotemporal connection between items within
the work's field of reality, each referentially motivated pattern or effect,
qua end, by definition outranks its motivators within the work as a
whole. Even the relationships of mimetic or rather quasi-mimetic determination that may inform the accent of the textual hierarchy (as character determines plot in the Aristotelian scheme) serve to realize, and
possibly to veil, the relationships of aesthetic determination that always
inform the descent. All this suggests no kind of division into artistic and
nonartistic components. On the contrary, the point of replacing an atomistic by a relational position largely consists in establishing quasi-mimetic motivation as part of the text's strategy and the fictive component
itself as amenable to both quasi-mimetic and aesthetic synthesis. Thus,
these is no reason why the patterning of elements into, say, a sequence
of events that progresses within the framework of reality inhabited by
the characters should either exclude or be excluded by their (and its)
coherence as a geometric or symbolic or persuasive design that unfolds
within the framework of the text addressed to the reader. On the contrary, that coherence must subsume as well as regulate the causal con-
catenation. Or take the reader's resolution of an ambiguity or an incongruity by way of attributing the problematic discourse to some fallible
channel of information, say a fictive observer of the scene: this process of
inference with its quasi-mimetic product is often the aesthetic point of
the whole device. The means-end linkage between these synthesizing
modes, therefore, reflects a necessary condition of representational art,
not at all a disparagement of representational structure or even realism,
which may well form the aesthetic end in question and thus determine
the choice of quasi-mimetic means. Mimesis, in short, operates as a

mediating rather than qualitative term; and its two faces also draw attention to the third requirement which follows.

An Asymmetry between the Two Motivational Modes

Of the two motivational modes, only the aesthetic can appear apart from as well as together with its complement. Always opposed and hence mutually illuminating in logic of operation, they do not necessarily coexist. The quasi-mimetic entails aesthetic patterning, referential choice presupposes functional intent; the fictive framework holding the dramatis personae must be (re)constructed with regard to the rhetorical framework holding author and reader, but the converse is not true. It is not merely that the aesthetics also marks nonrepresentational art—from concrete poetry to abstract painting—where motivational links and hierarchies indeed obtain between its varieties alone, for instance between graphic and prosodic design. There is nothing to prevent the teller from speaking straight to his addressee—from directing or misdirecting him, explaining his procedure, indulging in digressive commentary—with no reference to the represented world. All the resultant elements and effects will then be assimilated in rhetorical terms, pure if not simple.

MOTIVATION AND INTEGRATION: THE CONCEPT OF FUNCTIONAL MEDIACY

But if these two motivational modes are nothing but principles of assimilation, making sense of the text by incorporating and interrelating elements into patterns, what distinguishes them from other forms of integration? Aren't they just part of the text's unifying strategies or the reader's interpretive resources, and can't their sharp opposition be absorbed and refined by some more comprehensive scheme? A good way to answer these questions is to glance at the critical fortunes of Shklovsky's dogma, whose consistency is perhaps its strongest recommendation.

The Russian Formalists themselves seem as little aware as their followers and historians of their manifold divergence from the original approach—the conceptual ramification having been shrouded in terminological parity.[8] Thus, although on the face of it concerned to generalize and develop the earlier insights on which it obviously draws, Boris Tomashevsky's well-known account of "motivation"[9] in fact deflects and all but transforms them.

Not that these changes and twists are perforce for the worse. On the

contrary, even Tomashevsky's cursory reference at the start to the unifying or coherence-promoting role of motivation marks a welcome shift
from Shklovsky's focus on camouflage and local effect, with the resulting
fragmentation of the text into devices proper and motivating excres-
cences. Actually, as I argued, it is important to realize that such emphases may be rendered not just compatible but complementary. For to
camouflage a device (say, retardatory structure) is to foreground an alternative principle of organization (causality instead of suspense) that will
invite the reader to assimilate its components to a different network of
relationships (the exigencies of the hunt in the detective story or those
of love in comedy). Another promising initiative of Tomashevsky's is the
attempt to classify motivations into the "realistic," "artistic," and "compositional" varieties. Even the naming itself promises to supply an omis-
sion which at times led to ostensible self-contradictions: as when
Shklovsky states both that in *Tristram Shandy* "the artistic form is presented simply as such, without any kind of [realistic?] motivation" and
that Sterne lays bare his artifice because he considers "such [artistic?]
motivation an end in itself."[10] Not to mention the number of puzzling
references to motivated *vs.* unmotivated forms where the actual aim is
to indicate not the presence or absence but the basis of assimilation.

Unfortunately, however, these potential gains are more than nullified
by a wavering that has left its mark on later developments. Where
Tomashevsky gets into trouble will become manifest once we note how
his typology breaks down owing to a double confusion between the
particular and the general. On the one hand, his *compositional* motivation, justifying the introduction of material in terms of economy ("if one
speaks about a nail driven in a wall at the beginning of a narrative, then
at the end the hero must hang himself on that nail"), is in fact nothing
but a subtype of the *artistic* category. Where outside art do such peculiar norms and expectations of relevance operate? Within the domain of
art, moreover, this integrative constraint varies in line with different
conceptions of unity and sometimes (as in ancient epic and the Realist
novel) one finds it decidedly relaxed if not inverted: even works related
to the same literary tradition, like Biblical narrative and *The Gilgamesh
Epic*, operate with entirely different norms of economy as against
redundancy.[11] The "compositional" subtype therefore deserves no pref-
erential treatment at the expense of others belonging to the same popu-
lous category—thematic, generic, stylistic, affective, or for that matter
prosodic motivation. On the other hand, the treatment accorded to the
realistic mode, as well as bristling with internal difficulties, likewise
indicates the need to subsume it under a more general theoretical heading, which this time is conspicuously absent from the tripartite scheme.

Realistic motivation, we learn, arises in response to the reader's demand for "illusion."[12]

> Although firmly aware of the fictitious nature of the work, even the experienced reader demands some kind of conformity to reality. . . . Even readers fully aware of the laws of aesthetic structure may not be psychologically free from the need for such illusion. As a result, each motif must be introduced as a *probable* motif in the given situation.

Equally revealing is the stress laid on the clash between conventional and realistic techniques for introducing motifs, with a view to exposing "the irreconcilability of these absurd traditional techniques with realistic motivation." And given the criterial status of verisimilitude, no wonder that fantastic narrative and realistic motivation finally appear as diametric opposites.[13]

In view of its identity with the probable, Tomashevsky's "realistic" cannot correspond to Shklovsky's "motivated" variety, which (repeated occurrences show) accommodates what its ostensible analogue categorically excludes and even singles out the verisimilar for special dispraise. Unlike the discrepancy between unifying and veiling orientation, however, this one can neither be dismissed as just another instance of happy pluralism within the Formalist camp nor bridged in terms of some inclusive theory. If the fantastic contrasts with the realistic, does it constitute a separate, fourth (or, eliminating the compositional, third) type of motivation? And what about the intermediate degrees? Moreover, if realistic also contrasts with traditional motivation, along another axis of probability, where does the traditional belong? Hardly to the "artistic" category, whose paradigm is none other than the device of defamiliarization. It must then form a category of its own (and this still leaves unsettled, again, the whole range of possibilities between the newfangled and the stereotyped, historical dynamics and all). But with the exclusion of the conventional leaving room for the perceptually potent or viable alone, the realistic motivation suspiciously begins to look like the artistic.

Tomashevsky's main claim to interest thus consists in his having fallen between two theoretical stools, a fate that not many of his followers have managed to escape. Such accidents would deserve little more than passing notice did they not conveniently serve—and did their recurrence not stress the need—to disentangle two extremely important lines of inquiry converging on literary structure and structuring.

On the one hand, Tomashevsky's sporadic concern with unity might have developed into a general theory of textual coherence and integration, with its principles ranging through all the levels and contexts of the literary work. But such an undertaking presupposes, among other things, not just a wealth and specification of integrative procedures extending far beyond what is allowed for by his actual outline, but also the denial of any pride of place to reality and realism. In short, it presupposes a sharp dissociation from his fellow-Formalist's (or Aristotle's or James's or my own) concern with motivation, within which the relationship between art and reality (rather than between sound and sense, syntax and semantics, language and theme, character and plot, or beginning and ending) must hold the center of the stage. In fact, however, so far from his mind is the cutting of this umbilical cord that instead of widening he gratuitously restricts the scope of "motivation."

That he fails to provide additional forms of intelligibility even where logically indicated (as just shown) is only part of the story, and not the most telling part at that. Thus, there is surely no reason to limit motivational techniques to the "introduction" of material, or in other words, to accounting for its selection alone: What is this element doing in the work? Apart from negative (omissions, permanent gaps) and relative (redundancy, scene vs. summary) selectional features, it is no less important to explain combinatory features: temporary withholding (as with informational delay and distribution), presentational order (e.g., displaced chronology) and viewpoint (say, authorial vs. figural narration), etc.[14] Even more restrictive is the implied theoretical linkage between "motif" (as distinct from "motive") and "motivation." Regardless of etymological validity, this leads to the confinement of integrative operations to those irreducible fictive particles making up the sequence of events. All elements and structures outside the represented world are automatically excluded: whether phonic (like the sounds integrated into a rhyme pattern) or grammatical (recurrent constructions) or semantic (other than referential, like figurative fields) or ideological (thematic synthesis). What renders this implied condition so gratuitous is that for the "artistic" and "compositional" types in themselves it should make no difference whether or not the elements to be explained and assimilated are fictional—a syntactic unit being as amenable as a character to estrangement or economical exploitation. Whereas the "realistic" variety, strictly speaking, requires only that, of the two elements brought into a motivational pattern, the motivator(s), not the motivated device or effect, should belong to the fictive reality. But this of course makes the self-imposed limitation only more revealing.

On the other hand, Tomashevsky might have pursued a different—more sharply delimited but no less challenging—line of inquiry by revaluating and systematizing the scattered Formalist slogans into some theory of motivation proper. But for this the minimal requirement,

perhaps the only one equally met, after a fashion, by Shklovsky and
Aristotle, is the subsumption of motivational techniques under two appropriately opposed principles. With this in view, one must keep firm
hold of the elusive truth regarding the criterial force of the reference to
reality: it is the presence or absence of fictive mediation rather than
structural value that distinguishes the two principles. One is the aesthetic or rhetorical mode of motivation, organizing elements into patterns and effects addressed straight to the reader. The other is the
referential or quasi-mimetic mode ("realistic" in the widest sense possible), organizing elements in terms of the fictive reality interposed between author and reader and variously overlying or articulating the
text's functional ("aesthetic-rhetorical") design. So realism in the narrow
sense is still relevant here; but, just like surrealism, only as a special
case of quasi-mimetic motivation operating under certain aesthetic constraints. Simlarly, integration still remains of paramount importance—no
matter what the elements brought into pattern—but only insofar as
convertible or canalized into the issue of functional mediacy $vs.$ immediacy. For instance, how we make sense of figurative language by subject-
ing it to contextual operations may be, in itself, beside the point here;
how we make sense of a metaphor in relation to the fictive persona who
utters it (say, as unconscious self-relevation) and at the same time to the
hidden author who manipulates him into uttering it (as deliberate bet-
rayal), brings us to the heart of the matter. Given such distinctions,
there would have been nothing to prevent Tomashevsky from going on
to subdivide the primary modes and elaborate their implications for
textual coherence. But he observes none of them. Hence, quite apart
from all internal difficulties, the chasm that separates our ungradable
and exhaustive opposition from his trio or any other noncontrastive
analysis.[15]

More recent failures to appreciate this point, and thus delimit the
object and method of inquiry, have had further disruptive effects. In
"Vraisemblance et motivation," among the most influential of Structuralist essays, Gérard Genette explicitly follows the Formalists in defining
motivation as

> . . . la manière dont la fonctionnalité des éléments du récit se
> dissimule sous un masque de détermination causale: ainsi, le "con-
> tenu" peut n'être qu'une motivation, c'est-à-dire qu'une justifica-
> tion *a posteriori*, de la forme qui, en fait, le détermine: don
> Quichotte est donné comme érudit pour justifier l'intrusion de
> passages critiques dans le roman, le héros byronien est déchiré
> pour justifier le caractère fragmentaire de la composition des
> poèmes de Byron."[16]

But in fact he vacillates between this and an altogether different sense of the term, which comes to the fore in the division of narrative into three types:

(1) the *vraisemblable*, with its "implicit motivation" of the characters' conduct by reference to some generally accepted world-view to which it conforms throughout ("The Marquise called for her carriage and went for a drive");
(2) the *motivated*, which manifests deviations from that world-view but always justifies them through explanatory comments and maxims ("The Marquise called for her carriage and then went to bed, because she was very capricious");
(3) the *arbitrary*, tacitly refusing to account for what the public would regard as its improbabilities ("The Marquise called for her carriage and then went to bed").

Does this classification show any reasonable or even consistent basis? If designed (as suggested in the final summary of the argument [p. 21, n. 2]) to differentiate explicit from implicit motivation, it is rather trivial and certainly not tripartite but binary ("motivated *vs.* unmotivated narrative"). While if at the same time offered as a gradation marking a descending order of probability (pp. 8–10), it hardly makes any sense. It is then, to start with, theoretically narrow. For the location of a work upon the sequence leading from the verisimilar to the improbable depends here only on the institutionalized beliefs of the reading public—regardless of the complex of premises making up its own reality-model, whose interiority may establish its own verisimilitude and do duty for an increase in "motivation" at the points of divergence from the public norm. It is also empirically untenable, since both the "*vraisemblable*" (e.g., popular romance) and the "arbitrary" (e.g., the fantastic from Apuleius to Kafka) often resort to circumstantial or psychological explanation. To say nothing of the wholesale banishment of drama on purely presentational grounds—the awkwrdness and hence rarity of authorial exegesis compared with narrative—from the middle range of probability. And worst of all, it is logically fallacious, because the overtness of a motivation neither entails nor necessarily correlates with its probability, having in principle as little to do with public acceptability as with internal validity. No one who has threaded his way through the commentary of a Fielding, thick with ironies and double-bluffs, will ever be tempted to make such a linkage between formal elucidation and semantic lucidity.

Three independent features of representational strategy are thus yoked together here: (a) formal mode of articulation (the dichotomy explicit *vs.* implicit); (b) degree of probability (supposing it is amenable to a tripartite division); (c) referential context (external *vs.* internal, generic *vs.* empirical, conventional *vs.* original, etc., with their innumerable mixtures and variations). Still more disturbing is the fact that this typology, if possible to an even greater extent than Tomashevsky's, has lost touch with the very point at issue. Its three types are all referential, but it cannot count as an attempt to distinguish techniques of referential camouflage according to their distance from the most illusive one, namely, "realistic" motivation. This is precluded by two conceptual shifts transforming the term: the relapse into the traditional use of *motivation* as psychological intelligibility and the opposition of the *realistic* not with the functional or artistic but with the strange or nonverisimilar. In none of the three Marquise examples, not even in the one designated as arbitrary and hence expected to foreground the teleology of art at the expense of the conformity to reality, is the least aesthetic purpose either evident or assumed—certainly not as an *alternative* to the nominal mode of organization. The whole idea of what I called functional mediacy simply does not belong here. For the means-end relationship between world and function is entirely lost sight of; the notion of arbitrariness as the artificial logic regulating or underlying referential development gives place to arbitrariness as referential novelty, license, or sheer recalcitrance on the part of an artist refusing to play by the rules; and motivation becomes no more than an overt and/or moderately plausible technique for linking and illuminating a sequence of events.

And yet, the parts amount to more than the whole. Quite a few of the points do make sense; and were we to disregard the sections characterized by a nontraditional use of "motivation," the remaining argument would somehow hang together. From the viewpoint of narrative intelligibility, a work grounded in convention is doubtless more easily assimilable than one defiant of it; overt rhetoric may indeed (though, again, it need not) do much of the work that its dramatized equivalent leaves to the reader. It is not the novelty of these themes but their orientation that I believe suggestive. In Genette's references to Formalism, significantly, his definitions, examples, slogans, antirealistic bias, even the terminological pairing of "motivated *vs.* unmotivated," are all drawn from Shklovsky. But his wavering between illusion and intelligibility reveals a predicament similar to, and presumably descended from, Tomashevsky's.

This reinforces my claim that such inconsistencies in the handling of the inherited catchword partly reflect a radical division or shift of interest. The clinching evidence is provided by Jonathan Culler's synoptic account of "naturalization," whose lucidity and perceptiveness do more than justice to Structuralist work on this subject. He discriminates five levels of *vraisemblance*, in terms of which a text may be "naturalized" or made intelligible:

> (1) *The "real"* (naturalizing a discourse in relation to a model that "requires no justification because it seems to derive directly from the structure of the world. We speak of people as having minds and bodies, as thinking, imagining, remembering, feeling pain, loving and hating, etc., and do not have to justify such discourse by adducing philosophical arguments");
>
> (2) *cultural vraisemblance* (based on various categories, stereotypes, and generalizations that compose what the culture or public opinion itself recognizes as a valid, if not universally binding, conception of the world);
>
> (3) *models of a genre* (a set of literary conventions or world-views by virtue of which texts may deviate from the laws governing everyday reality and yet remain meaningful and coherent);
>
> (4) *the conventionally natural* (an attack on generic artificiality in the name of conformity to life, with a view to forestalling objections and gaining—or conventionally reinforcing—referential authority);
>
> (5) *parody* (the assimilation of one work in terms of another which it takes as its point of departure but literalizes and exaggeratingly imitates) and *irony* (likewise involving a contrast between two positions, one overt and incongruous, the other covert and deflationary).[17]

In contrast to the tripartite scheme just considered, Culler's straightforwardly develops and makes its point; but that point hardly coincides with mine. In fact, his consistency helps to bring out the extent to which the Structuralist concern with "motivation," "recuperation," "naturalization," etc. involves, for better or worse, a shift of emphasis from the means-end (i.e. referential-aesthetic) relations to the forms and conditions of intelligibility and the interplay of coherence-promoting and coherence-resisting factors; in short, from motivation proper to integration. And the sharper our awareness of the disparity of these cruxes— each lurking behind a wide variety of names and ostensibly unrelated or, worse, misrelated critical activities concerned with the linkage and interrelation of parts into a coherent whole—the better equipped we become to deal with either.

Integration emerges as much the more inclusive and amorphous of the two in that its object is nothing less than what makes a text hang together. Therefore, for instance, the fact that Culler's quintuple typology looks far more powerful than the motivational contrast in which it his-

torically originates is quite beside the point. The one's crudity, by nature redeemable only along oppositional lines, is left unaffected by the
other's refinement. While that refinement, in its own sphere, by no
means suffices to exhaust the range of factors that make and break a
literary text—the models and dimensions of integration.

Thus, the pride of place given here to fictive reality—as with Tomashevsky and for much the same reason—imposes serious restrictions of
scope. Why focus on the assimilation of referential elements at the
expense of the phonic, the lexical, the grammatical, the discursive, the
thematic, or any other textual dimension? Don't all these have their
conditions and conventions of coherence? And doesn't this coherence or
intelligibility likewise result from synthesizing operations that relate part
to part and part to whole? What is more, why focus on referential
models (texts, contexts, worlds) to the exclusion of, say, such omnipresent compositional and reconstitutive principles as analogy or logical and
chronological sequence? And why focus on referential relations rather
than literary interests and effects as sources of intelligibility, on static
configurations rather than dynamic processing and synthesis, or on naturalizing rather than disruptive forces?

Which simply points the moral that within a theory of integration the
clear-cut antithesis between referentially mediated and unmediated
patterning must give place to a crisscross of equipollent and variously
overlapping divisions, not necessarily marked by a functional logic. For
what informs the multiform activity I have called integration is not so
much a sense of purpose as a rage for order. If in other words such a
theory (like the interpretive activity it systematizes) always works with
an opposition, it is with the all-inclusive one directing the whole process of reading: between the coherent and the opaque, the fragmen-
tary, the incongruous. So any mechanism that serves to establish or
undermine, initiate or terminate, reveal or conceal, resolve or ambi-
guate a pattern (and thus to determine intelligibility) deserves equal
consideration, though its integrative role will of course vary in particular cases. Thus, the mechanism of integration may be functional (authorial strategy) or genetic (authorial slip), formal (including typographic
arrangement) or semantic (from co-reference to world-picture), sequential (like causality) or suprasequential (from rhyme to thematic counter-
point), extratextual (historical circumstance or philosophical system) or
intratextual (repetition, built-in probability-register) or intertextual
(from allusion to convention). It may be normative or empirical, lexical
or grammatical, psychological or ideological, perceptual or perspectival,
referential or rhetorical, logical or chronological or analogical, ubiqui-
tous or archetypal or generic or unique. And so on, till the whole

repertory of ordering resources and sense-making combinations available to humans has been covered.

To recognize the magnitude and complexity of the task is hardly to depreciate Culler's achievement, still less his purpose. But given the drastic shift from functional (im)mediacy to the adventures of reading, one might expect the former to be, if not jettisoned, then at least reserved for its proper context. And were it not for the Tomsashevsky-Genette (etc.) heritage, it would be surprising to discover how closely Culler relates Structuralist naturalization and Formalist motivation:

> These varieties of motivation represent different ways of naturalising the text, of relating it to models of intelligibility: realistic motivation involves my first and second levels of *vraisemblance* . . . and artistic motivation the second, third, fourth, and fifth. (pp. 159–160)

Though not groundless, considering the Formalist split, these equations turn out extremely problematic—even if we leave out more obviously unmatchable "naturalizing" devices.

The first identifies the *realistic* type, Tomashevsky-fashion, with the adherence to two external and intrinsically verisimilar models, excluding the conventional and otherwise *ad hoc*. But take, for instance, the work's justification of a referential ambiguity in terms of a naturally limited narrator like a child, a conventionally limited Watson, a fantastically limited observer from outer space, and a parodistically limited Catherine Morland. Given the common goal to produce and sustain an informational blur, aren't all these diverse tactics of harnessing the restrictedness inherent in the human condition revealed to be of a single, more or less "realistic" mode of motivation—especially when compared with the recourse to a freely omniscient teller, who could, if he would, enlighten us at once? A naturalizer may indeed prefer to oppose the child's narrative to the others on naturalistic grounds. A motivator, his first concern not with naturalness but with mimesis as a devised means-end complex, will unhestitatingly join it to the others, on the grounds that they all temper the bluntness of the final explanation "The author won't tell" with the referential indirection of "The narrator can't (or couldn't) tell." Again, the second coupling in fact identifies the *artistic* type with a series of models whose employment, just like that of the only one excluded, may no less serve to synthesize elements by recourse to some image of reality than to rhetorical strategy. Outside the Formalist tangle, then, our antithesis in no way subsumes but crosscuts the levels of intelligibilty that may seem to elaborate it.

INTEGRAL AND DIFFERENTIAL MOTIVATION:
THE MIMETIC FUNCTION

The protagonists of motivation are fiction and function rather than part and whole in general; its antagonist, the internal tensions between the two modes rather than simply looseness and incongruity; its arena, confined to the text's network of designed relationships rather than enlarged to encompass genetic contexts and symptomatic mechanisms as well; and its conflicts, always resolved and always by way of teleological explanation rather than of synthesis per se. Motivation thus reveals itself to be less a special area than a dimension of integration, one where much of the same range of phenomena is (re)grouped from a distinctive standpoint. Integration, as the overall quest for coherence, includes a variety of patterning and sense-making mechanisms common to all discourse, e.g., syntax, co-reference, stylistic register, Freudian slips, irony and point of view. Motivation, with its focus on the poetic license or presumption of fictionality, foregrounds the principles of order and ordering inherent, and indeed radicalized, in literary qua representational discourse. To give one of many examples, even a piece of language that is deviant to the point of virtual incoherence (as autonomous speech) may cohere on more than one level within a fictional context (as fabricated and mediated speech, from Mrs. Khokhlakov's grotesque transitions in *The Brothers Karamazov* to Benjy's infantile monologue in *The Sound and the Fury*). Moreover, while the integrational imposition of coherence may be, the motivational must be, regulated by a sense of the text's purpose: hence its exclusion of the unconscious, of the self-betraying, of the genetic—in short, of intelligibility in terms of the biographical as opposed to the implied author. And while integration has a thousand faces, motivation has no more than two: one turned to the text as a model of the world, the other to the text (notably including its world) as an artful structure, a transaction between author and reader. Hence, among other things, its power to reconcile the fiction of reality with the reality of fiction.

Nothing can better illuminate the first member of this pair than the nature of narrative—including the narrative dimension of all temporal art—as regards its distinctive representational constraints. Like the tragic hero caught in the consequences of his own acts, the artist's freedom of action increasingly narrows from the moment he has made his initial choices. Few decisions look so elementary as that to compose a narrative rather than, say, a descriptive or concrete poem. But even this decision already entails the development of a process of change within a referential framework or reality-model. Whatever else he does or fails to do, whatever the world he creates or invokes and the poetics guiding his procedure, whatever his repertory of means and ranking of ends, he must then "realize" (embody, objectify) his strategies in and through the dynamic interplay of character, event, and circumstance. It is therefore not the variable demands or preferences of readers or artists (e.g., for illusion, authenticity, verisimilitude) but the invariant logic and necessary condition of the art (actional dynamics) that dictates quasi-mimetic motivation in the most basic sense of the term: the appeal to some fiction of reality as an objectifying measure.

In the light of this common denominator, the disparities between particular forms of quasi-mimetic motivation turn out to be quite irrelevant to the opposition with the aesthetic mode as such. A case in point is the difference between the conventional and the original, whose undue emphasis by Tomashevsky leaves out of account the distinctive referential feature adhering to both alike. Another is Genette's motivated-implicit contrast, drawn, apart from its other problems, at a similar price. And most important, the same holds true for the (variously termed) distinction between the probable and the improbable. That to identify probable ("realistic") with what I call referential or quasi-mimetic motivation is to mistake the part for the whole leaps to the eye against the background of a system like Aristotle's, especially since he is the last person to be accused of slighting the claims of probability. Confronted by the necessity of bringing his hero to an unhappy (or happy) end, the artist may arrange a recognition or a providential interference, devise character-traits or external pressures, activate his own premises or draw upon popular tradition. The plot's shape, and hence its effect on the reader, will of course vary according to the nature and interrelation of its propulsive forces. (Since for Aristotle the work's value depends on the internalization of its structure of probabilities, such disparities may even have far-reaching normative consequences.) But regardless of all these variations in probability, each choice will be regulated by the inescapable logic of imitation, realizing the functional requirements of art (from unity to catharsis) in terms of referential processes and linkages analogized to life.

The probable and the improbable thus emerge as equipollent subtypes of quasi-mimetic motivation. At this level of generality, the actional progress of the most fantastic, convention-bound or even incoherent tales and dramas shows the same two faces and calls for the same double-edged operations as Jane Austen's *Emma*. And once we manage to extricate the universal opposition between modes from the clutter of vogues, genres, conventions, prejudices, and other red herrings, we realize that the motivational logic governing the fiction of reality is by no means confined to procedures deriving from the global necessary condition of actional dynamics—neither as global nor as necessary nor finally as an actional condition. Rather, it may apply to any pattern, any means-end relationship, any selective and combinatory measure in the literary text.

Thus, the metonymic principle of linking, in terms of spatiotemporal relatedness, informs both the referential dynamics of plot (as causality) or stream-of-consciousness (as associative sequence) and the referential statics of landscape (as material contiguity). So authorial strategy, including the distribution of subtle metaphorical or analogical links—whether the symmetrical shape given to the beginning and end of *The Ambassadors* or the network of correspondences unifying Balzac's minute descriptions—must in each case be realized in and through the spatiotemporal attributes of the represented object itself. Or from the reader's viewpoint, the process of aesthetic synthesis and explanation goes hand in hand with the piecing together of the fictive construct. To pass to a totally different area of motivation: in the *Odyssey* the rhetorical need to communicate to the reader some of the expositional premises is met first through the divine assembly and then through the civic assembly discussing the Odysseus affair. Needless to say, the distance between Olympus and Ithaca correlates with some variation in plausibility. But these distances are bridged in the common opposition to such aesthetically motivated devices as Homer's retrospect on Odysseus's scar, where the same function is performed by way of immediate communication from teller to reader. Just as the choice to delegate generalizing commentary to an authoritative agent, whether human (chorus or *raisonneur*) or supernatural (ghost, god, or God), contrasts with its authorial pronouncement: "This, as I could not prevail on any of my actors to speak, I was obliged to declare myself" (*Tom Jones*, III, 7).

The order of these examples goes to show, moreover, that as we move from functional necessity to choice, the fiat of quasi-mimetic mediation may give place to the license of purely aesthetic operation. Thus, the propulsion of fictive dynamics is inescapable, so that, however artificial the tale, the characters seem to be going about their own business in their own sphere of activity. Exposition, the basis of the referential structure of probabilities, can already be conveyed directly to the reader as well through fictive indirection; but even in the former case, though its communication is aesthetically motivated in terms of the need to enlighten (or mislead) the reader, the communicated material itself always assumes a quasi-mimetic guise in that it is patterned and explained as part of the represented world. Whereas normative commentary, say an interpolated discourse on ethics or literature, need not have any reference to that world, and its optional nature will then correlate with purely aesthetic motivation.

All this does not, however, affect my claim as to the amenability of any pattern and every means-end relation to quasi-mimetic distancing and hence to bi-modal synthesis. For even the most abstract commentary may be fictionalized through its delegation from authorial to figural speaker, as in the act of ventriloquism whereby Nabokov makes the narrator of *Sebastian Knight* voice parts of his own aesthetics: "The heroes of the book are what can be loosely called 'methods of composition' " etc. (Chapter 10). In fact, contrary to what is suggested by Fielding's pose of helplessness, it is only because he does not choose to "prevail" on any of his actors to formulate the novel's theme that he himself appears by way of chorus on the stage.

The disentanglement of the quasi-mimetic constant—the mediation of the text's fiction of reality existing, as it were, independently of the rhetorical frame occupied by author and reader—also reveals the true nature of its variables, notably that of the reality of fiction: the mimetic as the probable or verisimilar. The tremendous influence that mimesis in this more demanding sense has exerted on the theory and practice, thematics and development of literary art must not blind us to its status as *differential motivation*. However provocative-looking, this term implies no demotion within the work's scale of significance. The purpose is rather to indicate that each instance of quasi-mimetic motivation serves at least two distinct artistic aims or exigencies and separate its fixed or recurrent (e.g., mimetic in the widest sense) from its optional or divergent (e.g., mimetic in the narrow sense) features.

Briefly, instead of treating each case of motivation as a simple and isolated phenomenon, we can use the integral-differential contrast—on an *ad hoc* basis—to place it in some set(s) of analogous cases, actual or possible, break it down into the relevant aesthetic and quasi-mimetic features, and interrelate these features in functional terms against the background of its analogues. Within either mode, the integral feature or complex of features runs through the whole set and forms the ground for comparison—indeed, for putting the set together in the first place. Within the aesthetic mode, it consists in a common end or effect serving as a principle of organization: suspense, closure, redundancy, ambiguity, catharsis, intelligibility, cohesiveness, control of attitude, implicit characterization, semantic density, and so on. Within the quasi-mimetic mode, it consists in whatever aspects or components of the fictive reality can be explained in relation to the necessity or choice to actualize and mediate that end rather than give it up altogether (when mandatory) or give it over to aesthetic treatment (when optional). As such, again, that referential complex need not, and usually does not, overlap with any particular measure: it adheres, as common denominator marked by a smaller or larger degree of abstractiveness, to the whole set of motivating options eligible for that purpose.

These integral features may be as general as the positing of a world, a fiction of reality, in the set of representational art, and of an action as well in the less inclusive set of narrative art. They may also combine into overall patterns in more determinate sets: the process of investigation in the detective story, which must be enacted to fulfil the generic requirements of retardatory structure and chronological displacement, or the limited perspective which may be postulated to sustain the play of ambiguity in narratives otherwise as ill-assorted as those mentioned toward the end of the previous section. And these integral features may also be abstracted from local and either/or choices like that deliberated by Fielding in the preface to Book XVII of *Tom Jones*. Given the generic dictate to provide a happy resolution for the comic epic in prose, Tom's rescue from Tyburn tree must figure in any denouement, whether realized through "supernatural assistance" or "natural means."

Moreover, as suggested by the *ad hoc* nature of the analytical principle, much of whose power indeed springs from the resultant flexibility, the correlated integrals will vary with each change of grouping. This already appears when we shift a novel from the category of representational art, a lofty standpoint from which all images of reality are alike by virtue of their referentiality, to that of narrative. Within the variegated category of narrative, similarly, character must be reduced to a fictional means of launching and sustaining the indispensable process of change. Once we move to the set of psychological narrative, however, this unidirectional domination turns into a two-way motivation: the process of change now serves at the same time (as with Rastignac in *Père Goriot* or Densher in *The Wings of the Dove*) to bring out or develop character. And the more drastic or well-defined the shift, the more perceptible the variations. Thus, the fact that the Watson tradition of the detective story produces on the reader certain effects (heightened involvement, comic relief, an alleviation of our sense of inferiority *vis-à-vis* the sleuth) more specific than the generic integral calls for a corresponding specification of the quasi-mimetic integral: a process of inquiry narrated by a fallible eyewitness, usually of less than average intelligence. Just as on the other hand the placing of *Tom Jones* in the framework of comedy requires a despecification of the quasi-mimetic integral—from the rescue to the well-being of the sympathetic hero—and correspondingly an increase rather than a decrease in the work's differential features.

But in each instance, the (uniform and logically prior) recourse to quasi-mimetic motivation having been explained, the (contextually variable) recourse to a particular procedure out of the available or conceivable range still remains unaccounted for. And this is where differential correlation comes in. The selection and arrangement of quasi-mimetic differentials requires further aesthetic justification, again widely varying in line with the nature and point of the grouping. After all, from the essentially abstractive viewpoint of integrality, all tragedies will exhibit the same motivational structure, or else the category can exist only as a loose denomination or an open set but not as a functional pattern; what is more, a parody must exhibit the same features as the parodied text or else the parodic relations between a *Shamela* and a *Pamela* will pass unnoticed. But whatever their intrinsic interest, as in generic theory, from the differential viewpoint the establishment of such parities only provides a firm basis for the meaningful exploration of disparity. Given the common functional groundwork, what distinguishes Greek from Elizabethan tragedy; and to what specifying procedures does (or can) one subject the motivational base of a text to invert it into its parodic opposite? The accounting for quasi-mimetic in terms of aesthetic differentials may thus result in explanations of the most diverse kinds. But as with Fielding's preference of "natural" to "supernatural" unraveling, these often turn out to be the desire to enhance probability beyond the minimal fictionalizing, cohesive or dissimulatory effect equally producible by any of the alternative measures.

If each motivation appealing to the world must be multifunctional by virtue of the interplay between integral and differential features, it is the latter that determine its range of operation. Such variables not merely fill out the referential scaffold set up by the invariants; far more important, they may even promote the resultant synthesis, whether verisimilar or fantastic in tonality, from the role of means to that of end. Contrary to what is implied by Aristotle and roundly asserted in the Formalist-Structuralist line, each in the appropriate theoretical parlance, the referential-artistic does not overlap with the means-end, let alone the cost-gain distinction. In fact, motivational strategy in art reveals a whole complex of *mimetic functions*. They range from (1) the representational universal (the enabling function) through (2) the communicative exigency (the transmissional function) and (3) the narrative fiat (the actional function) to (4) the shaping of the referential key or tonality (the formative function, differentiating between the synthesis of, say, the tragic and the comic worlds) and (5) the rhetoric of realism with probability and verisimilitude as goal (the realistic and, in extreme cases, illusive function).[18] Most of these are widely pursued or observed in literature and only the last is optional in narrative: the fiction

of reality must imply an attitude, if not a commitment, to the reality of
fiction.

MOTIVATION AND COMMUNICATIVE STRUCTURE:
POINT OF VIEW AS CONSTRUCT

All we have seen so far, including the amenability of every functional
measure to fictive transformation, goes to show that the organizing principles called here motivational modes differ not so much in their materials and formal arrangement as in their locus and mode of existence: their
distance from the rhetorical relationship uniting author and reader. The
aesthetic mode relates the two directly through the text; the quasi-mimetic obliquely, through the mediation of the world of the text. But
regardless of its immediacy or mediacy, motivation as an explanatory
activity or process ultimately operates between author and reader.
Hence the question, which of these participants in the communicative
event performs the motivation?

To this there seem to be two primary answers, implicit under various
guises in critical practice and again perspicuously radicalized in the
approaches instanced above. To Aristotle, making sense is making plot;
and making plot is the business of the artist, not for nothing designated
as *maker*. To the Structuralists—contrary to the Formalist line—making
sense of a text by recourse to naturalizing models is part of the operations of reading. And such disparity between what I call author-oriented
(or encoding) and reader-oriented (or decoding) motivation often corresponds to more radical oppositions. These consist not just in the theoretical centrality of textual components (above all, world *vs.* language)
and the respective makers-of-sense, but even in the views of poetics
itself: as the art of production or the theory of re-production.

Each orientation is liable to such abuse or extremity as will carry it
beyond the pale of communicative structure. The reader-oriented variety may fall into the anachronistic, idiosyncratic, and otherwise textually
uncontrolled explications that the history of criticism is notorious for and
we are all so quick to discover in the enemy's camp. Is the Elizabethan
villain culminating in Iago a psychologically intelligible character in his
own right or, as the anti-Bradleyan school has it, little more than a
personified instrument for catastrophe? If the latter, then a whole interpretive tradition has been guilty of dissociating decoding from encoding
motivation, which can only reduce the literary text to a glorified Rorschach ink blot.

In contrast, the edges of the author-oriented variety merge into the concern with the creative act, environmental determinants, practical exigencies, obsessions having more to do with the man who suffers than the artist who creates—in short, into genetic integration. Why does Mrs. Proudie die in *The Last Chronicle of Barset?* The quasi-mimetic cause is a sudden heart attack; the aesthetic cause, the effect on both reader and plot; the genetic cause, the accident by which Trollope over-heard the strictures made on this favorite character by two clergymen at the Athenaeum Club and his consequent promise to them, "I will go home and kill her before the week is over."[19]

While the idiosyncrasies and blind spots of particular readers rarely have more than autobiographical interest, the status of genetic explana-tion is indeed somewhat problematic. This holds especially true where its factors cannot be sharply distinguished from established conventions or historical developments, or where it has not been fully transformed into, and thus superseded by, aesthetic and quasi-mimetic motivation. It is one thing to discount the pieces of dinner-party gossip that, by a process of elaboration designed to shackle accident and bolt up change through the internal mechanisms of art, germinated into James's master-pieces. It is another thing to ignore the manifold structural (selectional, segmentary, rhetorical) consequences of serial publication; or to wave aside the effects of social pressure on the coherence of individual works, as with Mrs. Proudie's untimely death or the altered ending of *Great Expectations* or the dark hints of the *Nibelungenlied*. But despite the fluidity of the borderline between the poetic and the genetic models of production, the shift to the genetic coincides in principle with a shift in the object and logic of explanation. And whatever sense this shift makes from the integrative standpoint—say, in the face of an otherwise stub-born incongruity—it hardly makes any from the motivational. As usual with all those textual features for which one cannot or will not find room within the text's world-design networks, the process of motivation is then simply suspended and other frames of intelligibility must take over. Like the purely reader-oriented approach, therefore, the author-ori-ented extreme disconnects itself from the functional model of communi-cation: the one because it fails to recognize authorial control as cause, the other because it fails to start from *and* correlate with the reader's response as effect.

Apart from these limiting cases, however, the two orientations are so complementary as to become inseparable. Within the communicative circuit of literature, after all, both author and reader are interpretive constructs that have no existence in isolation from each other: in a com-plex but nonparadoxical sense, each makes and shapes the other. No wonder that, throughout the development of his productive model, Aristotle hardly loses sight of the reader as recipient of effects. Conversely, short of the Rorschach extreme, even the most determined foregrounding of the reader's motivational activity cannot dispense with the regulating concept of author (as distinct from the term, whose anthropomorphic associations sometimes lead to its replacement by the neutral-looking metonymy, "text"). Thus qualified, the difference between these orientations proves a matter less of doctrinal substance than of methodological emphasis or even heuristic and expository effectiveness.

With author-oriented motivation, the typical movement is then from the general to the particular, from strategy to tactics, from referential context to verbal art, from rhetorical end to quasi-mimetic means. Take Poe's retrospect in "The Philosophy of Composition" on the series of selections and connections ("the progressive steps") that produced "The Raven." As befits a procedure aspiring to "the precision and rigid consequence of a mathematical problem," the first thing settled was the complex of effects to be generated: novelty and vividness, unity of impression, melancholy tone, semantic variety, etc. And then we observe the progress from desired effect to objective correlative: action, speaker, and situational framework. Given the need for a melancholy ("poetic") tone, the choice of a bereaved lover as the speaker hardly comes as surprise. But why is his interlocutor a bird, and of all birds a raven? Mainly, strange as it may sound, in the service of semantic variety. Seeking to produce "continuously novel effects, by the variation of the *application* of the *refrain*—the *refrain* itself remaining, for the most part, unvaried," Poe required "a pretext for the continuous use of the one word 'nevermore'": here "the idea of a *non*-reasoning creature capable of speech, and very naturally, a parrot, in the first place, suggested itself, but was superseded forthwith by a Raven as equally capable of speech, and infinitely more in keeping with the intended *tone*." And why do they meet in a room rather than, more naturally, in the open air? Again because, though the two motivations are equally serviceable from the integral viewpoint (dramatic collocation), the former has marked differential advantages (rhetorical focusing): "A close *circumscription of space* is absolutely necessary to the effect of insulated incident—it has the force of a frame to a picture . . . in keeping concentrated the attention."[20]

Whatever one's doubts about its genuineness and its validity as a model of actual creative construction, Poe's orderly "philosophy" certainly applies to the author-oriented process of theoretical and interpretive reconstruction. Roughly, that explanatory operation starts by reconstructing the work's hierarchy of interests and functions, its generico-historical constraints, and its range of choices; and only then does it proceed (or rather double back) to show how this abstract poetic system is embodied and deployed in a particular world, language, crisscross of patterns, and dynamics of presentation. Hence its advantages for the performance of certain critical tasks (comparative analysis, tracing the development of an author or a tradition, highlighting the one-many relationship between end and means or between the integral and the differential) and the counteraction of certain dangers (such as mistaking authorial choice for necessity, accident for purpose, convention for invention, and vice versa). Not the least of its virtues, to give one of many examples, consists in drawing our attention to the motivational significance of what, from the viewpoint of integration, might pass for casual, perfectly congruous, intelligible, indeed "natural," referential items or features: Poe's raven, Watson's obtuseness, the sex as well as the age of James's Maisie.

Reader-oriented motivation largely reverses this movement, stressing not the hindsight of full retrospection but the temporality and exigencies of the reading process as an experience entailing progressive discovery. Since what the reader directly encounters is a piece of language, it is the passage from (given) word to (conjectured) world and function that now comes to the fore. Since the reader starts by groping his way into the text's universe of discourse, the procedure foregrounds his hesitancy in the face of gaps, ambiguities, and discontinuities, his constant shifts of patterning under the pressure of new information, the trial-and error methods by which he distinguishes ends from means and incorporates or generalizes details into regularities. And since the sequentiality of the text ensures that that state of affairs should if necessary last to the very end, the explanatory process alerts us throughout to the dynamic rather than the static and the hypothetical rather than the objectifying or dissimulatory aspects of motivation. Of course, as later examples will show, the reconstitutive set of operations performed by the reader must again move between effect and cause, notably from aesthetic to quasi-mimetic inference. But this serves more to distinguish motivation from (possibly effectless and/or worldless) integration than to obliterate the disparities in inferential route, circumstances, and certitude between our motivating orientations—especially at the outset of the reading process, where we can hardly postulate a regulative purpose without first abstracting a world from the language.

As long as the reader's motivating activity is grasped as authorially controlled hypothesis-making, however, the two orientations converge in line with the text's gradual reconstruction (as shown in practice throughout my book on narrative) and ideally coalesce when the last page has been turned. Indeed, the control and manipulation marking this communicative structure justify my reference to "author-oriented" instead of the perhaps more expected "speaker-oriented" motivation and brings out an important difference between literary and nonliterary communication.

It is certainly not that ordinary discourse fails to have rhetorical intent, or to exploit situational factors, or even (*pace* traditional philosophies of mimesis, starting from the Aristotelian) to accomplish the one through and in the guise of the other. On the contrary, in order to unify our description of a person or a house we, no less than Balzac, resort to metonymic transitions following the natural make-up of the represented object, and often so devise them as to insinuate analogical links of equivalence and contrast. In our everyday storytelling, we invoke the natural dynamics of the action ("This is the way things happened") to propel and camouflage the artful dynamics of presentation (the sudden twist, the ascending order, the deferred punch line) in the best novelistic manner. We break idiomatic and allusive stereotypes with a variety of ends in view—surprise, ridicule, covert signaling—at times under the pretense of innocent slips or inadvertent garbling. Just as, from the selectional viewpoint, we conveniently forget things whose mention may interfere with our communicative purpose. Qua addressee, conversely, one is of course as much concerned in life as in literature to disambiguate and make sense of the message in terms of the speaker's intentions as well as his professions. Does the sequential arrangement of items, with its tendentious implications, merely follow after all a descriptive convention or associative habit? In suppressing that piece of information, is the speaker genuinely or diplomatically or perhaps affectedly forgetful, like Theophrastus's Ironical Man who "pretends he didn't hear when he did; that he hasn't seen when he has"? Is the misquotation due to malice or ignorance, wit or witlessness?

But this is not to say that the similarity is complete: that Longinus, for instance, is right to cut across all the boundaries of discourse in his attempt to demonstrate that sublime art veils its artfulness. The dissimilarity lies not just in the free referential play of literary motivation, but also in its dual reference or bi-dimensionality, resulting from the built-in discrepancy between speaker and author. In everyday discourse, above all in its face-to-face paradigm, whatever the motivations inferred—situational or psychological, conventional or idiosyncratic, expressive or persuasive—they must all ultimately apply to the speaker himself and for the most part to him alone. As the originator ("author") im-mediately responsible for the utterance he makes, there is normally no going beyond or behind him to explain his procedure. The speaker himself may indeed hide behind masks (as in irony) or secondary voices (as in all types of reported discourse); but once we have identified and penetrated these, we have reached the explanatory terminus. And in various contexts even the assumption of such masks, unless unmistakably signaled, is frowned on and penalized—which is to say, from the encoder's viewpoint, institutionally discouraged if not ruled out as an interpretive resource—in the interests of straightforward communication. Take a perjured witness who claims in his defense that throughout his testimony he was being ironical or was covertly using a friend of his as a persona: it would do that witness as little good to invoke a possible speaker as it would do a physicist or historian to say that his refuted theories were actually referring to some possible world.

All this means that the daily business of living imposes constraints on fictionality that affect both speaker and addressee, both the status of reference to the world and the distancing techniques by which either can shift the formal originator's responsibility for that reference to an intermediate whipping-boy. It also means that, whether these felicity-conditions are observed or violated, aesthetic-rhetorical functionality (and its referential motivation) belongs here only insofar as it is established or at least presumed to be intentional on the speaker's own part. If unwitting, the impression produced on the addressee, whether happy or incongruous, is accidental or symptomatic rather than properly communicative: it may indeed have effects and consequences but certainly no function. Hence the various possibilities of objective and irreconcilable noncoincidence in life between speaker-oriented and addressee-oriented motivation—notably those showing themselves wherever the decoder infers, integrates, and *genetically* accounts for (e.g., in terms of social station, mental state, ideological commitment) such information as the encoder is not at all aware of having betrayed.[21]

The only exception to this unitary responsibility of origination occurs where the formal speaker—the hired mouthpiece, the mimicked voice, the victim of brainwashing—is a puppet manipulated into saying in his own name ("motivating") whatever suits the purposes of some more or less invisible puppeteer. But that exceptional motivation behind motivation is the rule in literary, qua fictive, discourse. (And as far as the reading process is concerned, the same holds true for any text—from family anecdotes to scientific writing—subjected in this respect to a literary interpretation, regardless of its original nature: one, that is, where the constraints on fictionality have been relaxed or blocked in consequence of historical changes, generic relocation, personal whim, or whatever.) Whether obviously or subtly or only nominally distanced from his creator, whether an occasional monologist and dialogist or a full-fledged and seemingly autonomous narrator, the literary speaker is in principle as fabricated and his speech as mediated as any other textual component. Due to the interposition of the speaker between reader (as ultimate addressee) and author (as ultimate originator), the literary text postulates one communicative framework more than the corresponding nonliterary discourse: unmediated face-to-face exchange becomes direct quotation in the form of dialogue, inner speech becomes quoted monologue, quotation becomes quotation within quotation, and so on. And what underscores the distinctive value of this principle is that the additional context differs from all those it frames in constituting the locus of the work's art and meaning and rhetorical determination—in short, of the primary relationship between the reader and the disembodied ("implied") authorial power with whom the final authority and responsibility lie.

The intricacy of this communicative structure thus suggests why what might elsewhere count as mere genetic causes or symptomatic features of the speaker's discourse (accent, excitement, bigotry) should here be invested with functional significance: it is presumed to form a quasi-mimetic motivation for compositional choices, relating not to the interposed and foregrounded narrator (often facing his own addressee) but to the author who pulls the strings from behind the scenes for his various ends. Accordingly, what passes for a mistake or oversight on the part of the speaker within the framework of the fictive world (say, the sleepy Alice's garbling of "How doth the little busy bee" into "How doth the little crocodile") invites at the same time a purposeful explanation (say, in terms of Carrollian parody) within the rhetorical framework enclosing it. With that shift of framework, narratorial ignorance (Mrs. Slipslop's malapropisms or Huck Finn's innocence) likewise comes to signal authorial knowledgeability; redundancy and longwindedness (Nestor's in Homer or Abigail's in the Book of Samuel) to promote economy; immorality (like Jason Compson's) to reflect moral fervor; parochialism (as in James's fiction) to develop cosmopolitan themes; unconsciousness of audience (the diarist's, the interior monologist's) to highlight or dissimulate self-conscious artistry.

In each case, the shift involves not functional substitution but plurality and interplay. For the reader is led to integrate textual facts through the assignment of certain traits (ignorance etc.) to the speaker and to motivate their emergence as involuntary self-revelation; and this mimetically based process of inference and reconstruction forms part of the work's aesthetic strategy no less than any other authorial ends achieved by implying that speaker. It is not just that Mrs. Slipslop's malapropisms are Fielding's puns. The ease and confidence marking our decision that this is indeed the case, that she is obliquely characterized by his comic

strokes, prove as integral to the art of *Joseph Andrews* as are prolonged
or unresolved ambiguity and hesitant division of responsibility between
speaker(s) and author to the poetics of the modern novel. To define the
aesthetics behind a quasi-mimetic construct is always to combine the
final inference with the signposts and adventures along the devised
inferential route.

Of course, the text need not suggest a quasi-mimetic motivation (certainly none bringing a distinct speaker into play) for each choice and
design and procedure; and those left unfictionalized, like the incorpora-
tion of the prefatory chapters in *Tom Jones* or the abrupt transitions in
Joyce's *Portrait*, are then *immediately* related in aesthetic terms to the
author or his narrating plenipotentiary, the authoritative teller. On the
other hand, even a teller firmly situated in the fictive world may deliberately pursue certain artistic or communicative goals (as with Arkady
Dolgoruky's distaste for literary frills or Humbert Humbert's rhetorical
apologetics), which need not overlap with the author's. But the co-exis-
tence of the two "arts" by no means implies equivalence, nor does the
self-consciousness common to both "artists." Whatever the degree of
correspondence between them, the one is framed within the other,
devised and dominated by the other, and thus functions to motivate the
other.

In this their relationship does not essentially differ from that just
outlined between the far more removed frameworks of the unconsciously informative and the intentionally communicative: the narrator's
manifold art becomes another hypothesized trait, another more or less
opaque façade, another fictional means to various aesthetic ends, including the reader's probing for the status and limits of that art. In any such
system of motivation within motivation, therefore, even the figural inset's aesthetic motivations serve as the authorial frame's quasi-mimetic
motivations, regardless of the normative distance between them. This
holds as true for a paragon like Pamela as for John Fowles's monstrous
Collector, for a professional writer like Robert Graves's Claudius as for
the barely literate Huck Finn. The variables are thus many and crucial:
the combination of self-betrayal and intentionality peculiar to each inset
speaker; the nature and cogency of his own motivations; or even the
number of the insets, ranging from the zero-sign of such frequently
unrefracted short forms as the epigram and the fable to Conrad's Chi-
nese boxes. What remains constant is the overall control exerted by the
primary, purely aesthetic frame over the intermediaries that distance it
from the reader. And it is the rich potentialities for operating both
through the agency of the figures and behind their backs that invests the
literary text with a bi-dimensionality of motivation that distinguishes it

from all discourse with no inherent tensions between formal speaker(s) and covert manipulator.

That the fictive world serving as literature's functional mediator is itself mediated through speakers and reflectors, either wholly (as in the so-called first-person tale and lyric) or at least locally (as in discontinuous dialogues and monologues), begins to suggest the role played by point of view in this context. Since the two mediators relate to each other as object to subject, the referential sphere to which the literary text turns to effect and justify its strategies divides into two mechanisms or sublogics of quasi-mimetic motivation. One is the *existential*, grounded in what the reader comes to reconstitute as the objective makeup of the fictive image of reality, from the minutiae of character and event to general laws of probability; the other is the *perspectival*, grounded in the subjective makeup of the narrative situation in and through which this reality unfolds.

These mechanisms are theoretically distinct. Consider, for instance, the two mutually exclusive hypotheses that the reader of *The Turn of the Screw* is directed to construct so as to account for the apparitions of the dead servants. Either the fictive world is itself abnormal and the narrating governess only a lucid reflector, or the governess is abnormal and projects her supernatural hallucinations into a fictive world that in itself corresponds to our ordinary reality-model. Indeed, each of the hypotheses here held in suspension throughout, in the interests of the Jamesian play of ambiguity,[22] operates elsewhere as an independent motivation. We then find the clash between the existential and the perspectival either altogether precluded from the start or deliberately generated but sooner or later resolved and thus revealed as temporary rather than permanent. The one's primacy is by convention as much established in science fiction as the other's is in the Watson variety of the detective story; it takes as little time to decide that Esther Summerson's preternatural goodness is a fact in the world of *Bleak House* as that Blifil's is a delusion on Allworthy's part; and we have to work and wait as long to vindicate our trust in Fanny Price's priggish-looking views of her environment in *Mansfield Park* as to validate our suspicions of Elizabeth Bennet's image of Darcy.

Even drama, with its inherent perspectival constraints as a globally unmediated genre, in fact realizes, on a smaller scale, all these gap-filling options and shifts. Thus, the "objective" resolution of the ambiguity concerning the ghost in *Hamlet* (in terms of a deviant world) contrasts with its "subjective" resolution in *Julius Caesar* and, with still greater surety, in *Macbeth* (in terms of an overwrought perceiver). The same line of demarcation cuts clean across not the boundaries of genre alone but also of history, perceptibility, and above all, subject-matter or referential tonality. Take the conventional techniques of unraveling plot complications through some *deus ex machina* and through the disclosure that the whole imbroglio has been nothing but a dream: these mark the world-oriented and the transmission-oriented extremes as unmistakably as any corresponding innovations. And the question whether the fear of the bureaucracy, adduced as the reason for suppressing certain informa- tion at the beginning of Gogol's *Overcoat*, reflects an existential fact or a narratorial neurosis, parallels the more startling but equally Janus-faced ambiguity as to the predatory ghost showing up at the end.

What emerges is (1) that, once established or postulated as fictional, a text becomes referentially ambiguous throughout; (2) that the reader can then always resolve any peculiar (surprising, uncommon, incongruous, or otherwise problematic and hence actively ambiguous) feature located on the text's referential level by projecting and assimilating it into either fictional axis; and (3) that the decision between the resultant quasi-mi- metic constructs can be made (if at all) only *ad hoc*, on aesthetic grounds, like generic conventions and exigencies, situational probabil- ity, normative ends, simplicity and economy, etc. As in any interpretive process, we may describe the motivational interplay from the productive or the re-productive side; we may quarrel about the resolution of the ambiguity and the final meaning. But the potentialities for *making* fic- tional sense remain constant and distinctive. It is this that brings us to the heart of fiction as such: the dispensability of any special dispensa- tion, other than the text's own premises, to impose coherence in terms of a possible world and/or a possible observer, a more or less subjective reflector of that world. And if most of my opening examples have been drawn from ghost-ridden literature, this is only because the irruption of the supernatural dramatizes the explanatory duality inherent, and hence in principle omnipresent, in the quasi-mimetic mode itself. In conflict- ing with most everyday world-views, that irruption impels the reader— despite the temptations of the less demanding, because more literal, alternative—to look round for a perspectival loophole by which the imagined world may be drawn into his normal ken after all. And since to place and account for the deviant by assigning this feature to the repre- sented reality and to the representational prism is then to produce mutual incompatibles, the supernatural also brings home the distinct- ness of the two ordering operations.

Though distinct, however, the two closely interrelate far beyond their common opposition, as fictive constructs, to the underlying aesthetico- rhetorical logic that determines in each case their rise and fall, tempo- rariness or permanence, relative power at the start, and subsequent fortunes to the very end. Not unlike the primary motivational modes themselves, these operations are mutually implicative—as natural rivals always struggling all along the line for explanatory supremacy or at least for as large a share as possible in the process of making quasi-mimetic sense and its ultimate product. Hence also their mutual conditioning: the recourse to one must come at the expense of the other, whose coherence is thereby either flattened (if excluded) or (if concurrently posited and developed) complicated in excess of its aspiration to simple, firm intelligibility. Seldom are the objective and the refractive hypotheses so finely balanced (as well as permanently suspended) as in *The Turn of the Screw*; and even there the obtrusion of an alternative on our notice, by way of conflicting clues, not merely precludes the monopoly but threatens and disturbs the integrity of either. And this interaction becomes more—or differently—perceptible where we find the scales of referential hypothesizing tipped on one side or the other.

Thus in *Hamlet*, once convinced that the various observers of the ghost cannot all be deranged, we attribute the derangement to the world they inhabit, as a canon of probability, by reference to both dramatic convention and extraliterary belief as to the impingement of the supernatural on sublunary nature. The "subjective" explanation, with the correlative aesthetic motivation in terms of psychological insight and the like, has indeed been vanquished by an alternative coalition; but not without leaving its mark on the victor. In face of the divergent, the simpler the perspectival picture the more complex the world picture. A more intricate process of inference likewise yields the conclusion that the prodigies of Wonderland, long dismissed as figments of Odysseus's imagination, in fact belong to the Homeric world no less than the battlefields of Troy and the rocks of Ithaca. The ambiguity between the existential and the perspectival reading—each with its own aesthetic rationale and implications—does arise here. For the inset tale addressed to the Phaeacians (*Odyssey*, IX-XII) is indeed less verisimilar than the enclosing omniscient frame and its teller not exactly distinguished for finicalness about truth. But the epic's system of internal validation (including the factual correspondences between authorial frame and figural inset, in a work where precise as well as variant repetitions assume interpretive significance) establishes that the marvellous is after all due to Homer's and not Odysseus's inventiveness. In short, the existential mechanism of resolution prevails wherever the reader is impelled to minimize, if not to discount, the variables of communication—the distorting effect of such interposed prisms as narrators, personae, postures, dreams, vessels of consciousness, and other mediating agencies—and instead to assimilate the play of referents by appropriately adjusting his own reality-model or his conception of the fictive state of affairs.

On the other hand, when Brutus addresses Caesar's ghost or Ivan Karamazov his shabby devil, the supernatural can be registered as an objective fact (within the fiction) only if we are prepared to suspend disbelief in the supernatural as an existential premise while disregarding the features specific to the speech-event; and in Macbeth's banquet scene, at the additional price of supposing everybody but the hero struck blind. Hence the tendency to motivate these supernatural encounters by reference to their only observers *and* to another convention, this time more psychological or perceptual than metaphysical: the workings of the guilty conscience as action and theme. Again, though these examples may look extreme, the same perspectival mechanism for resolving ambiguity variously applies to a wide range of inferences and inference-promoting techniques, from irony and parody and ambivalence through unreliable narration to free indirect discourse.

In all these cases, the perspectival motivation of a gap or an incongruity often overcomes some existential hypothesis to which it stands in either sequential or simultaneous opposition. The sequential passage from one axis to the other takes place whenever the reader discovers that he has been lured into reconstituting the wrong state of affairs but can devise no satisfactory substitute without modifying the pattern of transmission as well. When in the opening of *Tom Jones* the omniscient narrator himself calls the hero Jenny Jones's "child" (I, 9), this is automatically registered as a cogent reference to an objective state of affairs. Tom's true parentage once divulged, however, we retrospectively shift the referring expression to an alternative, fallible, mediate source— relegating and assimilating it to the collective viewpoint of the environment, to which (we now say) the all-knowing teller restricted himself in the service of mystification.

An explanation along such lines is here clearly preferable to, because simpler and more integrative than, any other synthesis: the genetic (in terms of authorial oversight); the purely aesthetic (in terms of arbitrary misdirection, with no quasi-mimetic alibi); and the purely existential, which now becomes as far-fetched as it was natural prior to the denouement, since to sustain it within the same perspectival framework would be to postulate a reality-model accommodating double parentage and the like. It is not (hence the "purely") that the recourse to perspectival ordering excludes either the aesthetic mode or the existential submode. Aesthetic patterning, as indicated by the very concept of functional mediacy, not only attends but regulates all quasi-mimetic motivation. And the existential mechanism, while capable of excluding the perspec-

184   MEIR STERNBERG

tival by postulating a viewpoint identical with the author's and therefore
contextually objective by definition, cannot itself be excluded but only
modified in turn: a subject presupposes an object. On the contrary, the
more problematic the mediating perceiver (narrator, reflector), the more
marked both the field and the locus of perception as referential constructs: he is himself part of the world that he observes and that we
reconstruct through his observation. The point is rather that the emergence, let alone the prevalence, of a nonobjective viewpoint always
affects, and sometimes determines or reshapes, our existential and aesthetic reconstructions. And the further removed it is from the authorial,
the more drastic these adjustments and readjustments.

If inferential dynamics brings out the relations between the two sub-
modes by way of retrospective shift and revision, their simultaneous
occurrence further sharpens the point by collocating the different pros
and cons. In context, for instance, the following description gives rise to
a head-on referential clash: "P.C. Hardman tiptoed into the room. . . .
Light seeping through the curtain fabric revealed a sandy-haired boy
lying in the bed, breathing rather stertorously, a high flush on his
cheeks, a cloth pinned round his neck."[23] For we know that the child
lexically and pronominally referred to as a boy is a girl in disguise—as a
matter of fact, none other than the kidnapped girl the police are looking
for. The reading of the passage as straightforward ("objective") narrative
can be maintained only if we eliminate the factual clash through the *ad
hoc* postulation of a world admitting of sudden sexual metamorphoses.
But even such a counsel of despair, apart from its aesthetic pointlessness
in an earthbound tale, would at best substitute a global for a local
incongruity with the surrounding context. Therefore, the reader needs
must reorient himself not so much along the existential as the perspectival axis. And this negative indication is powerfully reinforced by a set of
positive clues pointing the same way. These include the girl's having
previously been disguised by her captors and the informational discrepancy between the enlightened narrator-reader coalition and the poor
constable who doesn't have the slightest idea of the criminal set-up in
the house. So the simple attribution to the official reporter, the omniscient teller himself, gives place to a more intricate hypothesis of mediated vision and divided responsibility: the narrator adheres to the constable's own view of the situation, mistaken references and all. Forced into
complicating the model of either reality or transmission, the reader
again opts for the second alternative as much superior in coherence and
explanatory power. Or to describe the quasi-mimetic motivation in
terms of free indirect discourse from the author's side, with the rhetorical end as starting-point: these integrative difficulties have been devised

in order to impress the ambiguity on the reader and manipulate him into discovering for himself the implicit communicative pattern that resolves them by way of perspectival montage.

As with free indirect, so with unreliable, ambivalent, ironized, and parodied discourse. These devices are likewise not givens but conjectures designed to deliver the text's world(-view) as well as its style and other nonreferential dimensions from the manifold weakness—looseness, incoherence, inconsistency, irrelevance, improbability, shallowness, or sheer silliness—that would vitiate it if taken to be straightforwardly presented by an authoritative speaker. The weakness is then accounted for as a clue of textual dissociation and plurality rather than an index of incompetence, as figural rather than authorial self-betrayal, as an invitation to inference rather than a ground for value-judgement. So what justifies the subsumption of that mixed bag under a single theoretical heading is this: each member forms an hypothesis that organizes the text, in line with certain aesthetic and functional assumptions, by recourse not (or not primarily) to a peculiar world but to a communicative structure other and more complex than that immediately apparent. For the interposition of some fallible perspective(s) between us and the author always involves a reshuffling, relocation, and distancing of the subjectively motivated material. This includes shifts from dialogue to dialogic monologue (as with Ivan and the devil or the Circe episode in the *Odyssey*); from external to internal action (as with Alice's dream of Wonderland); from authorial or authorially-backed to deviant or unprivileged narratorial discourse (as with Swift's Modest Proposer or the anonymous voice in Nabokov's *Pnin*); or from narratorial to figural viewpoint (whether the transition from Fielding's to the environment's or from the narrating to the experiencing self's in fictive autobiography).

All these motivational constructs are thus distinguished by their coupling of *quasi-mimetic mediacy* as the basis with *perspectival montage* as the mechanism for resolving ambiguity and making purposive sense. The quasi-mimetic basis distinguishes them from more variegated techniques like irony and parody, which similarly call for perspectival (re)orientation on the reader's part but do not necessarily presuppose fallible mediation from within the imagined reality. It is precisely this that separates Voltaire's ironic from Candide's ironized discourse. Though equally identified as such through inferential operations going below the surface, the former is addressed straight from authorial spokesman to reader, while the latter is fictionalized, obliquely refracted and placed at one remove (at least) from the rhetorical framework. What makes the difference is not so much the opacity or the transparency of the camouflage, the distance between surface and covert meaning, as its motivation. But whether rhetorically or also referentially camouflaged, their common anchorage in reconstructions and shifts of point of view discriminates all forms of irony and parody alike from all motivational resources that (like the happy ending in comedy) operate or (like the quest in the detective story) may operate on objective, existence-oriented grounds.

The two referential mechanisms having been distinguished, it only remains to emphasise once again their omnipresence as mutually conditioning alternatives. The existential mediator can be absent only in non-representational art—or segments—monopolized by the aesthetic mode; the perspectival, only where the author's position fully coincides with (and thus "aesthetizes") the speaker's *and* his delegates'. Even then these absences are significant not just as marking the zero-sign of unrealized potentiality but also due to their conjectural status: to say that a work (a concrete poem or an abstract painting) is nonrepresentational, or that it im-mediately reflects the objective world as posited by the author, is not to state a fact but to make an inference; and it is not till the reader has reached the last word that he can establish the neutralization of either fictionalizing mechanism, and again only on contextual, probabilistic grounds. But elsewhere, whatever our final hypothesis, we can make neither mimetic nor aesthetic sense of fictive reality without constantly moving between state of being and state of mind.

Notes

1. The following argument consists of a set of interconnected extracts from a work in progress on mimesis and communication. It also draws on some specific analyses and generalizes some points I made elsewhere, most recently in *Expositional Modes and Temporal Ordering in Fiction* (Baltimore and London, 1978), *passim*, especially pp. 246–305; "The Structure of Repetition in Biblical Narrative: Strategies of Informational Redundancy," *Hasifrut*, no. 25 (1977): 109–150; "Polylingualism as Reality and Mimesis as Translation," *Degrès*, no. 16 (1978): e1–26; "Point of View and The Indirections of Speech," *Language and Style* (forthcoming). A previous version of this essay was presented at the Porter Institute symposium on narrative theory (Tel Aviv and Jerusalem, June 1979).
2. A limitation emphasized, for instance, in E. M. Forster's *Aspects of the Novel* (Har-

mondsworth, 1962), Chapter 5, and Robert Langbaum's *The Poetry of Experience* (New York, 1963), Chapter 5.

3. For some pros and cons of such a reading see the comments *ad loc.* in Kenneth A. Telford, *Aristotle's Poetics* (Chicago, 1961) and Gerald F. Else, *Aristotle's Poetics: The Argument* (Cambridge, Mass., 1957), and further references there.

4. See my "Elements of Tragedy and the Concept of Plot in Tragedy: On the Constitution of a Generic Whole," *Hasifrut* IV (1973): 23–69.

5. Viktor Shklovsky, *Schriften zum Film*, trans. Alexander Kaempfe (Frankfurt, 1966), p. 20.

6. Viktor Shklovsky, "Sterne's *Tristram Shandy:* Stylistic Commentary," in *Russian Formalist Criticism*, trans. Lee T. Lemon and Marion J. Reis (Lincoln, Nebraska, 1965), pp. 38, 39, 44–46, 50–54.

7. Henry James, *The Art of the Novel*, ed. R. P. Blackmur (New York, 1962), p. 89. On the Jamesian doctrine of motivation, see my *Expositional Modes and Temporal Ordering*, pp. 281–305 (note 1 above); on the practice, with special reference to *The Ambassadors*, see my *Expositional Modes and Order of Presentation in Fiction* (Ph.D. dissertation, Jerusalem, 1971), pp. 299–431.

8. On this as on some other issues, the impression of theoretical uniformity given by Victor Erlich's *Russian Formalism* ([The Hague, 1965], pp. 194–199, 241–246) is a simplification of the facts. The only Formalist who seems to have both understood and adopted Shklovsky's position is Boris Eikhenbaum—for example in his illuminating essay on O. Henry (*Readings in Russian Poetics*, eds. Ledislav Matejka and Krystyna Pomorska [Cambridge, Mass., 1971], pp. 227–270). Among more recent studies in the same line, whose hallmark is the "motivated-unmotivated" antithesis, a notable instance is Benjamin Hrushovsky's *Segmentation and Motivation in the Text Continuum of Literary Prose: The First Episode of 'War and Peace'* (Tel Aviv: The Porter Institute for Poetics and Semiotics, 1976), especially pp. 23–29.

9. Lemon and Reis, *Russian Formalist Criticism*, pp. 78–87 (note 6 above).

10. Ibid., pp. 27, 30.

11. See note 1 re Biblical Repetition and Informational Redundancy, *passim*.

12. Another Formalist, Roman Jakobson, even identifies "consistent motivation" as one of the central meanings of "realism" ("On Realism in Art," in *Readings in Russian Poetics*, p. 45) (see note 8 above).

13. Lemon and Reis, pp. 80–84 (note 6 above).

14. For further discussion and various examples, see the references in n. 1 above.

15. A measure of the prevalence and deep-rootedness of this conceptual indecision among the Formalists is that it shows even in the work of a discriminating theorist like Jurij Tynjanov. In his remarkable essay "On Literary Evolution," motivation appears in the original Shklovskian sense: "The story might be used merely to motivate style or as a strategy for developing the material" (*Readings in Russian Poetics*, p. 70) (note 8 above). But little of this remains in a more extensive analysis he makes elsewhere: "Motivation in art is the justification of some single factor *vis-à-vis* all the others, the agreement of this factor with all the others (Šklovskij, Eyxenbaum). Each factor is motivated by its connections with the remaining factors. The deformation of factors is applied evenly. The inner motivation which takes place on the constructive level of the work tones down, as it were, the *specifica* of the factors, making the art work 'light' and acceptable" ("Rhythm as the Constructive Factor in Verse," ibid., pp. 130–131). Though Tynjanov's parenthesis invokes the appropriate authorities, the definition he attributes to them here actually reflects his own views and interests. Note in particular the shift from "justification" as addition to "justification" as welding of

elements; the replacement of the notorious "device" by "factor"; and the applicability of motivational linkage to all textual components, including meter and syntax. Even the normative bias noticeable in the equation of "motivated" with "light" (as opposed to difficult or perceptible) art has been given a radical twist, indeed almost turned upside down. For what makes such art light is not the subordination of the motivating to the motivated element but their balance and indistinguishability. As we move from the first to the second context, then, we again note the passage from motivation proper to (this time, undesirable) integration and intelligibility.

16. Gérard Genette, *Communications* 11 (1968): 19.

17. Jonathan Culler, *Structuralist Poetics* (London, 1975), pp. 131–160.

18. The whole issue requires much more detailed treatment than I can give it here. (For some further discussion, though, see "The Realism of James Bond," *Siman Kria*, no. 7 [1977]: 387–406.) Among the interesting problems to be resolved is whether to regard the transmissional as a mimetic function must mean to define fiction as a mimesis of a speech-act, along the lines persuasively suggested by Barbara Herrnstein Smith in "Poetry as Fiction," *New Literary History* II (1971): 269–282.

19. Anthony Trollope, *An Autobiography* (New York, n.d.), pp. 209–210.

20. Edgar Allan Poe, "The Philosophy of Composition," in *Poems and Essays* (Berlin, 1922), pp. 194–198.

21. For some points in what follows I am indebted to Tamar Yacobi's work in progress on narrative reliability, including her paper "Fictional Reliability as a Communicative Problem," presented at the Porter Institute symposium on narrative theory (Tel Aviv and Jerusalem, June 1979) and now published in *Poetics Today* 2 (1981): 113–126.

22. For an early discussion of gaps and multiple gap-filling in this paradigmatic Jamesian tale, see M. Perry and M. Sternberg, "The King Through Ironic Eyes: The Narrator's Devices in the Story of David and Bathsheba and Two Excursuses on the Theory of the Narrative Text," *Hasifrut* I (1968): 263–292. That analysis also leads to some general comments on point of view as an explanatory measure.

23. Nicholas Blake, *The Sad Variety* (New York, 1972), p. 88.

PHILOSOPHICAL CONCEPTS AND IMPLICATIONS WITHIN THE LITERARY WORK OF ART

Frank Gado

TOWARD A DEFINITION OF THE PHILOSOPHICAL IN LITERATURE

No pair of disciplines in the long history of the academy has found the attraction of each other's territory more irresistible than philosophy and literary criticism. These incursions divide into two general categories. The first, under the descriptive heading of "the philosophy of literature," includes among the numerous kinds of examination of literature employing the methods of philosophy the varied ramifications of literary aesthetics. The lines of address in such investigations present no basic confusions. The second category, with which this essay is concerned, focusses on philosophy in literature—i.e., it assumes that literature (or some precinct within it) is itself philosophical. Here the discussions, at least at the level of their implicit presumptions, are rather clouded, for, despite the frequency with which the term "philosophical" is employed in a literary context, its meaning blurs and wavers, sometimes even within the confines of a single study.

When George Santayana, reflecting the *Geistesgeschichte* movement that had been flourishing in Germany, nominates Lucretius, Dante, and Goethe as the three major philosophical poets, he is treating their writings as representations of the dominant systems of thought in the ages in which they lived. Whether the works directly incorporate philosophy (as in *De Rerum Naturae*) or merely serve as lenses revealing an extrinsic body of philosophical tenets (as in the case of *The Divine Comedy* and *Faust*) is for him an irrelevant distinction; it is the association with a great philosophy that makes the great poet philosophical, not the poet's mode of operation.[1] Other critics, perhaps wary of the implications of Santayana's approach, have sought to divorce the term from the history of ideas by locating its meaning primarily in the work. Rather typically, one philosopher announces at the start of his venture into literary criticism that he will pursue "the artistic treatment of philosophical ideas."[2]

But this strategy has its own dangers. What sets a "philosophical idea" apart from other ideas found in literature? Given the virtually infinite elasticity of philosophy's interests, the designation becomes almost useless. Furthermore, is it not the consideration of an idea from the perspective of philosophy, rather than the idea itself, that renders it philosophical in the sense implied by this criterion? And if so, where does this leave the artist—or the artistic?

The root of the problem lies in the undiscriminating shift from "philosophy" to "philosophical" (in reference to literature) as a merely morphological transformation of the same concept. Whatever the philosophical component of literature might be said to be, clearly it does not display philosophy *qua* philosophy. (To be sure, literature can take its subject matter from philosophy and dress it in a literary manner. The eighteenth century was especially fond of the practice—among the many and various examples it offers are Pope's "Essay on Man" and Rezzonico's *L'origine delle idee* in verse, Johnson's *Rasselas* and Diderot's *Jacques le fataliste* in prose. But these are instances of a conjunction without a true synthesis; the philosophy in such works retains a separate identity that does not impinge on how they function as literature.) That which distinguishes a work as literary proceeds from a different intention, conceives of argument in a different way, employs different methods in the fulfillment of its design, and is subject to different tests; even the most intricate themes in literature tend to concern the humblest truisms, presented without the least regard for rational scrutiny.

Most references to literature as philosophical, of course, recognize that it is not just philosophy in more appealing raiment; even so, the belief, at least as old as Longinus, that they nevertheless share a common substance persists.[3] Among modern critics, the designation of a work as philosophical tends to imply that it evinces attitudes and interests similar to those traditionally found in philosophic inquiry, and that this similarity makes the discourse appropriate to one also appropriate to the other. A brace of books published during the past decade illustrates several orientations in the practice. When Richard Kuhns calls *The Prelude* a philosophical poem, the judgment is based on the poem's concern with memory, beauty, and nature that describes a philosophic constellation.[4] Peter Jones approaches the subject from another angle: instead of examining *what* literature says, he analyzes *how* its statements are developed. Thus, when he discusses *Middlemarch* in his monograph on the relationship between novels and philosophy, he notes that George Eliot's procedure of concentrating on "the outward signs of men's inner lives" accords with the views of psychology found in treatises by G. H. Lewes, Hume, and Kant.[5] Gareth Matthews offers a simpler proposition: in reading stories written for children, he finds "a host of epistemo-logical and metaphysical questions familiar to students of philosophy"—leading to the inference that literature in its most rudimentary forms is a primal means of accommodating an urgency to engage in philosophcal inquiry that is already present in childhood.[6]

All three of these examples involve philosophy in their discussions, yet they supply virtually no guidance in determining what identifies a literary work as philosophical. Kuhns differs from Santayana in concen-trating on the affinity between literature's statements and philosophy rather than on the poet as spokesman from the peaks of intellectual history, but the result is essentially the same: literature becomes a document in the history of ideas. *All* art, however, in some respect and to some degree expresses the imaginative attentions of a mind that cannot avoid reflecting ideas current at an historical moment; some "documents" may be richer in the evidence they provide, or they may articulate that evidence more distinctly, but these qualities no more establish them as a kind of philosophy than the qualities of a period's philosophical discourses establish them as a kind of art. The same point can be stated in another way: architecture and music are no less indica-tive of the temper of an age than its poetry; if a poem that voices a period's ideas is thereby philosophical, should one not also be able to identify a philosophical building or a philosophical symphony?

Jones is vulnerable to similar objections even though he ignores the history of ideas *per se* and employs a different sort of argument. Imput-ing philosophical implications to the method by which life is imitated, he then attempts to prove his case by grounding that method in the texts of philosophers, but what does he actually show beyond parallel interests? In the instance of *Middlemarch*, how does the author's con-struction of reality through assessment of "outward signs" distinguish this novel from any other that takes into account the mental processes of the characters? Jones's citations of philosophers merely demonstrate that the dynamics of the psychological apprehension of the world has been a traditional concern of philosophy; they do not confer special status on *Middlemarch*. Even if he were to prove that George Eliot consciously incorporated their theories (which he does not try to do), how would that make *Middlemarch* more philosophical than other novels drawing on a set of assumptions about the reasons humans think and act as they do?

Matthews, despite the very narrow scope of his thesis and his neglect of critical questions, suggests the most provocative premise of the three: in an early stage of its development, the mind does not differentiate philosophy and literature (or, at least, some literature); both spring from

one impulse to formulate questions about the relationship between consciousness and the world it perceives. Unfortunately, however, Matthews contents himself with the proposition that children respond to a
kind of philosophical speculation contained in stories written for them;
he does not take the further step of demonstrating how the protophilo-
sophical elements he discerns radically relate to the aesthetic character
of the stories (i.e., how what makes them stories also impinges on what
makes them philosophical).

Admittedly, this brief is less than fair to the three scholars cited: in
addressing portions of their studies, it does not give adequate recognition to their larger theses; moreover, it seems to fault them for failing to
prove an argument they have not sought to advance. But chasing the
hares loosed by Kuhns, Jones, and Matthews—or by any other philoso-
pher-critic who approaches the issue as they do—is not the object of this
stage of the hunt; rather, it is to illustrate what invariably happens when
the philosophical element in literature is construed to mean that which
is subject to interpretation in the light of philosophy. Although the
semantic logic is unassailable, and although the practice to which it
refers is as legitimate as any other (such as the historian's recourse to
literature as a document of the times in which it was written), from a
taxonomic standpoint, this sense of the term is extremely problematical.
What fixes its limits? Not an intrinsic qualification but the interest of
philosophy. And since philosophy can shine its light on almost any facet
of any literary work and have it reflect back on itself, virtually all literature becomes potentially philosophical. If the term is to identify not a
susceptibility to a kind of analysis but a kind of literature, it will be
necessary to change the semantic apprehension of "philosophical literature" from one in which the adjective makes the noun dependent upon
the nature and operations of philosophy to one in which the two words
merge to form an independent concept.

As a descriptive term, "philosophical literature" presumably signifies
some relationship to philosophy, and given that a literary work will not
correspond to the practice through which philosophy defines itself, such
a relationship should be sought in the impulse to articulate a moral or
metaphysical vision that, in a sense, precedes its realization as either
literature or philosophy. Most casual references to literature as philosophical suggest no more than this common stimulus; yet, although it
offers a place to begin, it is too unrestrictive, too amorphous a concept
to furnish a basis for incisive distinctions. The essayist, in elaborating
even the most trivial subject, almost inevitably reflects a fundamental
structure of beliefs, and even a gathering of aphorisms becomes a cleres-
tory through which shines the aphorist's apprehension of the world. Yet

in neither instance does thinking of the work as philosophical lead to a new insight; the "philosophicalness" of such writing, although it may be expanded through inference, is principally coincident with its explicit statements. If the term denotes nothing more than this, its significance is too shallow to merit much discussion. The same difficulty attaches to statements couched in the discourse of philosophy that happen to be encased within a literary form—even when they are as magnificently expressed as in the Grand Inquisitor chapter of *The Brothers Karamazov*. If the "philosophical" is to have a literary meaning, it should refer to a peculiarly literary property—to some inherent means by which literature manifests content rather than to the nature of the content alone.

In turning away from the employment of language in an expository mode, one is led toward its employment as metaphor, and thus to consideration of poetry—in particular, that kind of poetry that speaks of one thing in terms of another, that creates a prism through which the flashings struck by attention to a limited subject illuminate a larger import. Just such a projection of meaning, linked to a concept of form, is what Robert Frost indicates by describing "the figure a poem makes" as that which "begins in delight and ends in wisdom";[7] although Frost's "figure" comes into sharpest relief in his own works, it is also present (given some license in the interpretation of "delight") in poems representing such diverse poetic practices as Herbert's "The Pulley," Keats's "Ode on a Grecian Urn," Dickinson's "The soul selects her own society. . . . " Even if one were to argue that Frost's formulation applies to too limited a range of poetry and, by redirecting the purpose from describing the progress traced by the poem to the process the poet follows, contend instead that the poem originates in the "wisdom" that is then expressed so as to delight, the upshot with respect to the question of the philosophical would be the same. To acknowledge that poetry's metaphors render a vision of some aspect of existence in images, however, is not only to restate a commonplace but also to restate one which has little taxonomic consequence. If "philosophical literature," or even "philosophical poem," means only that the language of metaphor is wedded to a philosophical impulse, the works so described are too diverse to constitute a class. Furthermore, the principle on which this classification is based mislays its emphasis. The *aperçu* contained in the poem's statement is relatively static; the dynamic element—the power and skill evinced in the manipulation of the metaphor—is judged according to the same criteria that apply to poems expressing different interests and in no significant sense yields to a more penetrating insight by virtue of being seen from a "philosophical"

perspective. To be useful, the term should indicate some special quality in *how* the literary work functions metaphorically.

Curiously, most casual references to literature as philosophical attach
to plays, narrative poetry, and (with greatest frequency) the novel or
novel-like fictions—i.e., genres in which story dominates. Although
such references are not surrounded by explanations of what the term
means, the practice suggests an intuitive recognition that some works
more than others display a heightened consciousness of an underlying
affinity between the impulse to construct a figure of truth and the peculiar way story operates as metaphor. Of necessity, all stories treat a
nexus of actions, every juncture of which manifests will and choice.
Either within or between the characters, the interaction of different
motivations produces conflict, and since a reflection of values is inevitable in the story-teller's manner of showing the resolution of the conflict, story inherently involves philosophical considerations. But the
story-as-metaphor does not consist in just the accumulation of the moral
and metaphysical implications in a series of events. Although all stories
in some sense "imitate" life, life itself does not define the form of any
given story—even the birth and death of an individual are merely sta-
tions in a succession of causes and effects that stretch infinitely in all
directions throughout time. In creating a story, the teller not only selects from life or invents on the basis of experience; he also arranges his
materials in an artificial construction having a beginning, an end, and a
middle that develops the meaning of the relationship between the beginning and the end. This conception of what makes a particular story
whole is grounded in a fundamental understanding of the nature of the
world; it is this set of assumptions that the story's design presents as
metaphor.

Given the premise that there are necessarily philosophical implications
in the designs of all fictions, does it follow that the designation of a
particular work as "philosophical" implies only a greater degree of self-
consciousness on the author's part in manipulating his story as a metaphor
of "truth"? Both *Jane Eyre* and "Cinderella" evince the ultimate triumph
of justice through essentially similar schemes (the marriage of a young
woman—humble, valorous in the performance of oppressive duties, and
endowed with true charity—to an exalted suitor who had apparently been
intended by society's unjust codes for someone else); should one pro-
nounce *Jane Eyre* more philosophical because its heroine, unlike her
fairy-tale counterpart, invokes moral principles in making the choices
leading to her ultimate reward? Is *The Portrait of a Lady*, an "anti-Cin-
derella" fiction that nonetheless bespeaks the same moral views, still
more philosophical than Charlotte Brontë's novel because James uses

more sophisticated means to elaborate the issue? The alternative to such a scale is to discriminate philosophical fiction as a separate phenomenon characterized by a different relationship between the story and the values to engages metaphorically. In each of the fictions cited above, although the actions and the plot they trace make a moral statement, that statement illustrates an orthodoxy; within the protocol of their encounter through the narrative, author and reader proceed from and end with shared moral or metaphysical presumptions. Philosophical fiction, in contrast, may be said to challenge the validity of pieties or, at the very least, to venture beyond a system of belief's familiar tracks; its core lies in intrinsic ambivalence, not certainty, and its power arises from the dubiety it exposes, not from proffered solutions.

In one the very few attempts to identify the writer of philosophical fictions—not as a philosopher *manqué*, nor as a writer who employs the insights of philosophy, nor as one whose methods and interests lend themselves to commentary by philosopher-critics, but as a special kind of interpreter of the world—Robert Penn Warren states that he is "one for whom the documentation of the world is constantly striving to rise to the level of generalization about values, for whom the image strives constantly to rise to symbol, for whom images always fall into a dialectical configuration, for whom the urgency of experience, no matter how vividly and strongly experience may enchant, is the urgency to know the meaning of experience. . . . For him the very act of composition [becomes] a way of knowing, a way of exploration."[8] Warren's description scarcely has the precision of a definition, but it nonetheless conveys a sense of what sets philosophical fiction apart. Although he obviously does not mean that it is literally "dialectical," he is indicating that it must generate dramatic tensions between valuative concepts, not with simple opposition but within a multifaceted "configuration"; furthermore, the stress on "striving" (instead of fixing) and on composition as "a way of exploration" (instead of exposition) suggests tentativeness, or a recognition of the elusiveness of a definitive resolution through the metaphor of art of the existential questions it develops. Once one grasps this fundamental difference in attitude toward the world and toward its relationship to art, it becomes possible to distinguish philosophical fiction not only from the general run of stories but also from that narrower range of literature that deliberately sets out to reflect a system of belief.

One might naively assume that allegory, by embodying abstract concepts in the elements of story and relating them to state a general truth, would inherently be the most philosophical of literary modes. To be effective, however, the allegory requires simplicity in the identification of the constituent parts of the narrative with the values they signify; any ambiguity in the relationship garbles the code in which the allegory speaks. Moreover, because the allegorist depends upon a ready recognition of his figurative meaning by his audience and on their ability to decode it in constant terms, he appeals to a framework of values that already resides, outside his fiction, in the society for which he writes. His imagery may be coruscating in its originality, but the concepts it illuminates mirror conventional values—in a sense, the worn conclusions of a society's priests and philosophers. In this respect, allegory stands at the opposite extreme from what agitates the writer of philosophical fiction. Can one conceive of Christian, on arrival at the Celestial Gate, contemplating turning back to celebrate the human folly he has met along his journey? Or Dante pondering the limits to divine charity as he gazes on Lucifer encased in ice? Were one to reinvent *The Pilgrim's Progress* or *The Divine Comedy* to accommodate these possibilities, it would be necessary to dismantle the footings of allegory on which they rest.

In the nineteenth century, a view emerged among dramatists and novelists that the methods of realism, beyond being employed to "report the news" of the remarkable in the midst of the quotidian, could provide a means of understanding the natural laws governing human behavior. The chief propagandist for this idea, Zola, went so far as to claim he was a scientist reporting on the "experiment" he had conducted in his "laboratory"; literature produced by the "experimental novelist" thus propounded a theory, a "philosophy" of life analogous to what contemporary materialistic philosophers were writing. Here we find a literature that, in Warren's phrases, strives for generalization in documenting the world, that seeks to transform image into the symbol of a greater truth, that seeks dialectical configurations, that quests for the meaning of experience. Should one, therefore, regard as prime manifestations of the philosophical not only the novels of Zola and Dreiser (who independently arrived at the same view in this country) and the plays of such adherents of Naturalism as Ibsen, Hauptmann, and (more distantly and eccentrically) Shaw but also any other work conceived to express an ideological position (such as the Marxism of Malraux's *Man's Fate* and Silone's *Bread and Wine*)? If so, would the term not also have to include works that evangelize a no less fundamental view of man, such as Henry Miller's *Tropic of Cancer*, Samuel Butler's *The Way of All Flesh*, François Mauriac's *The Knot of Vipers*? The more one considers the principle and expands the possibilities, the more attentuated the notion of the philosophical as a specific type of fiction becomes. The major objection to this broad application of the term, however, is not its impracticality but that the kind of fiction it would describe functions essen-

tially as an extension into art of a pre-existing thesis: the dynamic element lies in the composition and realization of that thesis, not in the
thesis itself. To cite Warren again, this time on the other side of the
proposition, such works are not "a way of exploration"; instead, they
illustrate a perception of life that has already been explored. Paradoxi-
cally, as an allegory, the "philosophy" precludes the philosophical.

A much stronger claim can be made for a rather large number of
works that go beyond exemplifying an ideology or a fundamental outlook
on underlying values in the conduct of life and, by means of the structure and development of the narrative, actively engage issues that also
have been traditionally examined by philosophers. John Barth's earliest
novels, *The Floating Opera* and *The End of the Road*—the former an
inquiry into the "reasonableness" of suicide given the gratuitous nature
of existence; the latter an investigation of moral responsibility in a world
without a code of moral imperatives—are paradigmatic instances of such
issues providing the *raison d'être* for the act of narrative. Another is
Hjalmar Söderberg's *Doctor Glas*, a test of the defensibility of altruistic
murder that is written as though it were progressively reporting a philosophical experiment. In these cases, the issue is narrowly construed,
and although its implications are far-ranging, the consciousness embodied in the fiction does not overtly seek to make universal statements
through the particular characters and circumstances it presents. Other
examples of the type, however, clearly exhibit such ambitions. Camus's
novels and plays speak as lucidly to his concerns as a philosopher as do
his essays and are central documents in what has been loosely called the
philosophy of Existentialism. Robert Penn Warren, while he would
loudly disavow the label of philosopher, repeatedly attempts to fill his
own prescription for the philosophical novelist, most notably in *All the
King's Men*—a complex psychological construction built upon the necessity of man's accepting the "truth" that he is "conceived in sin and born
in corruption and he passeth from the stink of the didie to the stench of
the shroud." And, leaping to the peaks of literary history, one finds
Milton's composition of *Paradise Lost* "to justify the ways of God to
man" and, perhaps (its heterogeneity presenting an obstacle to judgment on this point), Goethe's heroic conception of *Faust* as the enlarge-
ment of the human effort to overcome the "impulses of negation and evil
which reside in every normal man" and thereby attain redemption.[9]

That, in some legitimate, descriptive sense such works are philosophical is self-evident, and yet, if one insists that the term focus on the
uniqueness of literary art in how it poses a statement rather than on the
statement itself which can be arrived at through the means of literature,
the term is not wholly appropriate. The philosopher frames his problem,

develops his argument and tests the hypotheses that evolve from it, and then, consistent with his analysis, solves it; the route, from the introduction of the question to the final answer, is linear. From Milton to Barth, each of these examples conceives of its philosophical task in the same linear way and reflects a parallel procedure in its unfolding; indeed, although the force and merit of the work incontestably lies in its literary expression, its argument's metaphoric language can be translated into the language of philosophy. Also, although conceptions of literary form and the requirements of formal argument in philosophy respect different criteria, in these works the outcome of the conflicts that shape the story coincides with and metaphorically represents the conclusion to the philosophical argument. Neither occurs without the other; in this collision, the design of meaning that resides in the completed formal pattern is "closed."

In contrast, the authentically philosophical literary work is iconic in its response to the impulse to figure its sense of the world—its "philosophical" meaning rests primarily and irreducibly in the complexity of its particular representation and cannot be encompassed by paraphrase in the discourse of philosophy. As corollary to this premise, it follows that its design of meaning remains "open." Given the inevitability of all stories having endings, however, and the principle that endings should not be arbitrary terminations but resolutions of the conflicts preceding them, what does an open design imply? Because of the diversity of genres, the shifting conventions of different ages, and, most important of all, the freedom an author enjoys in inventing idiosyncratic ways of treating his subject matter, it would be folly to seek to distill one formula applicable in all cases, but essentially such "openness" involves setting the operation of the story as plot against a noetic dilemma arising from the disparity between the multiplex consciousness of experience and the mind's insistence on reducing that multiplicity to its categories of understanding. For want of a better term, that dilemma, which agitates the telling of the story and provides the perspective on its interpretation, is indicated by what might be called the "informing question"—it *in-forms* the story (i.e., gives shape and significance to its substance) yet remains beyond the story's capacity to resolve it. At this point, however, the argument is better served by some specific examples (inadequately brief though the confines of this paper force them to be) than by further discussion on an abstract plane.

That *Oedipus the King* is not usually thought of as a philosophical play is understandable—it broods no passage that resembles the disputations of philosophy—and yet not to recognize the philosophical question at its core—a question that can be verbalized in such various ways as *What is*

Man? and *Does truth save or destroy?* and still be, at bottom, the same question—is to miss its profoundest meaning. In Ode I of *Antigone*, the first-written part of the Oedipus "cycle," the chorus proclaims, "Numberless are the world's wonders, but none more wonderful than man," and then goes on to recite the mastery of his intelligence over nature in all respects but one—his mortality. Important as that passage is to *Antigone*, that same hollow boast becomes even more important when Sophocles picks it up again in *Oedipus the King*. Greeting his subjects, Oedipus accepts the praises the priest heaps on him as the deliverer who solved the Sphinx's riddle many years before, and he arrogantly vows to save them once more from their sickness-unto-death by again using his intellect. Ironically, "Man," the answer to the original riddle which stressed the advance of life toward death, is also the answer he is about to quest unwittingly after: the progress of the play is determined by his "unriddling" the riddle of himself as a man, a course that finds him retracing his way back—literally, in a sense—to his origin in Iocasta's womb. The detective-story plot drives to a clear-cut conclusion that complements the play's beginning: fulfilling his promise to find Laius' murderer by discovering that it is he, Oedipus earns expulsion from the city he had once rescued and causes Creon, whom he had accused of being a traitor, to become king in his own stead. The philosophical meaning of the play, however, is not only locked in a knot of ironies but it is also the figure of the knot itself. Representing human intellect that would undo fate, Oedipus, acting out of ignorance, has found the knowledge that spells his fate; from an initial seeking of deliverence from the scourge of death, the play finally arrives at the implication that death is a deliverance; blind to the truth at the start, the king ends being blinded by truth; to know too much leads to the abomination of oneself, yet not pursuing knowledge is tantamount to acquiescing to death.

Though often compared with *Oedipus the King* for other reasons, *Hamlet* strikingly resembles it in its generative center. Hamlet's taunting speech to Rosencrantz and Guildenstern—"What a piece of work is a man, how noble in reason, how infinite in faculties, in form and moving how express and admirable, in action how like an angel, in apprehension how like a god: the beauty of the world, the paragon of animals; and yet to me, what is this quintessence of dust?"—echoes, in a half-parodic way, the gloating over human intellect at the start of the Theban play, although by the time Hamlet makes it he already knows, even if he cannot fully face the knowledge, what hellish truth about himself his reason and faculties will lead him to. (One does not have to be Ernest Jones to see that Hamlet's obsession with his mother's "incest" with his

father's murderer indicts himself; that the Ghost's urgings to revenge
dramatize the guilt he feels as a result of his hidden knowledge; and that
the virtual suicide he enacts with Laertes, his alter-ego whose father he
has killed, executes the punishment he has pronounced on himself for
dreaming of taking his father's place in Gertrude's bed.) The fact that
Hamlet has spawned countless debates over what the play is about in
terms of the motivations and significance of its actions attests the impossibility of resolving its meaning through explication at that level of story;
at its heart, and radiating from it in manifold ways (not least of which is
the endlessly punning language of its expression) is the dilemma posed
by reason countervailing itself.

   Don Quijote, which stands on the threshold not only of the novel but
of the modern imagination as well, also rests on a final ambivalence—
although in this case the full reach of its philosophical impulse seems to
have been realized midway through its composition (ten years after
Cervantes had published Part One) instead of being planned as an intrinsic conceit from the start. The initial impulse was to mix the formula of
the romance (which Cervantes had previously employed unsuccessfully
himself) with that of the earthy, realistic picaresque tale then replacing
the romance in popularity. Cervantes varies the circumstances in which
these two views of the world collide comically, but the joke remains
essentially unchanged. So, too, does the reader's perspective on it. We
regret that the world does not yield to Quijote's nobility, yet we are also
enough part of the world to accept Cervantes's depiction of Quijote's
mad idealism as a disruptive, harmful force. But in Part Two, the
knight's madness becomes enveloped by a world made phantasmagoric,
and the nature of our response shifts.

   One can only wonder at Erich Auerbach's statement that

> both in part 1 and part 2, one thing is completely lacking: tragic
> complications and serious consequences. . . . [The satire and criti-
> cism] never goes to the roots of things and is moderate in
> attitude. . . . [Quijote's] activity reveals nothing at all. It affords an
> opportunity to present Spanish life in its color and fullness. In the
> resulting clashes between Don Quijote and reality no situation ever
> results which puts in question that reality's right to be what it is. It
> is always right and he wrong.[10]

Surely, when the Duchess (who, like us, has read Part One and been
charmed by Quijote's unwitting buffoonery) arranges the world of her
court to conform to his fantasy just for the sake of amusement, our
relationship to the narrative is transformed. In part, this is because the
Duchess stands in our shoes—or we stand in hers. The consequence of

the reader's position of condescension toward Quijote's idealism is a
theater of cruelty—all the more cruel because it is a gratuitous assault
on man's dignity, performed only for fun. The values of the society to
which we have given our assent become the target. (The ensuing
chapters about Sancho as governor extend the satire. His island—or,
more properly, the Duchess', and thus, figuratively, ours—is a microcosm of our world. Significantly, the simple peasant quickly has his fill of
his fellow man and abdicates his office in disgust.) But more important
than our discomfiture as we recognize the indictment of ourselves is
what the Duchess's make-believe does to our perception of Quijote.
Deprived of a tension with reality, he seems to lose his energy as a
character and to become, like any of us caught in his circumstances,
merely pitiable. From this point on, his eventual defeat by Don Antonio
seems inevitable, as does his deathbed renunciation of his knight-er-
rantry and his renunciation of books of chivalry as lies. This restoration
to sanity, which marks the noble fool's lapse into the tragic inheritance
of his humanity, closes the pattern that defines the limits of the plot but
opens up the ambivalence of its philosophical meaning. The reader,
having laughed at the absurdity in Quijote's substitution of illusion for
reality, is now brought to confront the desperate absurdity of life
stripped of those illusions. "Ah, master," Sancho cries in his final
speech, "dont' die, your Grace, but take my advice and go on living for
many years to come; for the greatest madness that a man can be guilty of
in this life is to die without good reason, without anyone's killing him,
slain only by the hands of melancholy." But it is precisely to that "greatest madness" that Quijote—and we—must succumb. The madness
cured is madness; this is not just an ironic reversal sprung at the end but
the figure subtending the metaphor of the tale in its entirety.

From *Typee* to *The Confidence Man* and *Billy Budd*, America's greatest philosophical novelist, Herman Melville, reveals an unavailing intellectual struggle with ambiguities, but it was only after his discovery of
Hawthorne's tales that he, in this "annihilating" personal struggle,
learned to devise literary structures to house the irreconcilably ambiguous. Yet strangely, the masterpiece he produced by rewriting an al-
most-finished *Moby Dick* in the light of Hawthorne's example has been
criticized as a technically naive work, bloated, furthermore, by an obses-
sive, encyclopaedic concern with whales and whaling. This betrays a
serious misreading that fails to take into account the full reach of its
philosophical base. If the novel pivoted solely on Ahab, then the prefatory material *would be* just an overly long joke, the introductory
chapters dealing with Queenqueg and Ishmael *would be* a separate narrative with thematic "loomings," and the cetological discourses *would be*

misdirected interruptions by a voice more appropriately Melville's than
Ishmael's. But the question posed by *Moby Dick* focuses on the limitations of the mind in its effort to comprehend the universe, and from that
perspective, even though Ahab is unmistakably the protagonist and
though it is his metaphysical quarrel with God that gives the plot its
thematic unity, the novel is as much about the accepting Ishmael as it is
about his rebellious captain.

   Already in the prefaces, Ishmael (for we are asked to regard the novel as
his composition) stands in awe of the whale as the emblem of God's
indefinable creation; as he will later in the cetological chapters, he looks
upon the attempts to fix the whale as pathetically comic. Melville's God—
the transcendent source and explanation of being—is ultimately unknow-
able. Recognizing the fatuity of seeking what cannot be found, Ishmael
instead devotes his mind to finding the basis for brotherhood ("the great
and everlasting First Congregation of this whole worshipping world")
beneath the apparent differences that separate men. The "sacramental"
expression of that brotherhood in the "marriage" of Ishmael and Queequeg is the high point of the introductory chapters, and after repeated
direct and indirect references to the "joint stock company" to which all
men belong during the account of the *Pequod's* voyage, the motif of
pan-humanism resounds again at the novel's end: in contrast to the lonely
Ahab, dragged down to destruction by the "coffin" prophesied for him,
Ishmael is saved by Queequeg's coffin-turned-lifebuoy and then picked
up by the *Rachel,* which, after having been spurned by Ahab in her
request for assistance (a plea based on their common membership in the
family of man), has continued searching for her "lost children." And yet,
restricting the book's final meaning to the schema traced by Ishmael as
the teller of the tale distorts Melville's position as much as the more usual
concentration upon the "No! in thunder" sounded by Ahab in the tale he
tells. If Ishmael represents the sanity of affirming the possibilities of life
within human limits, Ahab, willing to be destroyed before he will accept
those limits described by an unjust, indifferent God, represents (as he
himself states) the sanity of madness maddened. *Moby Dick* does not
choose between the two positions, nor does it retreat behind neutrality by
merely offering them as alternatives; rather, it pursues the question into
an ambivalence that admits no solution.

   If only because *The Brothers Karamazov* incorporates, to some extent
and in some manner, the questions that spin out of the vortices of
Oedipus the King, Hamlet, Don Quijote, and *Moby Dick* (and also,
by-the-by, *The Floating Opera, The End of the Road, Doctor Glas, All
the King's Men,* and *Faust*) but within the conventions of a more-or-less
"typical" nineteenth-century novel, it deserves its place at the end of

this short list of philosophical literature. Its plot deals with the circumstances of the murder of Fyodor and the trial of his son Dmitri for the crime; its main thematic element consists in the tracking down of guilt—not only in the search for the actual murderer but, more importantly, in the investigation of psychological guilt and of the metaphysical implications of human suffering. In the course of this intricate development, Dostoyevsky exposes an array of philosophical issues, sometimes, even, in dialectical form. But to seine for the novel's meaning by isolating any of these passages, or even by isolating the lot and all its complex thematic elaboration, would be to miss what makes it philosophical fiction at its deepest level.

The part of the novel, prior to its climactic scene, that revolves around Father Zossima only remotely engages the mechanism of the plot, and although what it reveals of his past and present parallels, at several key points, the story of the Karamazovs, its main function goes far beyond mere adumbration. Dostoyevsky presents Zossima as a cluster of ostensible contradictions that culminate, at his death, in the rapid putrification of the saintly monk's corpse. Since a saint's body is supposed by tradition to be immune to corruption, the stench rising from the bier seems to lend credence to his detractors, but the reader should, by this point, have surmised the real significance of the old monk's decay: Zossima's holiness lies in his humanity, not in his being above it. Just before his death, he had instructed Alyosha to "go forth into the world"—i.e., to experience the tumult of what it means to be human and, not in spite of what he will find but because of it, affirm life. The novel's quest for an understanding of this injunction underlies all the rest: the drama of the Karamazovs portrays the clashes among the manifold aspects of man—from his basest passions, to his Christ-like agony, to his regeneration through love. When the cry "Hurrah for Karamazov" closes the novel, it is an echo of Zossima's command, amplified by the intervening journey through the soul. And yet, as the novel's final pages emphasize, that experience in no way *proves* the validity of Zossima's teaching; indeed, the evidence documented by the world as mirrored in the novel and the inference one would draw from a mere recitation of the plot would seem to weigh against such affirmation. In this respect, Zossima's command becomes the challenge *to us* to fly in the face of the evidence and respond to the glorious agony of life with joy.

Obviously, one cannot, within the compass of one article, do justice to five examples drawn from among the greatest literary achievements in history, much less explore the various forms philosophical literature can take; if this article has only raised an important question and suggested some possible direction the answer might take, it will have accom-

plished its purpose. The point, of course, is not that philosophical literature is necessarily of higher quality than other literature but that it
springs from the highest ambition a writer can have. Like myth and like
the parables of religion, its motivating force belongs to pre-philosophy—
and in that respect, it is at once more primitive and more sophisticated.
It may be no accident that each of the works cited above as philosophical
was written at a moment in its society's history when it was being torn in
two directions by differences in the apprehension of values; perhaps the
only way to express that tension is through art. Philosophy is analytic; it
dissects, explains, and organizes what already exists. Philosophical literature, in contrast, answers a question with a story that only expands
the dimensions of the question.

Notes

1. George Santayana, *Thee Philosophical Poets* (Cambridge, Mass., 1910).
2. Morris Weitz, *Philosophy in Literature* (Detroit, 1963), p. 1.
3. Plato, of course, recognizes the argument in his *Republic*, but he disparages the poet
   for presuming to pass off as the same substance that which is not.
4. Richard Kuhns, *Structures of Experience* (New York, 1970), pp. 95–131.
5. Peter Jones, *Philosophy and the Novel* (Oxford, 1975), p. 48.
6. Gareth B. Matthews, *Philosophy and the Young Child* (Cambridge, Mass., 1980),
   p. 48.
7. Robert Frost, "The Figure a Poem Makes," *Collected Poems* (New York, 1939), preface.
8. Robert Penn Warren, "Nostromo," *Sewanee Review* 59: 391.
9. Edward H. Weatherly, *et al.*, *The Heritage of European Literature* (Boston, 1949), II,
   p. 8.
10. Erich Auerbach, *Mimesis*, trans. by Willard R. Trask (Princeton, 1953), p. 345.

Alain Mercier

LITERARY CRITICISM AND ESOTERISM IN THE HISTORICAL DESCRIPTION OF THE POETICAL MOVEMENTS OF THE NINETEENTH AND TWENTIETH CENTURIES (ROMANTICISM AND SYMBOLISM)

New perspectives, questioning and even upsetting traditional methods in literary criticism and history have for several years called upon psychoanalysis, dialectical materialism, linguistics, sociology, and even semiology . . . Much importance has been accorded to the *lecture* of texts, utilizing all possible decoding methods, relegating as almost useless both biographical research on the authors and source studies of the literary mainstream or the works themselves. Thus everything was discredited that was dependent on a henceforth suspect "historicism." It is especially this way in France under the pressure of what is called *la nouvelle critique* and of Roland Barthes, Julia Kristeva, Tsvetan Todorov, Jacques Lacan, Jacques Derrida, etc. . . . At the same time, particular attention was paid to elucidating the creative process, the *Poétique*, by laying stress on the structure of the work, while more or less giving up the thematic studies inspired by Gaston Bachelard or his disciples. I do not intent to neglect these recent developments in literary criticism—which sometimes go so far as to deny the very existence of literature. Nevertheless, the study and analysis—superficially or in depth—of the historical movements that produced decisive changes in European and American poetry, from the nineteenth century to the beginning of the twentieth century, required different methods of investigation. Indeed, methods are required which would allow me to better understand these more or less concurrent phenomena occuring in various countries, and to show texts and authors in a favorable light once again—many who were neglected until now.

Research into sources or origin and the relevation of relationships and legacies as part of the work of literary criticism does not appear to me to be illusory or out of date, insofar as neither tries to be systematic and exhaustive. Neither claims to reduce the genesis and the scope of works and historical movements to mere mechanical relations or simplistic influences. In his methodology, the literary critic and historian must respect the complexity and multiplicity of meanings inherent in all of creation.

Among the starting points which led me to a comparative study (to so simplify a relatively more complex work) on the development of the history of poetry and the so-called esoteric philosophers, I must mention the works of Albert-Marie Schmidt (*La Poésie scientifique en France au XVIᵉ siècle*), Auguste Viatte (*Les sources occultes du Romantisme*) as well as the convictions expressed by André Breton at the time of his *Discours aux étudiants français de l'Université de Yale (Address to the French students of Yale University)* and in *Arcane XVII* and *La clef des champs*. According to these opinions, university criticism was on the wrong track in evading the role of the occult sciences and doctrines—like alchemy, the Kabalah, magic, "animal magnetism' tarot cards, etc.—in the formation of movements which go from the end of the eighteenth century (Romanticism) to the twentieth century (Surrealism), by way of Symbolism. Why, wrote André Breton, do they overlook Martinez de Pasqually, L. C. de Saint-Martin, Fabre d'Olivet, Eliphas Lévi, Saint-Yves d'Alveydre. . . . ? In mentioning these names, I am confining myself to the French language, more familiar to the master of Surrealism; and everything led me to believe that in extending the scope of my study to the rest of Europe, I would arrive at closely related findings. Very much on the fringe of academic criticism at that time were the writings of A. Rolland de Renéville, one of the *Grand Jeu* theorists who since the thirties had compared the modern poetic experience to the spiritual experiences of the great eastern mystics. These works seemed to me to open up some interesting roads into comparative research, provided the work was done with great care. A detailed, serious and progressive examination thus led me to establish concomitances, points of similarity, or equivalencies between the varied esoteric conceptions—and even the thought structures—of the eighteenth and nineteenth centuries and a literary criticism that would primarily result in poetry but also showed up in Fantastic fiction, short stories, and novelettes. One *idée-force* set forth by Professor Gilbert Durand is that any given occult doctrine or legendary tradition corresponds to "structures of the imaginary" which, however coherent they may be, served as levers for creative and liberating adventures in the sphere of personal writing. The approach to literary works is not facilitated by this, however, for the simple reason that each creative process obeys aesthetic structures belonging to it alone. The study of the so-called esoteric philosophers will thus not be able to truly serve as a "decoding grid" (to use the terminology of current criticism) which would assure a clear understanding and *lecture* of works unopen to us because of their obscurity or their intrinsic finality. The study can only shift us towards evaluations or re—evaluations of texts brought into a new light. If it is striking to note that several of the great European poets of the nineteenth and twentieth centuries (Goethe, Novalis, Blake, Yeats, T. S. Eliot, Nerval, Hugo, Rimbaud) had, to varying degrees, a certain curiosity about the theories and practices of the occult, it is nevertheless very dangerous to try to systematize the interpretation of their works by using a key, one which might open all doors, according to certain recent attempts. In any case, the recourse to sources must not exhaust the layered or multi-layered potentialities of the works, especially when they are very valuable. It remains none the less true that there are a considerable number of texts that are practically inaccessible to us without some knowledge of occult philosophies and secret societies—for example: the poems of Blake, Nerval, or Yeats. The many critical analyses written in this spirit during the last fifteen years are often revealing and fruitful when they are not excessive.

The difficulty the critic and historian encounters when he approaches what we call the "occult philosophies" and when he wishes to establish relationships and interactions with literary products is the multiplicity of doctrines, theories, modes of understanding, and initiatory-type teachings for which the terms "secret sciences," "esoterism," "magical practices" are simply inadequate.

The more researchers of today are led to delve into a certain sector of these philosophies, and then decide upon the specificity of it from their own angle, the more these very designations divide and subdivide the domains of application. This is in contrast to the eighteenth, nineteenth, and the beginning of the twentieth centuries, where the effort towards unity—artificial or superficial as it may have been—was evident and differed greatly, in opinion from the current era of specialization.

I will now discuss hermeneutics, in a wide enough sense of the word to include the interpretation of sacred texts that more or less border on esoterism and theology. To a certain extent, hermaneutics also bears a resemblance to epistemology and patristics, which separates us even more from the nineteenth century poets. The expression "Jewish mysti-

cism" often replaces the word Kabalah—wrongly, in my opinion—under
the influence of Professor Gershom Scholem. That which used to belong
to either "animal magnetism," hypnosis, or telepathy, to use past terminology, has now become part of parapsychology or psychics, both scien-
tifically tested. Gnosis also lost its traditional meaning after the experi-
ments of the "Princeton gnosis," founded on mathematcal principles. As
for witchcraft, the various divinatory practices, and clairvoyancy, they
appealed more to folklorists and sociologists. The "occult" and the "esoteric," as such, are at present splintered apart, in divisions that no
longer seem connected to each other. As an example, did not Raymond
Abellio, a French writer, just entitle one of his books *La Fin de
l'esotérisme?* The modes of apprehension were, however, quite different
from the end of the eighteenth century until the beginning of the twentieth century, and the literary critic must still take into account the more
or less tenuous links which formerly united the following—the contemplative mystical doctrine of Boehme and Swedenborg, secret societies
with initiation rites, religious heresies, the divinatory practices (such as
astrology, fortune-telling, palmistry), spiritualism, white and black
magic, and alchemy, the *Ars Magna*. It is from the end of the eighteenth century—no doubt as a reaction against the rationalism of the
so-called Enlightenment, as much as in divergence from the official
religions—that activities judged to be "occult" or "esoteric" will succes-
sively appear, although on the fringe of the intellectual mainstream or
the current scientific philosophies. This will take place in quite different
ways—i.e. concentrated, unsteady, sporadic or nonexistent, depending
on that part of Europe or the Americas where the activities bore fruit.

The historian of the world's literatures will have to ask himself if this
phenomenon of resurgence and of strengthening of apparently irrational
thought patterns is peculiar to Western civilization alone (with much
more intensity in Russia than in the Americas, for example). Or is it
perceptible elsewhere in the world, even though economic and industrial development was far from being irrelevant to its evolution? In
considering Romanticism not as a simple literary or aesthetic movement
but as an historic event that basically disrupted all of Europe—especially
in the North—Auguste Viatte has brought to the surface the underlying
layer (with all its diverse components), going back to the middle of the
eighteenth century, which irrigated, watered, and promoted the hatch-
ing and birth of the works bearing the stamp of this historical trend in
Germany, France, and above all England. Illuminism, Theosophy, Rosi-
crucianism, hermetic philosophy or *Naturphilosophie*—such are the tendencies that Auguste Viatte synthesized, going from Swedenborg up to
Baader and Fabre d'Olivet in his essay on the *Sources occultes du*

Romantisme. He did not, however, indicate in what way and to what degree the literary works from 1750 to 1850 had really been affected by these tendencies, nor to what point they had eluded the grasp of the occult substratum. On the other hand, Viatte shortly thereafter dedicated to Hugo (*Victor Hugo et les illuminés de son temps*) a study that did tackle the problems of these lines of convergence and encounters of ideas as they happened in the case of this French Romantic poet. The study would have been nicely completed by some critical essay elucidating the illuminist or theosophic sources of the other European poets and prose writers.[1] Léon Cellier in France and Professor Brian Juden in Great Britain have given this a try, highlighting respectively the Romantic epic and the esoteric and mystical milieu in which Gérard de Nerval developed. The problematics of sources seems to me, however, to be so equivocal that it calls for a few remarks on whether or not Romanticism in itself constitutes a return to the roots—occult or not. The authors and writings that were on the fringe or in the background, presented by Viatte as embryos of major works—are they not just as representative of Romantic literature as what is generally classified under this label? Is not Franz von Baader a "Romantic" writer as much as Novalis or Tieck, and even more so than Uhland for example; do not Ballanche, L. C. de Saint-Martin, and Wronski have the right to this recognition in France—even more than Alfred de Musset or Henri Murger? Any given source study, without meaning to do so initially, can lead to many changes of viewpoint and courses of study—when it does not confine itself only to those influences close at hand or only those that are remote. Viatte's legacy has been greatly enriched by the critical studies of Professor Ayrault on German Romanticism and also by those of Professor Max Milner on French Romanticism. In reading them, one realizes how much the writings and ideas of philosophers—theosophists or illuminists—or even the anonymous treatises that are of little literary value about magic, demonology, "animal magnetism" and witchcraft, all blended together. This blending together—which took place during the very gestation period of Romanticism between 1750 and 1850–occurred to such an extent that one cannot always separate the wheat from the chaff.

In starting my own research into the "esoteric and occult sources of Symbolism in Europe," following the previously cited critical essays, I adopted a different methodology at the very start—a more pragmatic one, paying particular attention on the one hand to the history of revival movements descended from occult and initiate traditions, and on the other hand to the analysis of individual works and also works in journals and periodicals that are considered as a corpus. A rereading of these

works justified comparisons with esoteric themes and ideas, these having been too often neglected by the historical criticism of the 1860–1918
period—a trajectory going from Baudelaire to Apollinaire in France,
from Swinburne to Yeats in Great Britain, and from Wagner to Rilke in
Germany . . . . It seemed to me that as my approach widened in time
and space, that a new image of the "Symbolist" movement emerged—on
a European, perhaps American, but especially South American scale.
This image was going well beyond the literary school that was created in
France in 1886 and rapidly contested before later being salvaged by the
memorialists of the time. An extended and deepened image emerged—
one of an immense change of objectives, of the language used and also of
the poet's situation within Western society—changes delayed in varying
degrees according to the country in question. Moreover, this alteration
reached prose, by extending to the short story, the essay, and the novel,
and was characterized by an abundance and originality of journals, periodicals, and albums . . . all competing from Paris to St. Petersburg and
London to Madrid. My preliminary investigation into the conditions in
which the occult and esoteric renewal tallied with this transformation of
the *poétique* of the authors finally led me to the research the Symbolist
characteristics across Europe. This tallying also justified my abandonment of the traditional classifications in order to bring about some often
unexpected regrouping within the countries involved. Symbolism tried
to deliver a "poetic message" in France (according to Professor G. Mi-
chaud), all while undergoing a value crisis shortly after its appearance, a
crisis which caused it to become diluted in both important and minor
works at the beginning of the twentieth century (according to Professor
Michel Décaudin). It nevertheless spread across Europe and beyond,
for several decades. It left its imprint on personalities who then went
beyond its first fundamental ideas, like Rilke, Aleksandr Blok, Andreï
Biely, Endre Ady, T. S. Eliot, Ruben Darío, André Gide, Milosz, etc.
Later, this was the case of the poets who developed after a rather long
Surrealist period under the influence of André Breton. We have fol-
lowed the birth of works by those artists who were the forerunners of
the 1860–1880 years and those who were heirs to the 1900–1918 years.
All things considered, it is not very important ultimately if most of these
artists did not claim as part of their heritage the manifesto of Jean
Moréas. Either they wrote before the time of this succinct manifesto,
written in a Paris *brasserie*, or they did not recognize themselves in it.
Moreover, the popular notions—that Symbolism is supposed to be of
French origin or of a purely Nordic, Anglo-Saxon, or Slavic development—must be revised. These notions apply only to a limited part of
the movement under discussion. There is proof of this in the importance

of these so-called Symbolist imprints and their resurgences in a Latin country like Rumania, and their branching out as far as the work of the Italian Dino Campana, works that are closely related to those of Nerval and Rimbaud or even the Greek A. Sikelianos, in the very heart of the twentieth century. The recent publications and research on the art that derived from Gustave Moreau, the English Pre-Raphaelites, Böcklin, or Max Klinger (carried on in England, Belgium, and France), showed that there existed within these works an aesthetics of parallel destinies, depending on the area of Europe: Viennese Secessionism, the Parisian *Nabis*, English Aestheticism, Art Nouveau, etc.—all the possible nuances were there, according to the locale. This is without mentioning the unclassifiables—such as the American J. McNeill Whistler, who lived in Europe and was Mallarmé's friend and was also enamored of spiritualistic experiences, this being a characteristic not shared with the Impressionists.

At a certain point of this investigation into the "hidden" sources of Symbolism, it would be tempting to mark out its boundaries according to the ties and exchanges that these poets, prose writers, and artists maintained (or did not maintain) with each other. Indeed, was it not under the auspices of the Order of the Rose-Croix ("renovated" by Joséphin "Sâr" Péladan) that the annual art exhibits took place in Paris and even in Brussels? These Salons de la Rose-Croix brought together, as early as 1892 many painters and sculptors we now call "Symbolists." However, the Dutch Thorn Prikker did not exhibit there even though he was a friend of Péladan. The connections between these artists and the adepts, secret societies, brotherhoods, mystical orders, and groups claiming any kinship with esoterism, are as a matter of fact considerably less admitted—and less confirmed—than one would be inclined to believe. It may or may not be important to know that Saint-Pol-Roux, Elémir Bourges, and Erik Satie joined for a while Péladan's Order of the Rose-Croix, but at any rate I will not draw any conclusions that would permit a different reading of their works . . . . But it is not the same case if we note the membership of Yeats and Aleister Crowley in the Golden Dawn (taking into account the inferiority of Crowley as a poet), especially in light of the numerous and more and more elaborate essays and articles on this subject published in English during the past fifteen years. We should be very careful in our critical approach to the authors when we weigh the importance of their attitudes *vis-à-vis* esoteric circles or clubs. This is a principle that we must not lose sight of, while elucidating—with as much objectivity as possible—the literary value and scope of the texts, which really do not depend on the author's submersion into esoterism. This seems clear, but needs to be kept in mind. . . .

The concepts of marginality, suspicion, outlawing, and finally malediction seem to apply (as early as the 1860s, which saw the advance of scientism and naturalism) to a certain category of poets (best examples— Edgar Allan Poe and Baudelaire) and writings related to the *sciences maudites*—that is, not reducible to the official scientific policy. Parallelism is tempting and had, it just so happens, been emphasized by A. Rolland de Renéville. But it was, in effect, Stanislas de Guaita, author of the *Essais des sciences maudites*, the most scholarly summary of the material in the 1890s, also renovator (with and later against Péladan) of the Rosicrucians in France, who had as a friend and direct disciple the poet Edouard Dubus. And Dubus—who died young from a heroin overdose—can be counted as one of the "*maudits*" of Symbolism. Yet nothing in Dubus's elegiac poems allows the least trace of initiate knowledge to show through, nor any ambition to go beyond a musical and decadent intimism. Thus, the monumental work (as well as the library) of de Guaita remained quite outside the actual poetics of the adept, who was either little experienced or psychically too frail. Erudition, scholarly readings, and the frequenting of such company determines only relatively the poet's intrinsic creative power. Tristan Corbière, another *poète maudit*, appears to have had no dealings with the occultists and esoterists (except that he did listen to those Breton sea tales, often based on occult traditions), yet he wrote a unique work, of a force and verbal and syntactic originality that Dubus never attained in his relationship with de Guaita. Jules Laforgue, as spontaneous and individualistic as Corbière, had as a friend and favorite correspondent a certain Charles Henry, one of the scholars who was most open to esoteric philosophy and its new aesthetic applications. We are lost in conjecture however, as to the impact the ideas of Henry would have had on the texts of Laforgue; and it is a pity that the letters from Henry to Laforgue have not been preserved, whereas the letters from Laforgue to Henry (of little significance, after all) were all published . . . . [2] The examples I just mentioned show to what point individual creation can elude, or resist certain simplistic methods of literary criticism, which under the circumstances would explain the appearance of great works of the "Symbolist" times by the influence of (or general attraction to) the themes, myths, and problems of esoterism.[3]

In approaching any written work of the Symbolist era, it is not really essential that the critic seek to discover the degree of initiation the author reached in matters of alchemy, astrology, the Kabalah, "animal magnetism," etc. . . . It is however, essential to find out how and why— in what manner and toward what goal—the writer tackled, connected together, or delved into the works that were envisaged. The study of documents in archives, correspondence (published or unpublished), and of contemporary testimonies, can therefore be of appreciable assistance. Such is the case with Stéphane Mallarmé, who was not called the "sphinx of the Rue de Rome" for nothing. In his published work there are few manifestations of his tastes or his later aspirations towards traditional esoterism, except for the rare use of words like "arcane" and "alchemy," which certainly did not appear by chance in parts of his important prose works. Was not poetry the only possible religion for Mallarmé? Attempts have been made to interpret the syntax (especially verb position) of Mallarmé's verse and also the ideal of the one and only "Book" towards which the entire work of a poet must lead, by means of the Kabalah and its derivatives. The constant presence of allusions to funeral rites in *Poésies* gave rise to varying conjectures. We learn several things from the *Correspondance* published by Professor L. J. Austin: that Mallarmé was in correspondence with the Egyptologist Eugène Lefébure; that Villiers de l'Isle-Adam had recommended the reading of Eliphas Lévi to him; that he wrote a brief but significant commentary to the poet and hermetist Victor-Emile Michelet concerning Michelet's essay *De l'Esotérisme dans l'art*; and that he wrote in warm words to Edouard Schuré to congratulate him on his *Grands Initiés*. We know also that he associated with the bookseller Edmond Bailly, who specialized in esoteric books and was an intermediary between artists, poets, and occultists of the time. On the other hand, the completely published correspondence between Mallarmé and Henri Cazalis (Jean Lahor) reveals nothing about the neo-Buddhism this Parnassian poet-doctor shows in his writings. These facts are useful if collected together or linked up with other more well-known facts, but obviously do not exhaust the complexity of Mallarmé's works.

The theory of the poet or narrator finding almost intuitively the ways and truths that would be indicated by esoteric conditions and occult practices is certainly not without foundation. There are examples in ancient civilizations and early societies of identification between the sacred text reserved for adepts, the magical formula, the incantation or exorcism, and what we consider today to be the very essence of poetry (the Orphic hymns, the Egyptian *Book of the Dead* . . .). Language, thus cut off from its utilitarian or didactic function, assumes an initiating quality, accessible to only a few, a tangible link between the invisible world—the "supernatural"—and the immediate surroundings. The poet is thus quite naturally a sort of "medium," more or less unconsciously, someone who translates according to his genius what the "*bouche d'ombre*" says, to go back to Victor Hugo's expression. This concept of the poet as a messenger, a prophet, a clairvoyant, an interpreter, or a magus, was current from Hugo to Surrealism, by way of Rimbaud and Symbolism; but it was strongly attacked by Roger Caillois (*Les impostures de la poésie*) and René Etiemble (*Poètes/Faiseurs*). In the name of rationalism, they both denounced the idea that the poet possesses a quasi-irrational creative power, one that is driven by "supernatural," "semidivine," or "diabolical" forces over which he has no control. Rimbaud's idea that the "*Je est un autre*" is once again called into question, but with no resulting clarification of the particularities of the author's approach, nor of those characteristics which saw it overtake, in certain inspired moments, the methods of the hermetist and the sorcerer.

Whether we be philosophers, esoterists, linguists, semiologists, psychoanalysts, or critics from the school of Kristeva and Todorov, we risk misunderstandings when we use the words "Symbolism" or "the Symbolic" as nouns that suggest a whole network of multiple signifiers. Would not these misunderstandings in fact prevent a consensus—even a partial one—on the signifiers? Ernst Cassirer and Jung have shown the coherence of symbols in both literary creation and in the "collective unconscious." The works of both men have the rigor and the required breadth of vision that is often characteristic of German Swiss scholars. Bachelard has more subtly linked up the major universal symbols (water, earth, fire, air) to the intuitions and reveries of modern poets. This criticism confines itself to the application of a set of themes to a text in order to "decode" it. The themes, or sets of themes, are the results of generalities about these symbols. Without a certain Bachelardian finesse, however, there is an obvious danger in this type of criticism—narrowness of the field of application. Personally, I am more attracted to the type of criticism done by Jean-Pierre Bayard (*La Symbolique du feu, La Symbolique des Rose-Croix . . .*). Bayard is an historian who is devoted to the values of traditional hermetics but at the same time is open to those parts of civilization and culture that are outside the boundaries of esoterism. I also like the works of René Alleau—whose initial scientific background (and the support of Breton) saved him from extrapolations and simplifications that were just too standard, too run-of-the mill, for those who write about hermetic subjects. This period of the nineteenth century was, essentially, the subject matter of my research. In looking back, we must remember the often vastly different efforts of theorists and poets who tried to establish a network of analogies between human nature and the symbols which surround it. From Wronski to Lacuria, by way of C. Fourier, J. A. Vaillant, and E. Lévi, it is the same endeavor—to re-establish a *lost unity*. This is the goal, no matter what is involved—physics, linguistics, math, sociology, or the Kabalah; and methods are used which go beyond rationalism or the logic of contemporary philosophical systems. These tendencies do not just come to the surface with the French authors that I just cited. Confining myself to nineteenth-century Europe, I find them in Great Britain, Russia, Poland, and Germany. Messianic reveries, austere treatises, frenzied ideas of utopia—tendencies that are either contradictory, oblivious of one another, or sometimes even complementary. Despite the differences, they all hope to attain a certain Absolute. Wronski's "prognometer," a forerunner of Saint-Yves-d'Alveydre's "archeometer," is the perfect materialization of this Absolute. Letters of the alphabet, numbers, vowels and consonants all refer to a whole system of signifiers, of a symbolic or rather an analogical nature. The stars, the elements, animals, plants, minerals—they too form part of the general framework of "*correspondances*" or correlations with the psychophysiological image of man: feelings, sensitivity, imagination. Hermetists identify this correspondence with the relationship between the macrocosm and the microcosm. Analogical thought suggests correlations between colors, odors, sounds, flavors and the sense of touch—in the hands of a poet this became Baudelaire's sonnet "*Correspondances*."

Analogical thought does not develop freely when one is fully awake— changes must be made in order for the mind to truly soar, changes which free the Imaginary and permit the rediscovery of basic archetypes. The mind must be plunged into a dream state—induced or unintentional—or placed in one of those states between the waking dream and heightened mental concentration. It is from this point of view that the numerous teatises published since the 1850s about hypnosis, "animal magnetism," sleepwalking, etc. seem so valuable to us. The treatises by Cahagnet, Deleuze, Delaage and especially Albert de Rochas are important, however incorrect or faulty they would seem to a twentieth-century scientist. Around 1860 the works of Alfred Maury were very widespread in France. He studied sleep and dreams, and also fairy tales and folk legends, books that concern the occult while avoiding its most irrational aspects. Maury (recently republished) is in more than one way the precursor of Freud, Jung, and modern psychoanalysis. It is not really essential to know whether or not the poets of the 1860s, 1870s, or 1880s even read any of this abundant literature. Baudelaire and others felt the need to resort to mild drugs (hashish) in order to have free access to the zones of "free circulation of the spirit and of the sensations," which supposedly favored poetic inspiration. Théophile Gautier and the little known poets Antoine Monnier and Ange Pechméja also used drugs for inspiration and must be mentioned as being among those rare forerunners of Symbolist poetry.[4] Philosophical considerations based on the use of drugs, transcendental meditation, or mysticism of

the Timothy Leary/Alan Watts type would certainly not be found among
the Romantics of the second or third generation. The interests of many
of these poets stood in contrast with other concerns—"readability," formal recognition, and of course, artistic lucidity. These concerns were
the lot of a large part of European poets, whether they aim for commu-
nicability with the masses or whether they stayed with *"l'Art pour l'Art"*
theory of the Parnassiens.

The role of mediator between the environment of esoteric theories
and that of the poet was transmitted to a handful of authors. Between
1848 and 1870 their position was ambiguous, difficult and sometimes
uncomfortable—I have already discussed Eliphas Lévi. The French and
comparative literature specialist might for example be interested in Al-
phonse Esquiros and Ange Pechméja, both of whom were in touch with
Baudelaire for some time. Both wrote in French, but were driven out of
France for political reasons; Esquiros traveled to Holland, Great Britain,
and Ireland, Pechméja to Rumania and Turkey. Esquiros was one of the
first to advocate the principle of creation by *analogy* and to bring the
idea of "animal magnetism" to the attention of the poets. In Bucharest,
Pechméja explored in long, unfinished segments "the world of dreams,"
as he called it, and also hashish. In *L'Oeuf de Kneph* (Bucharest, 1864),
he applied the ideas of the Kabalah and the *"epoptique"* of his teacher
(Vaillant) to linguistics and the symbolics of words. Politics interested
Esquiros and Pechméja more than literature and esoterism, and their
poetical writings did not go as far as their theories foreshadowed. In his
own way, each demonstrated the difficulty of being a major poet and a
true adept in hermetism at the same time. Towards the end of the
nineteenth century, there were quite a few specialists in esoteric subjects who also wrote poems according to the current fashion, especially
in France. Except for Marc Haven, however, a neo-Martinist who published a beautiful lyric suite, and the Russian Vladimir Soloviev, most of
this poetry was of small value for today's reader. Soloviev is an exceptional case and is worth being pointed out. He was a philosopher satu-
rated with gnosis and theosophy and a major poet of the Russian Symbolist movement, a mentor of Alexander Blok and Andreï Biely. The
amazing thing with Soloviev is that the profound knowledge and scholarship reflected in his extensive prose work did not hamper poetic sponta-
neity. Moreover, he was not the only who was doing this in the literary
circles of St. Petersburg or Moscow.

As the nineteenth century wound towards its finish, and communications methods became modern, these "intermediaries" became pilgrims
of a sort, lecturers, people with a message to deliver. While they did
not have the same contacts with the public that the ideologues or

revolutionaries did, they were no longer hermits or the recluse ancho-
rites which people conjured up when they thought about hermetics, at
least until the end of the eighteenth century. The Italian Angelo de
Gubernatis lived in India and the Far East for long time before spread-
ing his ideas in Rome and Florence. Joséphin Péladan, the Sâr, traveled all over Europe, from the Netherlands to Rumania, in order to
disperse his ideas about the Rosicrucian revival, and everywhere he
went he met artists and poets. Edouard Schuré's works and actions
extended well beyond the *Grands Initiés* to touch upon Wagnerism,
tales of the fantastic, and the idealist theater. He too was a tireless
traveler and lecturer: from Berlin to Bayreuth to Greece, Sicily, and
the Middle East, he accumulated impressions and experiences that
confirmed his interpretations of Germanic legends, Orphic hymns, or
even of Fabre d'Olivet. His sensitivity as an artist and his intuitions as
a reformer of the theater made Schuré (a product of both German and
French cultures) a rather remarkable example of those mediators who
facilitated the circulation of esoteric ideas among poets and aesthetes.
The span of his dispersal of ideas was perhaps limited by the few
contacts he had with the Anglo-Saxon world, although he had met
William Crookes in London.

After 1900, it was Rudolf Steiner who organized lecture cycles in
Germany, Scandinavia, and France. These lectures drew large audiences until he withdrew to Dornach to build his Goetheanum. The
artists and poets who received the full Steinerian teaching belonged to
vastly different linguistic fields; they never truly formed a Steinerian
school of poetry, and in many cases were oblivious of each other. It is
only because of their common attraction for the esoteric philosophy of
Steiner that I have combined the German Christian Morgenstern, the
Russian Andreï Biely and the Italian Arturo Onofri. Except for Biely,
the post-1900 relations of the other poets with French Symbolism are
tenuous. Morgenstern is linked with "cosmic poetry," closer to Novalis's
German Romanticism than Mallarmé's works. Onofri, aesthetically related to Valéry, was almost as isolated in Italy as Dino Campana. All
things considered, they seemed to me to be more truly representative of
Symbolist poetry than many other "Symbolist" poets. At the risk of
deviating from the chronological and geographic limits given by literary
history, the critic needs to use these comparisons—with an intermediary
like Steiner for example—in order to splinter the frozen molds of
schools, manifestos, and movements.

The ideas, practices, and doctrines of an esoteric nature were spread
relatively easily across Europe and even from continent to continent,
adapting to the ways of the country involved. This gave them an interna-

tional scope that often erased the language barrier, local traditions, and to a certain extent religious or nonreligious customs (Catholicism, Protestantism, Orthodoxy, and Islam in Turkey). The case of the Czech poet Julius Zeyer is typical here; in spite of his Slavic background he became interested in Druidic rites of the Celts, just as were people in Great Britain, Ireland, or Brittany. August Strindberg, first under the influence of the eighteenth-century visionary Swedenborg, met in Paris his initiator into alchemy, P. Jollivet-Castelot. In addition, he had read Vial and Tiffereau—all before writing *Inferno* and *Légendes*. Both of these works are masterpieces of Symbolist prose in my opinion, even though Strindberg is usually classified with the Naturalists or the Expressionists. In Europe, only Spain remained apart, suspicious of heterodox tendencies, refusing any intrusion which could attack its strict Catholicism.

There were certainly some occult philosophies and secret fraternities which thrived only in Anglo-Saxon territories and had very little hold elsewhere. For example, there was the Theosophism (the term coined by René Guénon) of Madame Blavatsky, which had some adepts in Russia, but spread essentially in England and the United States. This form of neo-Buddhism or esoteric Buddhism probably found most of its adepts in the English readers of Leadbeater, Olcott, and Annie Besant. The Irish poet Æ (George Russell) seems to have been more influenced by her than his countryman Yeats. The Golden Dawn, by which Yeats was even more impressed, remained strictly British, although its founder "MacGregor" Mathers had lived in the Paris literary milieu and although "Le Vril" and the "OTO," both offshoots of the Golden Dawn, had started out in Germany. The neo-Martinism of Papus (Dr. Encausse) sought to find correspondents throughout the world, especially in Czarist Russia, where Joseph de Maistre, an adept of Saint-Martin, had lived and disseminated his doctrines at the beginning of the nineteenth century. Around 1900, however, his influence affected mostly the Paris and Lyons regions. It nevertheless indirectly affected spiritualist Freemasonry (the unofficial variety which was not affiliated to the *Grand Orient de France*) which was stronger in Western civilization.

The considerations set forth here led me, as I widened my fields of research, to a comparativism on two levels. The first concerns traditions, organizations, fraternities, teachings, etc., all related, in one degree or another, to esoterism and the occult. The other concerns literary (especially poetic) products, according to the usual methods of

comparative literature—by specific linguistic or geographic "domains."
I like the term "domains" because it reminds me of Valery Larbaud's
cosmopolitanism, in spite of the fact that these domains are far from
coinciding with the separation or binding together of esoteric
"sources." The main stumbling block of such a double-acting methodology is that it produces many useless repetitions. This can be avoided
by determining from the very outset the actual level of impregnation—
semantic or philosophical—of so-called occult themes in the text being
read.

I would like to say that there are a number of "Symbolist" poets and
prose writers who were only superficially preoccupied with all these
matters. That is, they really did not investigate them deeply. Thus it
was with satanism, witchcraft, and sorcery, with their spell casting and
their picturesque witches' sabbaths; although the "demoniacal" aspect
was inwardly lived by some of them, especially in Portugal. In France,
I have pointed out poets such as Maurice Rollinat and Jean Richepin. I
have done so in spite of the oblivion into which these poets have
fallen, because they had, outside of France, a much larger influence
than Rimbaud, Cros, or Corbière, who were unknown for a long time.
Widely spread and translated, Rollinat and Richepin, for example, had
readers in Central Europe (e.g. Hungary). Among those readers were
poets who belonged more directly to "Symbolism." The climate of
witchcraft, black magic, and malediction was more discernible in the
so-called decadent authors, like Jean Lorrain or the Belgian Iwan Gil-
kin. With the Swedes, Norwegians, Poles, and Lithuanians, this climate was related to folk legends. At this level, it is still possible to
speak of "occult sources" although it is a question of a substratum with
no specifically stated intellectual or philosophical contents. The recurrence of certain terms from witchcraft and diabolism justifies treating
these works in my study, although true "verbal alchemy" is often absent. The occult, and not only its dark side, thus had only one importance with European poets—it is of a decorative value, i.e., outside the
content. When the satanic or luciferian background of the poem sub-
sists on a deeply felt anguish, we reach the Fantastic, a genre illustrated by the short story, novelette, or novel more often than by true
poetry. This was the direction taken by the English writer James
Thomson in *The City of Dreadful Night*, Victor Hugo in *La fin de
Satan,* Lautréamont in *Chants de Maldoror,* and quite differently by
Alexis Tolstoï and Sologub in Russia. The Italian Carducci and the
Sicilian Rapisardi introduced too much rhetoric and too little mystery
to interest the modern reader.

At other levels of cultural impregnation or inner experience, we are face to face with poets of one of two persuasions. First there are the poets who totally assimilated the lessons of the hermetists, gnostics, and Kabalah experts, having read some of these works before composing their own *"poétique;"* for example, Louis Ménard (*Rêveries d'un payen mystique*), who has been "re-established" by Henri Peyre.[5] Then there are those poets who almost instinctively adopted an approach that in writing and in ethics recalls that of the initiate, undergoing several tests, such as passage through inferno, before reaching the supreme moment when poetry and enlightenment are one. This is called Orphism and is illustrated by Rimbaud, Mallarmé, Rilke, G. Fröding, and somewhat doubtfully Claudel (at least in his early period).

In tackling the investigation into esoteric and occult sources of a period and of linguistic zones that were of necessity somewhat restricted, I did not want to indulge in a mere game that would have no other purpose than the game. I have tried to show that "Symbolism" (if indeed one is forced to limit oneself to a term which served only as a reference) was not a sealed movement, closed in on antiquated affectation, the last offspring of Romanticism. This idea has been asserted on several occasions. To the contrary, it had deep roots in all of Western culture and was a major contribution to the birth of modern revolutions in poetic writing—expressionism, imagism, Surrealism, etc. . . . What is more, one can recognize these same features, ones which give a fresh dimension to the esoteric background, in certain works of major twentieth-century poets such as Apollinaire, Milosz, Cendrars, L. P. Fargue, Antonin Artaud, André Breton, J. L. Borges, and Ezra Pound. A long and patient study could be envisaged for the critic who would like to introduce one or several comparative methodologies into his own problematics. What I tried to establish, *vis-à-vis* European poetry, was a sort of progressive synthesis that could be applied to North and South American literature, and if need be, on a worldwide scale. Certain isolated works and those mediators who were neglected are worth being reread and rediscovered. With the necessary perspective and a new approach, contemporary poetry could also conceivably be lectured from this angle. The question of the presence of esoteric roots also poses the problem of the final purpose of poetic writing in the writer's own destiny and in his rapport with society. Is not the search for the Word a sort of quest for the Holy Grail or the Philosopher's Stone? Some might wonder "what good is it?" And when all is said and done, is it wisdom or folly?

Translated from the French by Joyce J. Sulger

Notes

1. Special studies are always useful when they establish unknown connections between great works and esoterism; for example, a recent study by Professor Jean-Pierre Lassalle of the University of Toulouse on *"Alfred de Vigny et la Franc-Maçonnerie."*
2. Very few of Charles Henry's letters—published or unpublished—can be found in French archives. It would have been useful to know something about his correspondence with Gustave Kahn and Paul Valéry, for example. Note that it is American (and not French) researchers and academics who pay particular attention to the personality, the work, and the influence of Charles Henry, both in literature and in art.
3. Notice, however, that T. S. Eliot, the main heir in English to Laforgue and Corbière, placed *The Waste Land* in the context of the search for the Holy Grail.
4. A French researcher, M. Arnould de Liederkerke, recently wrote a paper *"Les drogues et les poètes symbolistes et décadents"* ("Drugs and the Symbolist and Decadent Poets"). This was directed by Professor Décaudin and merits publication.
5. And during true Symbolist period: the Belgians Max Elskamp and M. Maeterlinck.

Works by Alain Mercier Related to this Article

Les Sources ésotériques et occultes de la poésie symboliste.
    Vol. I: *Le Symbolisme français*, Paris, 1969.
    Vol. II: *Le Symbolisme européen*, Paris, 1974.
Eliphas Lévi et la pensée magique au XIXe siècle, Paris, 1974.

M. E. Grenander

MACBETH AS DIAPHTHORODY: NOTES TOWARD THE DEFINITION OF A FORM

Macbeth poses a fundamental problem for the aesthetician. Modern readers as disparate as the composer Ernest Bloch, the anthropologist Loren Eiseley, the poet Kenneth Rexroth, and the cinéaste Roman Polanski have testified to its enduring power. And yet the recurring challenge, as A. C. Bradley long ago recognized and as Rexroth has reaffirmed, is that Shakespeare's play does not fit the criteria for a tragedy laid down in Aristotle's *Poetics*. Lily Bess Campbell, who referred to *Hamlet, Othello,* and *King Lear* as "tragedies" (of, respectively, Grief, Jealousy, and Wrath in Old Age), neatly sidestepped the issue in *Macbeth* by calling it a "study" (in Fear). Most critics have nevertheless tried to explain this drama (and other similar works) according to the Aristotelian theory of tragedy. Their attempt is subsumed under a larger problem, outlined by Bernard Beckerman: the disproportion in critical refinement between the *Poetics* and the primitive theories attempting to describe alternate dramatic species. Beckerman therefore calls for "a comprehensive theory which encompasses but goes beyond the Aristotelian and yet within which individual works can be located."[1] This can be developed only by examining those dramas which do not yield to Aristotelian analysis. For this reason, *Macbeth* raises questions of a special kind, perennially fascinating to those who wish to extend critical theory in the direction of greater flexibility and subtlety. If one assumes that criticism must follow creation—that the critic's job is not to lay down *a priori* rules, but to examine the workings of a play which experience has shown to be effective—then evidently *Macbeth* requires us to develop some aesthetic principles that have not heretofore been formulated.

In recent years, four critics—Francis Fergusson, Julian Markels,

Wayne C. Booth, and R. S. Crane—have essayed Aristotelian examina-
tions of *Macbeth*. The attempts of Fergusson and Markels are unsatisfac-
tory, for reasons I shall point out. Those of Booth and Crane, which rest
on a penetrating understanding of Aristotle, are good but limited. As
both Campbell and Virgil K. Whitaker have demonstrated, a discussion
of *Macbeth* according to Aristotle must include the *Nicomachean Ethics*,
since certain concepts and terms not mentioned in the *Poetics* are necessary if one is to grapple successfully with *Macbeth* according to Aristotelian criteria.[2] This paper therefore undertakes to examine the grounds
for this necessity, to discuss those concepts required for an adequate
Aristotelian analysis of *Macbeth*, and to propose the term *diaphthorody*
for its form.

Fergusson's attempt to interpret *Macbeth* according to Aristotle is
inadequate largely because he misinterprets *action* as the "purpose" or
"motive" governing the psyche (85–86). It is true that the following
passage occurs in Chapter 6(2) of the *Poetics:* "All human happiness or
misery takes the form of action; the end for which we live [i.e., happiness, explained in the *Ethics* as living in a virtuous way] is a certain kind
of activity, not a quality." Aristotle, however, makes abundantly clear
that by dramatic action he means a sequence of incidents or episodes.
He refers explicitly to the action as "the combination of the incidents, or
things done in the story." A tragedy, he says, "is an imitation of an
action that is complete in itself, as a whole of some magnitude . . .
which has beginning, middle, and end . . . , with its several incidents so
closely connected that the transposal or withdrawal of any one of them
will disjoin and dislocate the whole."[3]

Markels' essay also rests on a misinterpretation of Aristotle, in his case
a double one. He ignores Aristotle's threefold division of the sciences,
and he expands Aristotle's term *Spectacle* to include imitation. The first
of these confusions is fundamental. Aristotle applied different criteria
and different rules of evidence to different kinds of disciplines: the
theoretic sciences (like metaphysics, mathematics, and the natural sciences); the practical sciences (ethics and politics), which deal with action
and conduct; and the productive sciences (such as poetics), which aim at
making artificial things.[4] Aristotle never lost sight of this distinction. For
example, at the beginning of the *Nicomachean Ethics*, he says: "Every
art and every inquiry . . . is thought to aim at some good . . . . But a
certain difference is found among ends; some are activities [as in ethics
and politics], others are products apart from the activities that produce
them [as in the *Poetics*]. Where there are ends apart from the actions, it
is the nature of the products to be better than the activities."[5] For
Aristotle, then, a tragedy was a made object that resulted from the

poetic process, and he described the way in which it was constructed by an examination of actual artifacts, or existing tragedies.

Markels' failure to understand the place of the productive sciences in this basic division underlies his challenges (pp. 294–295) to Aristotle's "ambivalence of conception" concerning tragedy. He is also guilty of a second oversimplification of the *Poetics*, a reduction of imitation to Spectacle. Aristotle points out that once the poet has chosen the incidents of his action he then decides how to represent them (*Poetics*, 17). In Markels' version, this becomes the ground for saying (p. 297) that "Spectacle is a functional element" because "probability and the arousal of the tragic emotions depend upon the poet's choice of episodes to represent directly rather than to narrate." But the "choice of episodes to represent directly rather than to narrate" is a function not of Spectacle but of imitation. Once the confusion between them is firmly fixed in Markels' mind, however, he charges Aristotle with underplaying the importance of Spectacle.

Aristotle does indeed regard it as the least important and least artistic element of tragedy; and it occupies sixth place on his list (plot, character, thought, diction, melody, and spectacle). As Markels (pp. 301, 296) finds particularly annoying, he considers it part of the "visual trappings and machinery" whose mounting is more the province of the stage manager and the costume-maker than the poet. Believing that every discipline should be handled on its own terms, he thought that Spectacle was not something to be treated in detail in a treatise on poetics. The limit of a play's length, "so far as that is relative to public performances . . . , does not fall within the theory of poetry." But Aristotle is perhaps not quite so contemptuous of Spectacle, even in its true sense, as Markels seems to think. He speaks of both Spectacle and Music as "not inconsiderable" additions to the other elements of a tragedy, and he drops his discussion of them because, he says, he had already said enough elsewhere about rules "for such points of stage-effect as directly depend on the art of the poet" (his reference is to the lost dialogue *On Poets*).

Nevertheless, he felt that it is better to arouse the tragic fear and pity and achieve their catharsis through the "very structure and incidents of the play" than through the Spectacle. "The Plot in fact should be so framed that, even without seeing" the movement of actors on the stage, anyone who hears an account of the events, or reads the play, will feel horror and pity at the incidents. "To produce this same effect by means of the Spectacle is less artistic, and requires extraneous aid" (*Poetics*, 6[2], 7, 14, 15, 26). Markels can accept none of this. His animadversions on Aristotle's discussion of Spectacle draw him into the *cul de sac* of saying (p. 295) that in *Macbeth*, "the gross visual trappings of the imita-tion" are *"indispensable"* (italics mine) to the tragic catharsis—a state-ment that contradicts not only Bradley (p. 284), but all experience and common sense, as anyone who has read the play can verify. And his position leads him eventually to the curious conclusion (pp. 302–303) that Spectacle usurps the function of Plot at the close of *Macbeth*, a usurpation he regards as necessary because "the degenerative tragedy must end in a wild spectacle that signifies merely nothing."

Markels nevertheless makes one statement with which I am in whole-hearted agreement. He says (p. 294) that if Aristotle's *Poetics* is "to retain and perhaps enlarge its relevance," we must be aware of its limitations in order to develop its potentialities. Precisely. Granted that Aristotle has given us a perceptive and useful account of the way trage-dies are constructed and how they operate, he could not, by the very nature of his approach, describe a kind of play which had not yet been written, for the data of his investigation were always existing works of art. Obviously an examination like his can go only as far as the empirical data on which it rests; that is, extant dramatic works. If different kinds of works come into existence, we cannot apply the *Poetics* to them without change. But what we can do, if we understand the method of Aristotle, is to approach them in the spirit of Aristotle, modifying certain princi-ples of the *Poetics* in order to arrive at a deeper understanding of dra-matic forms unknown to the Peripatetics of the Lyceum.

It is for this reason that *Macbeth*, rather than—say—*Lear* or *Othello*, which *can* be handled with the criteria of the *Poetics*, is of special interest to the critic interested in broadening the scope of theory. But our scrutiny of Aristotle must result first in a comprehension of what he says, for surely we cannot arrive at any awareness of his limitations if we cannot interpret what he has already done. And it is at this point that both Fergusson and Markels have failed. When we turn to the essay by Booth, however, and the remarks by Crane, we find critics who do, indeed, pick up where Aristotle left off.

I

Certain assumptions about the nature of knowledge underlie the *Poetics*. One of Aristotle's greatest contributions to human thought was the doc-trine of multiple causation: the explanation of a given effect in terms of four causes: (1) the material cause, the "matter or substratum" from which a thing comes; (2) the formal cause, its essence, form, or arche-type; (3) the efficient cause, the "source of the change or coming to rest"; (4) the final cause, the good which is the end or purpose for whose sake generation and change occur.[6] We might explain this theory as it relates to the productive sciences—the ones we are interested in—by using it to account for some common object like a chair. The material cause of our chair is the wood out of which it is made; the formal cause, the blueprint or other design followed in its construction; the efficient cause, the carpenter who makes it; and the final cause, getting something we can sit on. In the productive sciences the final cause is of overriding importance. We would never be content with a chair we could not sit on, no matter how precious its material, how beautiful its design, or how skilled its carpenter. We would prefer a sturdy upturned box to a chair too small, or too fragile, or too uncomfortable to implement the final cause which motivated its construction.

An understanding of this complex causation is particularly important today, for since the Renaissance, the theory has been gradually eroded until most of us, when we think of cause-and-effect, think in terms of the efficient cause only.[7] In the *Poetics*, however, Aristotle uses all four causes to describe the way in which tragedies are made. The efficient cause (the poet) operates with the material cause (object, means, and manner) according to the formal cause (appropriate principles of construction) to effect the final cause (a catharsis of pity and fear). The objects are plot, character, and thought; the means are diction and melody; and the manner is a dramatic mode of imitation, including spectacle. The final cause is the purgation, through pity and fear, of those emotions. The *Poetics* is thus an account of the design, or pattern, which informs the material in order to produce a work which will effect a catharsis of pity and fear. If other emotions are involved, then we will not have a tragedy; for example, amusement will result from a comedy, whose design or formal cause will be quite different from the one outlined in the *Poetics*, even though we may have a somewhat similar material cause.

Aristotle (*Poetics*, 14, 13) makes quite clear that by "tragedy" he means *only* a work which will arouse pity and fear, "its own proper pleasure." We should not require other kinds of pleasure from a tragedy, since the imitation of actions arousing fear and pity is its distinctive function. The *Poetics*, then, is an analysis showing how those plays have been constructed, with what kinds of plots and what kinds of characters, which do in fact arouse and effect a catharsis of pity and fear. A work that does not arouse these specific emotions is not a tragedy, by Aristotle's definition, and his criteria do not fit it. This is not to say that parts of the *Poetics* may not be salvaged in order to deal with it; but other parts must be changed or modified if we are to have an analysis, *using*

Aristotelian methodology, of a kind of work which Aristotle himself did not describe.

II

Both Crane and Booth were well aware that however much convention may have dictated calling *Macbeth*, a tragedy it is not one in the classic Aristotelian sense. Certain modifications must accordingly be made in the critical apparatus with which we approach it. And both critics treated its emotional effect very gingerly, for it is just here, as they obviously realized, that the distinction lies between such a play and those works described by Aristotle as tragedies. Crane used the terms *pity* and *fear* in describing *Macbeth*, but he was clearly not happy with them. He said (pp. 171–172) that although the form cannot be stated in "strictly Aristotelian terms," it involves "the arousal and catharsis of painful emotions . . . for which the terms pity and fear are not entirely inapplicable." Again, he said that we can "feel fear and pity *of a kind*" (my italics) for such a person as Macbeth. Booth went further (pp. 20–21): "Our emotional involvement (which perhaps should not be simplified under the term 'pity' or 'pity and fear') is thus a combination of two kinds of regret. . . . We lament the 'bad fortune' of a great man who has known good fortune. To this [Shakespeare] adds the much more poignant pity one feels in observing the moral destruction of a great man who has once known goodness."

I shall go beyond Booth, discarding the terms *pity* and *fear* completely, and indicating that the final cause of *Macbeth* can be expressed in some such terms as *anguished concern at morally repellent character deterioration involving human waste on a grand scale, and relaxation of tension when it has come to an end*. This definition fits not only *Macbeth*, but other works constructed on similar principles, such as Moussorgsky's opera *Boris Godunov;* Eugene O'Neill's trilogy *Mourning Becomes Electra;* and, if we extend the scope of our inquiry to include commercial fiction as well as high art, even Spiro Agnew's recent novel, *The Canfield Decision*. Heeding Beckerman's plea (pp. 34–35) for an extension of our critical vocabulary to cope with new dramaturgic demands, I propose to call this form *diaphthorody*, from λύπαι καὶ φροντδεσ πεπί τῆσ διαφθοπᾶσ τῶν ἀνθπὠπων (grief and concern over human destruction; literally, griefs and concerns over the destruction of human beings).[8]

Such a work is constructed on somewhat different principles from those laid down in the *Poetics*. Crane says in another context that the plot of any nondidactic novel or drama is a synthesis of action, character, and thought (what Aristotle calls the "objects" of imitation).

> Plots will differ in structure according as one or another of the three causal ingredients is employed as the synthesizing principle. There are, thus, plots of action, plots of character, and plots of thought. In the first, the synthesizing principle is a completed change, gradual or sudden, in the situation of the protagonist, determined and effected by character and thought (as in *Oedipus*, [James's *The Ambassadors*,] and *The Brothers Karamazov*); in the second, the principle is a completed process of change in the moral character of the protagonist, precipitated or molded by action, and made manifest both in it and in thought and feeling (as in [Thackeray's *Pendennis* and] James's *The Portrait of a Lady*); in the third, the principle is a completed process of change in the thought of the protagonist and consequently in his feelings, conditioned and directed by character and action (as in Pater's *Marius the Epicurean*).[9]

Using these distinctions, one sees immediately that *Macbeth* has a plot of character; it is what James Kirsch (p. 397) calls a *Seelendrama*. Operating within such a framework, Crane points out the ways in which the development of *Macbeth* differs significantly from tragic action: "The change is not merely from good to bad fortune, but from a good state of character to a state in which the hero is almost, but not quite, transformed into a monster." Moreover, Crane (*Languages*, p. 171), Whitaker (pp. 291, 299), and Campbell, emphasizing Macbeth's complete awareness of the evil he does, agree that discussions of the play must focus on its ethical implications. It therefore becomes necessary to examine the moral character of a protagonist like Macbeth in order to see how this differs from the moral quality of the *tragic* protagonist, as outlined in the *Poetics*.

According to Aristotle, dramatic agents are "necessarily either good men or bad—the diversities of human character being nearly always derivative from this primary distinction, since the line between virtue and vice is one dividing the whole of mankind." They must be "either above our own level of goodness, or beneath it, or just such as we are." In this significant division, Aristotle leaves no doubt that the tragic hero is better than ordinary persons (although he may have such infirmities as a quick temper), revealing his character as a good man by demonstrating moral purpose in his speeches and actions (*Poetics*, 2[II], 15).

But is the Macbeth who wades through a river of innocent blood a good man? Surely not. Booth gives him far too much credit in suggesting that he has "potentiality for greatness," that his life—"a tragic error, one big pitiful mistake"—could easily have been otherwise (p. 25). With the kind of character Macbeth had, which does not really contain much potential for greatness, it is extremely probable that he would have succumbed to evil, in one form or another, at some time or another. And his life is much worse than a "tragic error" or a "big pitiful mistake." The problem is that we cannot fully explore Macbeth's character if we confine ourselves to the meager outlines given in the *Poetics* for making moral distinctions. But Aristotle had no need to go into detail on this question there, since it was one he explored minutely in the *Nicomachean Ethics*. It is simply not true to say, as Fergusson does (p. 97), that Aristotle would have found Shakespeare's "vision of evil hard to understand," since the play "shows modes of the spirit's life" he had not dreamed of. Both Whitaker and Campbell repeatedly stressed that although Shakespeare was dealing with a Christian system of ethics, it owed much to Aristotle. Even the New Testament word for sin (*hamartia*) is the Aristotelian term for the tragic hero's mistake. In fact, Aristotle understood very well the nature of the evil in a character like Macbeth. And his careful discriminations, as Elder Olson recently pointed out, are more useful to the aesthetician than the reductive blurring of most modern psychologists.[10]

III

Aristotle believed that the soul includes passions, faculties, and states of character. By passions he meant feelings, accompanied by pain or pleasure, that affect the judgment. Examples include anger, appetite, confidence, emulation, envy, fear, friendship, hatred, joy, longing, and pity. Faculties are what make an individual capable of experiencing the passions. States of character are settled dispositions, good or bad, with respect to passions: in brief, the moral virtues. "Virtue, then, is a state of character concerned with choice" as it would be determined by a man of practical wisdom following a rational principle. Ordinarily the virtue is a mean between two vices, one an excess, the other a defect, of the passion under consideration. In some cases, however, this principle is not applicable; some passions (like spite, shamelessness, and envy) and some actions (like adultery, theft, and murder) are bad in and of themselves, not in terms of excesses or deficiencies. It is impossible ever to be right with regard to such passions and actions. There is no mean, no excess, nor any deficiency with regard to them; they are simply and always wrong.[11]

For Aristotle the habitual performance of good or bad actions, regulated by either our emotions or principles, or both, determines whether

	MORAL TYPE	EMOTIONS	PRINCIPLES	ACTIONS
[Assuming a good society]	Superhuman, heroic, godlike	Superhumanly good	Superhumanly good	Superhumanly good
	Temperate	Good	Good	Good
	Continent	Bad	Good	Good
[In an evil society]	[Naturally good; Huck Finn would be an example]	[Good]	[Bad]	[Good]
[Assuming a good society]	Incontinent	Bad	Good	Bad
	Intemperate	Bad	Bad	Bad
	Bestial	Subhumanly bad	Subhumanly bad	Subhumanly bad
[In an evil society]	[Socially bad; Adolph Eichmann would be an example]	[Good]	[Bad]	[Bad]

we are good or bad. But this is a description of virtue, not a workable set of discriminations which can be applied to actual men and women. Even in the *Poetics*, with its crude refinements, the distinction between "good" and "bad" men is no simple black-and-white one. In the *Ethics* Aristotle makes much subtler discriminations, describing three types of "good" men and three types of "bad" men. The quotation marks indicate that, strictly speaking, only one of these is truly good or truly bad. Aristotle also assumes a good society. In an evil society, one more type would have to be added on each side of the moral barrier. The division that results can, perhaps, best be shown by means of a table.

For Aristotle, only the temperate man is truly good; and only the intemperate man is truly bad. As George Bernard Shaw quipped in *Man and Superman*, "Virtue consists, not in abstaining from vice, but in not desiring it."[12] The temperate man may commit a rare bad action, and the intemperate man may commit a rare good action, but it is his settled *disposition* that determines whether he is a good or bad man. These distinctions allow us to refine the description of the tragic protagonist according to the *Poetics* (13). Since the final cause of tragedy is a catharsis of pity and fear, and since we feel pity for undeserved misfortune and fear for the misfortune of one like ourselves, or a trifle better, the tragic hero is a good man, but a good man of a specific kind—a *temperate* good man. "An extremely bad man" (the intemperate man) should not "be seen falling from happiness into misery. Such a story may arouse the human feeling in us, but it will not move us to either pity or fear." The tragic hero is "the intermediate kind of personage" or better, although he is not "pre-eminently virtuous and just" (i.e., the superhuman type). Initially he enjoys "great reputation and prosperity"; the change in his fortunes is brought about not by any vice or depravity on his part, but by some great error of judgment.

Clearly this does not describe Macbeth. His misfortunes are not undeserved, but the just requital of the evil he has committed. And that evil is not the consequence of some error of judgment, but of his own growing depravity and vice. "We are masters of an action of ours from start to finish, and it is present to our minds at every stage, so that we know what we are doing. But with dispositions it is otherwise. Their beginning is something we can control, but as they develop step by step the stages of their development elude our observation—it is like the progress of a disease. They are, however, voluntary in the sense that it was originally in our power to exercise them for good or for evil."[13]

On the other hand, Macbeth is no Richard III; he does not claim that evil is his good. Judged in moral terms, then, what kind of character does he have? It cannot be described statically, since we are dealing with a plot of character which shows a change from one state to another. But it is an oversimplification to say that Macbeth is a good man who becomes a bad man. He is, rather, a continent "good" man who becomes an incontinent "bad" man. But even a continent good man is not the type of good man described in the *Poetics* who is like ourselves, or a trifle better. Again, we may turn to the *Ethics* for clarification. "Now incontinence and continence are concerned with that which is in excess of the state characteristic of most men; for the continent man abides by his resolutions more and the incontinent man less than most men can."[14] Thus it is not true to say of Macbeth, as does Markels, "There but for the grace of God go I." Nor is it quite true to say, as Crane does more temperately: "He is only doing upon a grander scale and with deeper guilt and more terrifying consequences for himself and others what we can, without too much difficulty, imagine ourselves doing, however less extremely, in circumstances generally similar." And even though he has done nothing bad until he murders Duncan, up to that point he is not really, as Booth and Crane call him, "basically" a noble man with "every potentiality for goodness."[15]

True, he is, at the beginning of the play, "admired by all who know him," as Booth says, but that is because he is a brave man who has as yet committed no overt bad actions. He is neither "basically" good, nor does he have much "potentiality for goodness." The reason lies in the fact that a character like his is essentially unstable, and herein lies its psychological fascination. He can be neither firm in his goodness, for his evil desires are continually at war with his good principles; nor, if his desires eventually win out and he commits evil actions, can he be stable in his badness, for his good principles are continually torturing him for what his evil emotions have driven him to. Aristotle says: "Both the continent man and the temperate man are such as to do nothing contrary to the rule for the sake of the bodily pleasures, but the former has and the latter has not bad appetites, and the latter is such as not to feel pleasure contrary to the rule, while the former is such as to feel pleasure but not to be led by it."[16] Thus we *can* say, with Booth and Crane, that he is not naturally "a true son of evil," but "incontinent." Booth says he is "a 'good' man who, though he has become a 'bad' man, still thinks and feels as a good man would." He is "perfectly aware, in a way an evil man would not be, of the moral values involved" in murdering Duncan.

What makes a continent good man become an incontinent bad man? As I have indicated, such a character will be unstable, no matter which side of the moral line he occupies. Someone like Macbeth, when he eventually crosses that line, "is driven from his considered course of action by a flood of emotion contrary to right principle. He is prevented by overmastering passion from acting in accordance with that principle, yet not so completely as to make him the kind of man to believe that it is right to abandon himself to such pleasures as he seeks." Since incontinence is only a bad *quality*, and not a settled disposition, the incontinent man "is morally superior to the intemperate man [e.g., Shelley's Count Cenci] and is not to be called bad without qualification, for he preserves his noblest element—that conviction on which all morality is founded." While the incontinent man "does not sin against his will—for in a way he does know what he is doing and why—he is not a wicked man. His *choice* is morally sound, so that he is only half wicked."[17] Whitaker, who had pointed out that Shakespeare's moral system had a rational underpinning emphasizing right choice based on intelligence, says of Macbeth (p. 292) that "he is not good enough to escape sin, but he is good enough to feel its horror and to imagine its consequences." For Crane, he "commits monstrous deeds without becoming wholly a monster, since his knowledge of the right principle is never altogether obscured."

But it now becomes necessary to add a few stipulations to this description of Macbeth's character. For he is not, in the most precise sense, a continent good man who becomes an incontinent bad man, since incontinence refers only to excess in the pursuit of the bodily pleasures:

eating, drinking, and sex. Malcolm has this strict meaning in mind when, describing his pretended lechery to Macduff, he says:

> my desire
> All continent impediments would o'erbear
> That did oppose my will. (IV, iii, 63–65)

Macbeth, however, is not driven by gluttony, alcoholism, or lust; rather, the change in his character is initiated by ambition and shame. He therefore becomes a qualified type of incontinent bad man: an incontinent bad man with respect to ambition and shame.[18] (To be exact, as I shall show, he is incontinent with respect to ambition and intemperate with respect to shame.)

IV

Let us now apply these principles to a detailed examination of the moral character of Macbeth. At the beginning of the play he is a continent "good" man. And he has one outstanding virtue: bravery. Aristotle tells us that the brave man "is fearless in face of a noble death, and of all emergencies that involve death; and the emergencies of war are in the highest degree of this kind." When the brave man fears, it will be "as he ought and as the rule directs, for honour's sake."[19]

This describes Macbeth at the beginning of the action exactly. The Sergeant, reporting on his exploits, tells Duncan he "well . . . deserves" the name of brave, as he hacked his way through the battle, his sword smoking "with bloody execution / (Like valour's minion)," in order to reach and kill the rebel Macdonwald (I, ii, 16–23). "O valiant cousin!" Duncan exclaims; "worthy gentleman!" (I, ii, 24). Deciding to make him Thane of Cawdor, the king refers to him as "noble Macbeth" (I, ii, 67). But the alert reader notices the quality of ferocity in Macbeth's bravery: the passage he had carved to reach his enemy had been through human flesh, and he had slit Macdonwald's body open from navel to jaws.

The praises of Macbeth continue in the next scene, but ironically this time, for meanwhile he has already been tempted by the three witches, and Banquo was struck with the startled and fearful way in which he reacted to the prophecy of "Things that do sound so fair" (I, iii, 51–52). As Bradley points out (p. 288): "No innocent man would have started, as he did, with a start of *fear* at the mere prophecy of a crown, or have conceived thereupon *immediately* the thought of murder. Either this thought was not new to him, or he had cherished at least some vaguer dishonorable dream, the instantaneous recurrence of which, at the moment of his hearing the prophecy, revealed to him an inward and terrifying guilt." As yet, however, Macbeth has taken no overt action, and Ross gives us further evidence of his bravery:

> The king hath happily receiv'd, Macbeth,
> The news of thy success; and when he reads
> Thy personal venture in the rebels' fight,
> His wonders and his praises do contend
> Which should be thine or his. Silenc'd with that,
> In viewing o'er the rest o' th' selfsame day,
> He finds thee in the stout Norweyan ranks,
> Nothing afeard of what thyself didst make,
> Strange images of death. As thick as tale
> Came post with post, and every one did bear
> Thy praises in his kingdom's great defence
> And pour'd them down before him. (I, iii, 89–100)

But the deterioration of Macbeth's character in respect to bravery had already begun, when he seriously contemplated the commission of dastardly actions for the wrong end. For the brave man openly faces danger and death; and he faces them for a noble purpose, "in the right way and at the right time."[20]

We may next ask what "black and deep desires" (I, iv, 51) drive Macbeth in the destruction of his character, and how these operate. He is swayed initially by two passions: ambition and shame. Since the continent good man is an unstable character who maintains his precarious moral balance only by dint of tremendous self-control, his emotions may at any time overwhelm him, and it will take very little to activate them. It makes small difference what hand pulls out the control rod inaugurating the chain reaction within him; indeed, the possibility of a spontaneous explosion can never be discounted.

Thus I am not quite in agreement with Booth's statement (p. 24) that Macbeth has "two spurs 'to prick the sides' of his intent, besides his own vaulting ambition," the witches and Lady Macbeth, without whom "he would find himself incapable of the murder." This view requires a little refinement. As Bradley says (p. 292), the witches' words are fatal only because something in Macbeth "leaps into light at the sound of them." And he picks out from their forecasts only those that will further his ambition, rejecting and trying to change the prophecy that the ruling line will be of Banquo's issue, not his. It is this aspect of his response Loren Eiseley has noted, drawing a perceptive parallel with the lure of modern science. He ascribes the "almost unbearable" power of the scene to the fact that Macbeth's malevolent character change introduces a future he

himself creates. Like the technologists who are today's style in necroman-
tic projections, the witches are "smoking wisps" of their auditor's "mental
vapor," proclaiming what he subconsciously wants and bolstering his own
desires with their "Delphic utterances." His conscious acceptance of
these half-truths establishes their power. The "fixed, static, inflexible"
future such juggling fiends present is "fated beyond human will to
change" precisely because it is brought about by human will.

Thus the witches' prophecy would be meaningless—as Banquo's very
different reaction demonstrates—if it did not activate Macbeth's own
latent ambition, which he has heretofore been able to suppress. Aristotle
regarded ambition as a dangerous passion, and used the word pejora-
tively. "We call a man 'ambitious,' " he says, "when he shows an inordi-
nate desire for honour or desires it from an improper source."[21] Ambition,
then, is a bad emotion which Macbeth, as a continent good man, has been
able to control. But with the prophecy of the witches, he becomes incontinent in respect to ambition, and the change in his moral character is
initiated. This takes place first as an intrapsychic struggle, before he
commits any overt action, and he is alarmed and repelled by the horrify-
ing picture his unleashed passion paints on his soul. Man's greatest problem, according to Eiseley, in Shakespeare's time as in our own, is that we
get what we wish for. What Macbeth wishes, and what his ambition
suggests to him, is so violently contrary to his principles that he is shaken
to the depths at the prospect before him:

> This supernatural soliciting
> Cannot be ill; cannot be good. If ill,
> Why hath it given me earnest of success,
> Commencing in a truth? I am Thane of Cawdor.
> If good, why do I yield to that suggestion
> Whose horrid image doth unfix my hair
> And make my seated heart knock at my ribs
> Against the use of nature? Present fears
> Are less than horrible imaginings.
> My thought, whose murther yet is but fantastical,
> Shakes so my single state of man that function
> Is smother'd in surmise and nothing is
> But what is not. (I, iii, 130–42)

The other emotion that drives him, once it gets out of control, is
shame. Here the issue is more complicated, for Macbeth is not incontinent in respect to shame; he is intemperate in respect to shame; and, as
Macduff points out later in another context: "Boundless intemperance /
In nature is a tyranny" (IV, iii, 66–67). Macbeth does not feel shame
with regard to the proper objects, for what he is made to feel ashamed of

is not wanting to commit a murder. It is Lady Macbeth who activates this shame.

The modern psychiatric scholar, Thomas S. Szasz, has indicated that "the feeling of shame is closely related to what other people think of one. Exposure and humiliation are feared both as punishments for shameful acts and as stimuli for increasingly intense feelings of shame." Eric Hoffer has also pointed out that shame "involves an awareness by the individual of being watched and judged by the group. . . . The more compact the group, the more pronounced the sense of shame." Aristotle had probed this emotion in even more detail:

> The people before whom we feel shame are those whose opinion of us matters to us. . . . We feel most shame before those who will always be with us and those who notice what we do, since in both cases eyes are upon us. . . . And before those who have never yet known us come to grief, since their attitude to us has amounted to admiration so far. . . . Generally, we feel shame before those for whose own misconduct we should also feel it. . . . And we feel more shame when we are likely to be continually seen by, and go about under the eyes of, those who know of our disgrace.

Since this passage is a perfect description of Lady Macbeth in relation to her husband, she is a person before whom he can easily be made to feel shame. But when we examine what kind of emotion shame is, we face certain complexities. It is pain or disturbance at a mental picture of disgrace, past, present, or future, to ourselves or those we care for, discrediting us with people about whose opinion we care. But even under the best of circumstances shame—a fear of dishonor—is not a very worthy emotion, nor is it characteristic of a good man, since he should not be contemplating the bad actions on which it is dependent.[22] Macbeth, however, under the prodding of his "fiendlike queen," feels shame not at the prospect of committing a shameful deed—the murder of his king, friend, guest, and kinsman—but rather, shame at the prospect of *not* committing this deed. As Booth says (p. 24), "she shifts the whole ground of the consideration to questions of Macbeth's valor." Twitting him for cowardice, she makes "him fear to seem cowardly" so that his "whole reputation for bravery seems at last to be at stake." We must say, therefore, that Macbeth is not incontinent with respect to shame; he is, rather, intemperate with respect to shame. He feels ashamed of not wanting to commit a particularly shameful murder. Not only is his emotion a bad one; his principle is bad, too.

Yet we do not lose all sympathy with him at this point, for we realize that, left to his own devices, he *would* feel shame at Duncan's murder. His wife, when she receives his letter, considers his character. She, who should know him best, fears his nature because "It is too full o' th' milk of human kindness / To catch the nearest way." She apostrophizes him in a soliloquy:

> Thou wouldst be great;
> Art not without ambition, but without
> The illness should attend it. What thou wouldst highly,
> That wouldst thou holily; wouldst not play false,
> And yet wouldst wrongly win. Thou'ldst have, great Glamis,
> That which cries "Thus thou must do," if thou have it;
> And that which rather thou dost fear to do
> Than wishest should be undone. (I, v, 17–26)

Whitaker comments (p. 291) that "he has already been established as brave; Lady Macbeth. . . . adds the data that he is ambitious but is humane and has moral standards, qualities which are abundantly evident as he approaches his first crime." When, alone, he ponders the murder, he comes up with four good reasons against it: Duncan is his kinsman, his king, his guest, and a good man. Against all these, Macbeth can place only his "vaulting ambition"—and it is not enough:

> He's here in double trust:
> First, as I am his kinsman and his subject—
> Strong both against the deed; then, as his host,
> Who should against his murtherer shut the door,
> Not bear the knife myself. Besides, this Duncan
> Hath borne his faculties so meek, hath been
> So clear in his great office, that his virtues
> Will plead like angels, trumpet-tongu'd, against
> The deep damnation of his taking-off;
> And pity, like a naked new-born babe,
> Striding the blast, or heaven's cherubin, hors'd
> Upon the sightless couriers of the air,
> Shall blow the horrid deed in every eye,
> That tears shall drown the wind. I have no spur
> To prick the sides of my intent, but only
> Vaulting ambition, which o'erleaps itself
> And falls on th' other side. (I, vii, 12–28)

When Lady Macbeth comes on the scene, he tells her: "We will proceed no further in this business" (I, vii, 31). But immediately she goes to work shifting the ground of his shame:

> Art thou afeard
> To be the same in thine own act and valour
> As thou art in desire? Wouldst thou have that
> Which thou esteem'st the ornament of life,
> And live a coward in thine own esteem . . . ? (I, vii, 39–43)

Macbeth's answer ("I dare do all that may become a man. / Who dares do more is none"—I, vii, 46–47) is, as Bradley points out (p. 300), one of which he himself is "half-ashamed." And, as Lady Macbeth continues her verbal assaults, he is won over to Duncan's murder without too much difficulty, since his evil passions were already on her side. Yet even in the moment of his capitulation, his resolve firm to go through with the assassination, he characterizes it as "this terrible feat" (I, vii, 80).

Macbeth, the diaphthorodic protagonist, is now ready to embark on the murderous career that will translate into action the moral defeat his character has already suffered. While we do not continue to experience the suspense and anxiety evoked by his first struggle, our anguish escalates during his downward plunge. As he pursues his bloody course in Acts II, III, and IV, his character degenerates through successive stages on all three fronts indicated in the chart on page 00: actions, emotions, and principles. His murders grow increasingly brutal and unnecessary, progressing through Banquo's and culminating in the completely unwarranted slaughter of Lady Macduff and her children. The passions that motivate them grow more diffuse and concomitantly more compulsive.

As Shakespeare understood long before Freud, it is the nature of emotions to operate most powerfully when they are least comprehensible. Macbeth's murder of Duncan had been triggered primarily by ambition; it was, from an amoral point of view, "necessary" if he was to reach the throne. But his plot to murder Banquo and Fleance is sparked by vague worries shading into the irrational. For this very reason, he is more strongly impelled to kill Banquo and Fleance than he had been to kill Duncan. Three interwined passions drive him to this murderous scheme. The first is fear for his life; he himself has set the pattern for regicide, and he judges Banquo, not by objective evidence about that upright warrior, but by projections of his own character. Second, he is troubled over whose decendants will occupy the throne, even though this is a concern for the distant future: Fleance is, after all, still only a boy. Finally, and most irrational of all, is his vain hope of gaining surcease from psychological torment by committing further murders. Afflicted with terrible dreams that shake him nightly, his mind full of scorpions (III, ii, 18–19, 36), he believes "Things bad begun make strong themselves by ill" (III, ii, 55). When he learns that Fleance has escaped, his immediate reaction is that his "fit" will come again, that he will be "cabin'd, cribb'd, confin'd, bound in / To saucy doubts and fears" (III, iv, 21–25)—as indeed he is, for his mental turmoil projects itself almost immediately as Banquo's ghost. Psychologists tell us that such hallucinatory visions may be produced by acute anxiety and expectation.[23] Not only have Macbeth's passions become more inchoate; only a faint echo remains of the principles by which he had condemned Duncan's murder. His recognition of evil in the Banquo-Fleance plot was revealed only in his desire to keep the details from his wife until after the deed was done.

But worse is to come, as his character degenerates still further. Even these rags of scruple are torn away as he contemplates Macduff's absence from his feast. He decides to eliminate all considerations of principle from his future murders by the simple expedient of not examining them morally; he will carry out every bizarre whim, without stopping to think about it:

> I am in blood
> Stepp'd in so far that, should I wade no more,
> Returning were as tedious as go o'er.
> Strange things I have in head, that will to hand,
> Which must be acted ere they may be scann'd. (III, v, 136–40)

No principles are left to deter him from murdering Lady Macduff and her children. And as his faculty for normal emotional responses withers away, his driving passion becomes random blood-lust:

> The flighty purpose never is o'ertook
> Unless the deed go with it. From this moment
> The very firstlings of my heart shall be
> The firstlings of my hand. And even now,
> To crown my thoughts with acts, be it thought and done!
> The castle of Macduff I will surprise,
> Seize upon Fife, give to the edge o' th' sword
> His wife, his babes, and all unfortunate souls
> That trace him in his line. No boasting like a fool!
> This deed I'll do before this purpose cool. (IV, i, 145–54)

Shakespeare, however, has handled Macbeth's deterioration with such consummate art that, even while we abhor his vicious actions, we never completely lose our solicitude over the destruction of his essential humanity. Although we are horrified at the degeneration of his character, we are at the same time deeply concerned as we watch the progressive brutalization of this once honored man. There are several reasons for this. One is that he is never portrayed in the direct act of committing a murder with his own hands; another is that Shakespeare continually reminds us of the horrendous conflict taking place in Macbeth's soul; and still another lies in those traits pointed out by Booth (p. 23) which are quite apart from his moral qualities: his gift for poetic expression, "his mammoth sensitivity, his rich despair," all of which add powerfully to the effect of the play.

And it is also true that, toward the end of the action, some of Macbeth's bravery reasserts itself, as he goes out to meet the forces of Malcolm and Macduff on the battlefield. But certain stages in his show of "bravery" here need to be drastically qualified in the light of Aristotle's discussion of the five types of false courage. When Macbeth first goes forth to fight, he thinks he is invulnerable because of the witches' prophecies that he has nothing to fear until Birnam Wood comes to Dunsinane, and that no one born of woman can harm him. Both principles and passions buoy him up: "The mind I sway by and the heart I bear / Shall never sag with doubt nor shake with fear" (V, iii, 9–10). His condition thus fits Aristotle's fifth type of false courage: that "displayed by those who face a danger without realizing that it is a danger."[24] Macbeth "will not be afraid of death and bane / Till Birnam Forest come to Dunsinane" (V, iii, 59–60). Then he gets shocking news, in the very midst of his furious preparations for battle: his wife, the partner of his degradation and the one consolation he might have looked forward to in old age, is dead. His famous response is one of the most quoted speeches in all of Shakespeare:

> She should have died hereafter;
> There would have been a time for such a word.
> To-morrow, and to-morrow, and to-morrow
> Creeps in this petty pace from day to day
> To the last syllable of recorded time;
> And all our yesterdays have lighted fools
> The way to dusty death. Out, out, brief candle!
> Life's but a walking shadow, a poor player,
> That struts and frets his hour upon the stage
> And then is heard no more. It is a tale
> Told by an idiot, full of sound and fury,
> Signifying nothing. (V, v, 17–28)

I follow Elder Olson[25] in my interpretation of this speech. If only the news of Lady Macbeth's suicide had come at a later date, he could have called up psychological resources to handle it. Now, at the very moment of his frenzied efforts to cope with external enemies, he must somehow cope also with this terrible assault on his psyche. His feeling for his wife is the last vulnerable area where he can feel direct human emotions; all else in his soul has become hardened and callous. The news of her death hence arouses such despair in him that, as he considers the solitary waste his own life has become, he can reflect only on the meaningless-ness of all life.

And yet he must continue to fight. Aside from the one speech with which he reacts to Seyton, there is no time for his private grief. It is interrupted by a messenger, who reports that Birnam Wood is, indeed, coming to Dunsinane. Macbeth then shows another form of false cour-age. He says:

> I pull in resolution, and begin
> To doubt th' equivocation of the fiend,
> That lies like truth. "Fear not, till Birnam Wood
> Do come to Dunsinane!" and now a wood
> Comes toward Dunsinane. Arm, arm, and out!
> If this which he avouches does appear,
> There is nor flying hence nor tarrying here.
> . . . .
>
> Ring the alarum bell! Blow wind, come wrack,
> At least we'll die with harness on our back! (V, v, 42–52)

And later:

> They have tied me to a stake. I cannot fly,
> But bear-like I must fight the course. (V, vii, 1–2)

Macbeth's mood at this point is to be compared with Aristotle's discus-sion of the third type of false courage, "the fighting spirit." Men who are animated by it, like

wild beasts when they charge the hunters who have wounded them, are generally reckoned courageous, because the courageous man has the fighting spirit which is always ready to àdvance in face of danger. . . . The motive of the brave, however, is the nobility of what they do; their high spirit merely contributes its aid to their efforts. But when wild animals are "brave" it is the result of some pain they are feeling. When they turn on their hunters it is because they have been wounded or frightened. It is not then courage that they display, because they need the spur of pain and fury to make them rush into danger blind to the risks they run. . . . Of the moods which resemble courage this which has a high spirit for its driving force seems the most natural; indeed, when it includes deliberate choice and purpose it is hard to distinguish from cour-age. . . . But the most one can say of those who fight from no higher motive than anger is that they are good fighters; one cannot call them brave. For they are not moved by honour or guided by principle; simply they are swayed by their feelings. Still some resemblance does exist between them and the brave.[26]

But Macbeth's "courage" at this point continues to rest also on Aristotle's fifth type of false courage, for he still believes that he cannot be harmed by anyone born of woman. Buoyed up by this false hope, he rejects the idea of suicide: "Why should I play the Roman fool and die / On mine own sword? Whiles I see lives, the gashes / Do better upon them" (V, viii, 1–3). We are, it is true, rather impressed with this decision, and Aristotle would have been, too. He says: "To kill oneself as a means of escape from poverty or disappointed love or bodily or mental anguish is the deed of a coward rather than a brave man. To run away from trouble is a form of cowardice and, while it is true that the suicide braves death, he does it not for some noble object but to escape some ill."[27]

When Macbeth faces Macduff immediately after his decision against playing the Roman fool, he still thinks he cannot be harmed. This conviction adds poignancy and sincerity to the remorse he feels at facing the man whose wife and children he has had murdered. Moreover, Lady Macbeth's suicide has taught him what it means to be a bereaved husband. When Macduff accosts him as "hellhound!" Macbeth's answer is freighted not only with guilt, but also with the distressed empathy he has just acquired through his own pain and grief: "Of all men else I have avoided thee. / But get thee back! My soul is too much charg'd / With blood of thine already" (V, viii, 4–6). When Macduff insists on fighting, however, Macbeth engages him, then says:

> Thou losest labour.
> As easy mayst thou the intrenchant air
> With thy keen sword impress as make me bleed.
> Let fall thy blade on vulnerable crests.
> I bear a charmed life, which must not yield
> To one of woman born. (V, viii, 8–13)

Macduff quickly disabuses his opponent of this error with the information that he was a product of Caesarian birth. At this point Macbeth almost loses his few shreds and patches of bravery. Hearing Macduff's news, he says:

> Accursed be that tongue that tells me so,
> For it hath cow'd my better part of man!
> And be these juggling fiends no more believ'd,
> That palter with us in a double sense,

That keep the word of promise to our ear
And break it to our hope! I'll not fight with thee! (V, viii, 17–22)

Here his reaction fits exactly that described by Aristotle when those who have false courage based on ignorance of their danger realize the true situation. "Those who have been deceived about the facts fly if they know or suspect that these are different from what they supposed."[28]

But when Macduff taunts him with being a coward who will be captured and displayed as a sideshow monstrosity, Macbeth finally shows something approaching true courage:

I will not yield,
To kiss the ground before young Malcolm's feet
And to be baited with the rabble's curse.
Though Birnam Wood be come to Dunsinane,
And thou oppos'd, being of no woman born,
Yet I will try the last. Before my body
I throw my warlike shield. Lay on, Macduff,
And damn'd be him that first cries "Hold, enough!" (V, viii, 27–34)

As Szasz says, "Courage is the willingness to play even when you know the odds are against you."[29] Our last sight of Macbeth is of a man who, at the end of his life, exhibits some remnants of a virtue, incomplete though it is because his cause lacks nobility. "When things go wrong," says Aristotle, "the brave man . . . comes out in his true colours when he has with his eyes open to face dangers as great as human nature can endure."[30] And we may say, with Crane (*Languages*, p. 173), that we "take satisfaction, at last, in the manner in which Macbeth himself behaves."

We have now traced the deterioration of his one outstanding virtue, bravery, in the progress of the change in his character from the continent "good" man to the incontinent "bad" man. We have indicated how he was driven over the moral dividing line, under the influence of evil passions which got out of hand: his own latent ambition, activated by the witches' prophecy; and false, unprincipled shame, activated by his wife. We have traced two further stages in his progressive debasement: with his principles fading into mere shadows, he is motivated by ill-founded fear and an irrational hope that somehow more murders will set his unquiet mind at rest; and finally, he kills aimlessly, at whims he refuses even to examine. At the very end of the play, however, we see a remnant of his devotion to his wife, expressed in the quiet anguish and hopeless despair with which he reacts to the news of her suicide. And, before he dies, some simulacra of his one outstanding virtue, bravery, assert themselves, though even here Macbeth is not acting with true nobility, for his cause remains an evil one: fighting to prevent the lawful government of Scotland from reestablishing itself, and fighting against good and honorable men.

To sum up, what we have in *Macbeth* is not a tragedy, but what I have named a *diaphthorody*. A diaphthorody I define as a non-didactic drama or novel which imitates a serious and complete action of appropriate magnitude, in either dramatic or narrative form, with incidents revealing morally repellent character deterioration that arouses horrified fascination, anguished concern, and grievous regret at human waste on a grand scale; and release of tension when it has worked itself out. The plot is a plot of character, or *Seelendrama*, showing the change in moral disposition of a continent good man (or woman) to an incontinent bad man (or woman), with an accompanying change in his or her fortune from great to low. The protagonist is initially driven across the ethical boundary by evil passions, at the same time that he maintains his good principles. In full awareness of how wicked the deed is that he proposes doing, he commits it anyway. After perpetrating unforgivable harm, he is finally justly punished and his depredations are brought to a conclusive end. All possibilities for any further injuries he can do to good men and women, and all possibilities for any further moral deterioration on his part, are exhausted. His character must be represented in such a way as to have demonstrated his intrapsychic conflict. The more terrible it is, the more powerful the emotional impact of the diaphthorody. At its conclusion, he himself recognizes, as does the reader or spectator, that he has become a damned soul inhabiting a hell of his own creation; and the best we can wish for him is the surcease from his torments only death may bring.

Notes

1. Eiseley, "The Uncompleted Man," *Harper's Magazine* (March 1964), pp. 51–54; Rexroth, "Classics Revisited—XXX: Macbeth," *Saturday Review* 49 (June 25, 1966): 17; Bradley, *Shakespearean Tragedy* (1904; London, 1961), p. 15; Campbell, *Shakespeare's Tragic Heroes: Slaves of Passion* (Cambridge: Cambridge University Press,

1930), p. 208; Beckerman, "Dramatic Theory and Stage Practice," *Papers in Dramatic Theory and Criticism*, ed. David M. Knauf (Iowa City: University of Iowa, 1969), pp. 28–29.

2. Fergusson, "*Macbeth* as the Imitation of an Action," in *Explication as Criticism, Selected Papers from the English Institute, 1941–1952*, ed. W. K. Wimsatt, Jr. (New York, 1963), pp. 85–97; Markels, "The Spectacle of Deterioration: *Macbeth* and the 'Manner' of Tragic Imitation," *Shakespeare Quarterly* 12 (Summer, 1961): 293–303; Booth, "Macbeth as Tragic Hero," *Journal of General Education* 6 (October, 1951): 17–25; Crane, *The Languages of Criticism and the Structure of Poetry* (Toronto, 1953), pp. 169–173; Campbell, pp. 208–239; Whitaker, *Shakespeare's Use of Learning: An Inquiry into the Growth of His Mind and Art* (San Marino, California, 1953), pp. 291, 296, 299. Fergusson's essay was reprinted in his *The Human Image in Dramatic Literature* (Garden City, N.Y., 1957), pp. 115–125; in Alfred Harbage, ed., *Shakespeare: The Tragedies* (Englewood Cliffs, N.J., 1964), pp. 105–112; and in Terence Hawkes, ed., *Twentieth Century Interpretations of MACBETH* (Englewood Cliffs, N.J., 1977), pp. 67–68. Crane's remarks were reprinted in Hawkes, pp. 69–73, as "The Structure of *Macbeth*." Among other studies of *Macbeth* I have found particularly helpful are J. V. Cunningham, *Woe or Wonder: The Emotional Effect of Shakespearean Tragedy* (1951; Chicago, 1969) Paul Jorgenson, *Our Naked Frailties: Sensational Art and Meaning in Macbeth* (Berkeley, 1971); and Dennis Biggins, "Sexuality, Witchcraft, and Violence in *Macbeth*," in *Shakespeare Studies VIII: An Annual Gathering of Research, Criticism, and Reviews*, ed. J. Leeds Barroll III (New York, 1975), pp. 255–277. James Kirsch offers a Jungian analysis of the play in "Macbeth's Descent into Hell and Damnation," in his *Shakespeare's Royal Self* (New York, 1966), pp. 321–422. Barroll's thoughtful and extended discussion of Aristotle in "The Structure of a Shakespearean Tragedy," *Shakespeare Studies VIII*, pp. 1–27, is of general interest.

3. *Poetics*, 6 (1), 7–9, trans. Ingram Bywater, in *The Basic Works of Aristotle*, ed. Richard McKeon (New York, 1941). All subsequent references to the *Poetics* are to this edition.

4. For a discussion of this division, see McKeon's Introduction to his *Basic Works of Aristotle*, p. xxii.

5. Trans. W. D. Ross, in *Basic Works of Aristotle*, p. 935. Subsequent references to the *Ethics* are either to this edition, or to J. A. K. Thomson's translation, *The Ethics of Aristotle* (Baltimore, 1955), which is more graceful, but not as accurate.

6. This account is based on the *Physics*, trans. R. P. Hardie and R. K. Gaye; and on the *Metaphysics*, trans. W. D. Ross; both in McKeon, pp. 240–241 and 693.

7. For a succinct account of this erosion, see Willard O. Eddy's essay, "The Scientific Bases of Naturalism in Literature," *Western Humanities Review* 8 (Summer, 1954): 219–230.

8. I am indebted to Donald W. Prakken, Professor of Classics at the State University of New York at Albany, for assistance in constructing the name for this species of imitative literary art.

9. *Critics*, pp. 620–621; reprinted with the bracketed examples in "The Plot of Tom Jones," *Essays on the Eighteenth Century Novel*, ed. Robert D. Spector (Bloomington, Ind., 1965), pp. 92–130.

10. Whitaker, pp. 11, 43, 204, and 241; Campbell, *passim*, especially pp. 210 and 212; Olson, "Art and Science," *On Value Judgments in the Arts and Other Essays* (Chicago, 1976), p. 306.

11. *Ethics*, II, 5–6; *Rhetoric*, II, 1, trans. W. Rhys Roberts; McKeon, pp. 956–957, 959, 1380.

12. "Maxims for Revolutionists," *Man and Superman* (1903; Baltimore, 1974), p. 257.

13. I have chosen the Thomson translation of Aristotle for this passage; see his *Ethics*, p. 93. The Ross translation, *Ethics*, III, 5, is found in McKeon, p. 974.

14. Ross translation, *Ethics*, VII, 10, McKeon, p. 1052. Cf. the Thomson translation, p. 217: "Both continence and incontinence go farther than the character of most of us permits us to go, the continent man showing more, and the incontinent less, power of moral resistance than the generality of mankind possesses."

15. See Markels, p. 293; Crane, *Languages*, pp. 171–172; Booth, pp. 17, 19–20.

16. Ross translation, *Ethics*, VII, 9, McKeon, p. 1051.

17. Again I have chosen Thomson's translation, pp. 213, 216. The Ross translation, *Ethics*, VII, 8, 10, is in McKeon, pp. 1050, 1052.

18. Thomson, pp. 202–205; Ross, *Ethics*, VII, 4, in McKeon, pp. 1042–1044.

19. Ross, *Ethics*, III, 6, 7; in McKeon, p. 975.

20. Ross, *Ethics*, III, 7, in McKeon, p. 976.

21. Thomson, *Ethics*, p. 126; cf. Ross, *Ethics*, IV, 5, McKeon, p. 995. See also Kristian Smidt, "Two Aspects of Ambition in Elizabethan Tragedy: *Doctor Faustus* and *Macbeth*," *English Studies* 50 (February, 1969): 235–248.

22. The discussion of shame is based on Aristotle's *Rhetoric*, II, 6; and *Ethics*, IV, 9 (Ross translation), in McKeon, pp. 1392–1395 and 1001. See also Szasz, *The Myth of Mental Illness: Foundations of a Theory of Personal Conduct*, (1961; New York, 1974), pp. 51–52; and Hoffer, "Long Live Shame!" *New York Times*, October 18, 1974, p. 41.

23. Nicholas P. Spanos and Jack Gottlieb, "Ergotism and the Salem Village Witch Trials," *Science* 194 (24 December, 1976): 1393.

24. Thomson's translation, *Ethics*, p. 101; cf. Ross, *Ethics*, III, 8, McKeon, p. 979.

25. *Tragedy and the Theory of Drama* (Detroit, 1961), pp. 113–125.

26. Thomson's translation, *Ethics*, pp. 99–100; cf. Ross, *Ethics*, III, 8, in McKeon, pp. 978–979.

27. Thomson's translation, *Ethics*, p. 97; cf. Ross, *Ethics*, III, 7, McKeon, p. 977.

28. Ross, *Ethics*, III, 8, McKeon, p. 979.

29. *The Second Sin* (Garden City, N.Y., 1974), p. 39.

30. Thomson, *Ethics*, p. 100; cf. Ross, *Ethics*, III, 8, McKeon, p. 979.

LIST OF CONTRIBUTORS

FALK, EUGENE HANNES
Born: August 10, 1913, in Czechoslovakia.
Present position: Marcel Bataillon Professor of Comparative Literature and Professor of French, University of North Carolina at Chapel Hill.
Books: *Renunciation as a Tragic Focus* (1954); *Types of Thematic Structure* (1967); *The Poetics of Roman Ingarden* (1981).

FIZER, JOHN
Born: June 13, 1925, in Mircha, Ukraine.
Present position: Professor of Slavic and Comparative Literature, Rutgers University, New Brunswick, New Jersey.
Books: *Psychologism and Psychoaesthetics: A Historical and Critical View of Their Relations* (1981).
Co-author: *Linguistic and Literary Studies in Eastern Europe* (1979); Vol. 1: *Philosophy in the Soviet Union: A Survey of the Mid-Sixties.*
Editor: *Selected Tragedies of Sumarkokov,* (1970).

GADO, FRANK
Born: November 15, 1936, in Fairview, New Jersey.
Present position: Professor of English and American Literature, Union College, Schenectady, New York; editor of the Union College Press.
Editor: *First Person: Conversations with Novelists on Writers and Writing* (1973).

GRENANDER, MARY ELIZABETH
Born: November 21, 1918, in Rewey, Wisconsin.
Present position: Professor of English, State University of New York at Albany.
Book *Ambrose Bierce* (1971).
Editor: *A Record of Research and Creative Activity, State University of New York* (1958); *Helios: From Myth to Solar Energy* (1978); *Apollo Agonistes: The Humanities in a Computerized World* (1979); *Asclepius ar Syracus: Thomas Szasz, Libertarian Humanist* (1981); —with John C. Gerber: *Contemporary American Literature 1900–1941* (1950).

MAGLIOLA, ROBERT
Born: 1940, in the United States.
Present position: Professor of Comparative Literature and English, Purdue University; member of advisory board of the International Circle for Research in Philosophy, deMenil Foundation, Houston, Texas.
Book: *Phenomenology and Literature* (1977).
Forthcoming: *Phenomenological Approaches to Literature: An Annotated Bibliography, with Introductory Monograph; Derrida on the Mend;* —with Vernon Gras, an anthology of literary criticism.

MERCIER, ALAIN
Born: January 7, 1936, in Compiègne, Oise, France.
Present position: Research Fellow at the French National Research Center in Paris, section 36.
Books: *Les Sources ésotériques et occultes de la poésie symboliste en Europe*, vol. 1 (1969) and vol. 2 (1972); *Eliphas Lévy et la pensée magique au XIX siècle* (1973).

MUELLER-VOLLMER, KURT
Born: June 28, 1928, in Hamburg.
Present position: Professor of German Studies and Humanities, Stanford University; member of the Board of Counselors of the Humboldt-Gesellschaft; co-editor of "Literature and the Human Sciences" series, Urizen Books, New York; co-editor of Stanford German Studies, Verlag Peter Lang, Bern and Frankfurt.
Books: *Towards a Phenomenological Theory of Literature, A Study of Wilhelm Dilthey's Poetik* (1963); *Poesie und Einbildungskraft: Zur Dichtungstheorie Wilhelm von Humboldts* (1967).
Editor: *Humboldt Studienausgabe*, vol. 1, *Ästhetik und Literatur* (1970) and vol. 2, *Politik und Geschichte* (1971); *Return from Italy, Goethe's Notebook 1788* (1970).
Forthcoming: *The Essential Hermeneutic Reader: The German Tradition. From the Enlightenment to the Present.*

NAEHER, JÜRGEN
Born: April 11, 1947, in Chemnitz, Germany.
Present Position: Assistant Professor, University of Düsseldorf, West Germany.
Books: *Walter Benjamin's Allegorie-Begriff als Modell. Zur Konstitution philosophischer Literaturwissenschaft* (1977); *Einführung in die idealistische Dialektik Hegel's* (1981); *Oswald Spengler in Selbstzeugnissen und Bilddokumenten* (1982).
Editor: *Die negative Dialektik Adornos* (1982); *Dialog Philosophie* series.

STERNBERG, MEIR
Present position: Associate Professor of Poetics and Comparative Literature, Tel-Aviv University.
Books: *Expositional Modes and Temporal Ordering in Fiction* (1978).
In print: a book about the poetics of Biblical Narrative.
In preparation: a book on the artistic representation of reality.

WASIOLEK, EDWARD
Born April 27, 1924, in Camden, New Jersey.
Present position: Distinguished Service Professor of Slavic, English, and Comparative Literature and Chairman of the Comparative Literature program, University of Chicago; Cultural Exchange Research Fellow in the Soviet Union; visiting professor at several universities.
Books: *Dostoevsky, the Major Fiction* (1964); *Tolstoy's Major Fiction* (1978);—with Raymond Bauer: *Nine Soviet Portraits* (1955).
Editor: *Crime and Punishment and the Critics* (1961); *The Notebooks for "Crime and Punishment"* (1967); *"The Brothers Karamazov" and the Critics* (1967); *The Notebooks for "The Idiot"* (1968); *The Notebooks for "The Possessed"* (1968); *The Notebooks for "A Raw Youth"* (1969); *The Notebooks for "The Brothers Karamazov"* (1970); *"The Gambler" and Polina Suslova's Diary* (1972).

WEITZ, MORRIS
Born: July 24, 1916, in Detroit, Michigan.
Last position: Richard Karet Professor of Philosophy and History of Ideas, Brandeis University.
Books: *Philosophy in Literature* (1963); *Philosophy of the Arts* (1964); *Hamlet and the Philosophy of Literary Criticism* (1964); *The Opening Mind: A Philosophical Study of Humanistic Concepts* (1978).
Editor: *Problems in Aesthetics* (1960).

INDEX OF NAMES

Whitehead, Alfred North, 42, 43, 61
Wiggershaus, Rolf, 62
Willard, Penelope, 108
Williams, Raymond, 134
Wimsatt, W.K., viii, 247
Winch, Peter, 42, 43, 61
Wittgenstein, Ludwig, 33, 34, 35, 36, 37,
    38, 42, 96, 110, 118, 131
Wolf, Christian von, 61
Woodmansee, M., 61
Wordsworth, William, 3, 9, 10, 11, 12, 13,
    15, 17, 18, 39
Wright, Georg Henrik von, 62, 63

Wronski, Józef Maria, 211, 216, 217
Wuchterl, K., 109
Wunderlich, D., 110

Yacobi, Tamar, 188
Yeats, William Butler, 209, 212, 213, 220

Zeitlin, J., 39
Zenck, M., 111
Zeyer, Julius, 220
Zimmerli, Walther, 62
Žmegač, V., 61
Zola, Emile, 198